THE SEVEN KEYS TO COMMUNICATING IN JAPAN

THE

7

KEYS TO COMMUNICATING IN

JAPAN

An Intercultural Approach

HARU YAMADA

ORLANDO R. KELM

DAVID A. VICTOR

Georgetown University Press | Washington, DC

The publisher is not responsible for third-party websites or their
content. URL links were active at time of publication.

Library of Congress Cataloging-in-Publication Data
Names: Yamada, Haru, author. | Kelm, Orlando R., 1957- author. |
    Victor, David A., 1956- author.
Title: The Seven Keys to Communicating in Japan : An Intercultural
    Approach/Haru Yamada, Orlando R. Kelm and David A. Victor.
Description: Washington, DC : Georgetown University Press, 2017. |
    Includes bibliographical references and index.
Identifiers: LCCN 2016048386 (print) | LCCN 2017003769 (ebook) |
    ISBN 9781626164765 (hc : alk. paper) | ISBN 9781626164772
    (pb:alk. paper) | ISBN 9781626164789 (eb)
Subjects: LCSH: Business communication—Japan. | Business
    communication—United States. | Communication—
    Japan. | Communication—United States. | Intercultural
    communication—Japan.
Classification: LCC HF5718.2.J3 Y36 2017 (print) | LCC HF5718.2.J3
    (ebook) | DDC 658.4/50952—dc23
LC record available at https://lccn.loc.gov/2016048386

All photos were used with permission and are acknowledged in the
caption. Those without acknowledgment were taken by the authors.

♾ This book is printed on acid-free paper meeting the requirements
of the American National Standard for Permanence in Paper for
Printed Library Materials.

18 17   9 8 7 6 5 4 3 2   First printing

Printed in the United States of America

Text design by click! Publishing Services
Cover design by Connie Gabbert Design + Illustration
Cover image courtesy of the authors

For the future generation of intercultural
explorers, Beni and Sébastien.

HARU YAMADA

For my German father, Wolfgang, and my
Canadian mother, Aline, who exemplify
effective intercultural communication.

ORLANDO R. KELM

For my wonderful family, who
complete my world.

DAVID A. VICTOR

CONTENTS

Figures

Tables

With one author, it is difficult to thank everyone who helps bring a book to completion. With three authors, this difficulty is exponential—however, we are going to try!

In chapter 8 of this book, you will read the story of Dallin Bates, an American who works with a team from Japan and who visits them for the first time in Japan. In actuality, we changed the names of the company, the people, and the places. The story, however, is based on "Dallin's" real work experience. We thank him for sharing his story, even if we do not publicly recognize him by name. (We can say, however, that "Dallin" is his son's real name, and we used this name in the case study by special request.)

We can and do openly recognize our guest executives who commented on the case study. We thank Howard Cash, Mitsuo Hirose, Thomas Mally, Scott Stegert, Junji Taniguchi, and Ko Unoki for taking time from their busy schedules to comment on the vignette. Readers will notice that each executive added a unique style, which gives the chapter a personal feel and particular perspective.

Special thanks also go to Mina Ito, who did much grassroots coordinating in Tokyo. And as a picture speaks a thousand words, we thank Sandrine Burtschell. Readers will notice that she supplied a lion's share of the photos.

This book is the second in a series where we use the LESCANT approach to discuss the keys of intercultural communication. After we completed the first book about Brazil, Hope LeGro and her team at Georgetown University Press encouraged us to use the same format for other countries. This is how our Japan focus began. We thank everyone at Georgetown University Press for being open to the idea of continuing the series.

Thank you, too, to all our friends and family, from London to Michigan to Texas, where we live. And of course we do not forget those who live in Japan as well. Your "Is it done yet?" helped pull us through. Here it is, and thank you!

Dawn. Kyoto. A male senior monk rakes the stones at Ryōanji, Kyoto's iconic rock garden, so the namesake dragon and its accompanying meditators can be at peace.

Dusk. Tokyo. A female middle manager clicks on a screen, so a robotic arm can lower an urn in a high-rise mausoleum to join the deceased with the visiting family.

At once ancient and hypertechnical, symbolic and actual, ritual and practical, this contrast is present in the lives of many Japanese on a daily basis. Mirroring the synergy of the dual faces of humans and nature, the Japanese regulate public behavior and prescribe communication, all the while guarding the free-flowing exchanges of intimate feelings for insiders at home, in school, and in the workplace.

As baffling as all this may seem at times to North Americans, there is no confusion about its importance. At present, Japan is the third-largest economy (after the United States and China), and on its own represents 7 percent of the world's gross domestic product.[1] Japan is the United States' fourth and Canada's fifth-largest trading partner.[2] Japan's business importance stretches across the globe, ranking third in the world (behind China and the United States) both in the service sector and in industrial output.[3] Japan is home to 129 of the world's 2,000 largest companies, including the world's largest automotive company (Toyota), convenience store chain (7-11), tire maker (Bridgestone), security service provider (Secom), and business supplies maker (Canon), as well as the top three consumer electronics companies (Sony, Panasonic, and Fujifilm) and all five of the largest trading companies (Mitsubishi Corp., Itochu, Mitsui, Marubeni, and Sumitomo Corp.).[4]

Given the importance of Japan, and its position in international trade, the purpose of this book is to provide a guide for North Americans on how to conduct business and otherwise interact culturally with their Japanese counterparts. At this point, it is important to note that while this book uses the United States and Canada as its point of comparison in discussing Japan, we hope that the book will be useful for any number of other nationalities as well. For that matter, we hope that this book may also be of value for those Japanese trying to understand North America.

To give structure and focus to our analysis, we follow what we call the "LESCANT approach."[5] LESCANT is a simple acronym that represents seven areas where intercultural communication may differ from one group of people to another; it was developed by one of our authors, David Victor, to categorize intercultural communication. These seven areas are:

- **L**anguage
- **E**nvironment and technology
- **S**ocial organization
- **C**ontexting
- **A**uthority conception
- **N**onverbal behavior
- **T**ime conception

Using the LESCANT approach in this book, we walk you through seven doors to Japanese communication. We examine Japan and the Japanese by following each of the seven letters of the acronym in successive chapters. Each chapter explores the key characteristics that define Japan and its people. Using examples that illustrate the key in question, we highlight points to remember and make recommendations for interacting with the Japanese. We hope this friendly introduction to communicating with the Japanese unlocks a few doors for you.

Chapter 1 examines the **L** of the LESCANT acronym, Language, revealing significant aspects of the Japanese language in intercultural communication. The language barrier is perhaps the most easily recognized barrier because the Japanese, of course, speak Japanese, a language that very few North Americans can speak. We start off by looking at a language that is essentially unrelated to any major language group. We then explain how the fact that Japanese is only spoken in Japan has an impact on how the world perceives the Japanese and likewise on how the Japanese view the world. English, increasingly the world's common linguistic currency, is one such instrument that the Japanese use for communicating outside Japan.

Following a general description of selective elements of the Japanese language, we point out some aspects that may confuse intercultural communicators. For example, an interesting but often frustrating aspect of Japanese grammar is that it is structured so that the verb comes at the end of a sentence, and any affirmation or negation comes even after that. Sometimes the Japanese use this native sentence structure in English, adding to the growing impression that they are being intentionally ambiguous, cryptic, or worse—hiding something.

Learning about the structure of the Japanese language thus can become a first step toward uncovering the linguistic tools the Japanese use in intercultural communication. Even something as small as this can help those who do not speak Japanese understand what is actually going on, and eventually help in their own communication with those Japanese communicators who have made the effort to speak in English (or other languages, for that matter). In this way, an understanding of the mechanics of language helps us understand how the Japanese put together their thoughts in sentences, and is therefore more than just a dictionary for content or vocabulary. It helps us understand the Japanese, and this can have a direct impact on our relationships with them.

Chapter 2 discusses the **E** of the acronym LESCANT, the Environment and technology, and their effect on Japanese society. This chapter deals with the sense of human harmonization of the human-made and the natural worlds. The Japanese word for "space" is *ma*. The character for *ma* is 間, which itself combines the characters for the *sun* 日, and a *gate* 門. The combined character, then, shows the sun filtering through a gate—which is just how the Japanese view space as their human translation of the natural environment. This notion is in contrast to the North American idea that people control the environment rather than living in harmony with it, and it is this difference that runs through this chapter, as we address the issues of the Japanese view of the environment.

In this chapter, we first examine Japan's islands and its regions, and then examine its physical environment and its impact on the Japanese population. We then discuss Japan's enormous population density. Japan, for instance, is roughly the size of California but contains more people than the entire United States west of the Mississippi River. Greater Tokyo alone has more people than all of Canada. The Shibuya crossroads in Tokyo is emblematic of just how crowded Japan is; with 73 percent of Japan's territory uninhabitable due to mountains, 873 people are squeezed into a square mile (337 per square kilometer). This is a massive contrast to the United States, which has a population of 83 per square mile (32 per square kilometer), let alone Canada's 8.8 per square mile (3.1 per square kilometer). Add earthquakes, tsunamis, and typhoons to the mix, and it is easy to see the impact that the physical environment has on Japan.

As with other urban environments, the Japanese have taken on physical challenges by building highly efficient infrastructure. High-speed bullet trains cut through mountains, subways descend five stories below cities, and buildings sway with earthquake-resistant civil engineering. A lack of natural energy sources has also had an effect on Japanese livelihood and businesses, providing evidence for how the physical environment has shaped Japanese trade and commerce.

Publicly, the Japanese manage crowded space by promoting rule conformity. Subway stations are wallpapered with public service messages that each person must obey to allow enough space for everyone. In chapter 2, we examine some of these messages aimed at influencing train station behavior, and discuss the impact of limited physical space on Japanese interaction and aesthetics.

Chapter 3 investigates the **S** of LESCANT, examining the Social organization that structures personal and professional interactions in Japan. We broadly define social organization as the common institutions and collective activities that members of a culture share. These include such areas as family, views toward work, individualism (and collectivism), religion, education, sports, the role of women in society, and how we use our leisure time. The influence of these social institutions and collective activities form the foundation on which each culture builds the behavioral norms that govern our lives, from business to education to family relationships.

Many of the variables that we examine in this book take place without our even being aware of them. In the case of social organization, we generally *are* aware of the differences with other cultures, but often are *not* aware of the implications. Perhaps because these differences are overt, it is sometimes easy for us to be condemnatory or critical when others deviate from our own system of social organization. The reality is that such matters are neither right nor wrong—just different. In this chapter, then, we begin by showing how Japan's social structure focuses on others while the North American social structure focuses on individuals. We take a look at how these two dynamics set the stage for different relationships and interactions in Japan and North America. We then explore how differing inside and outside organization permeates social structures throughout Japan. By understanding how the Japanese use back faces for insider feelings and front faces to display public ones, we explore how this dual organization is present at home, at school, and at work. With an awareness that the Japanese have and use inside and outside faces in every domain, we can see how they categorize relationships differently from the North America division between personal and professional interactions.

Following these principles of face management, we then look at an ideology that has persisted in Japan from ancient times to the present, that of *ikkaichimon*, which translates as *one house, one crest*. This symbolic image of a house united as a clan is replicated and played out in daily interactions in all areas of Japanese organization, from home to school to work. We conclude this chapter on social organization with a brief discussion of three underrepresented groups in the workforce in Japan: women, immigrants, and robots.

Chapter 4 addresses the **C** of LESCANT, **C**ontexting. Although we try throughout this book to keep away from using much technical terminology, in the case of "contexting," there is simply no good equivalent term. The great cultural researcher Edward T. Hall coined this term to describe how much of what we say or do is understood directly or implicitly by understanding the context surrounding the communication.

Hall used the term "high-context" communication to refer to cultures where we depend more on gathering information that we share in common, which then does not need to be specifically stated because it is understood. By contrast, Hall described "low-context" communication for those cultures in which we depend more on actual words or gestures, so we need to state them specifically. On the contexting scale, North American culture is on the low end of the scale. Japan, conversely, has the highest level of context of any major culture. This makes the cross-cultural gap in contexting between North Americans and Japanese among the largest anywhere.

Building on Hall's theory, one of our authors, Haru Yamada, terms the North American preference for speaker-led content and clarity in communication "speaker talk," and calls the Japanese preference for listener-led focusing on relationships and context "listener talk."[6] Because fluency in Japanese therefore involves contexting literacy, we examine the anticipatory work of listeners and then present five examples of strategies that the Japanese use in their high-context conversations: feedback, interpretation, silence, saying "no," and handy verbal expressions for daily conversation.

In short, this chapter compares the principles of North American and Japanese contexting. Adding to our knowledge base of communication content that we sometimes call "facts," this chapter examines the skill of using listener talk in Japanese, and examines what happens in the absence of such context literacy in intercultural communication.

Chapter 5 explores the **A** in LESCANT—how Authority and power are conceptualized in Japan. This topic deals with how we define power and authority, who has power, and how power is shared or exchanged. This category also brings up issues of leadership style, how decisions are made, and how titles are used to show status. Because many of the issues related to authority are culturally based, we examine how authority and power are perceived among the Japanese.

We begin this chapter with a brief look at the Japanese hierarchical authority conception, including its origins both in the influence of Confucian thought and of Japan's old feudal system. Next we discuss the notion of loyalty and the concept of *amae* interdependence that we began discussing in chapter 3, on social organization. After this, we compare and contrast concepts of power and leadership in Japanese and North American organizations. Finally, we discuss how to communicate and achieve a consensus within the framework of the Japanese hierarchical system.

Chapter 6 focuses on the **N** of LESCANT and thus dedicates itself to the many aspects of **N**onverbal communication. The way we move when we speak, how we use our eyes, how we dress, and what our various symbols mean are all part of nonverbal behavior. We begin by examining the way we use our body to communicate, ranging from almost subconscious hand gestures and head-nods to deliberate signals used in place of a verbal message, such as bowing or pointing to signal "you!" We then explore how eye contact and gaze are interpreted in North America and in Japan, followed by our expectations toward dress and general appearance. We close the chapter with a discussion of signs and symbols in Japan that differ from those in North America.

Chapter 7 explores the final key of the LESCANT categories, **T**, for the concept of **T**ime. Although we often think of time as something immutable and universal, in reality our views of time are actually shaped by our culture. We can see this most clearly when contrasting cultures such as those of Mexico, India, and Brazil, which have a relaxed view of time (called polychronic) with cultures such as those of North America, Germany, and the Netherlands, which have a fixed view of time (called monochronic). The difference between North American and Japanese views of time, however, are somewhat more subtle than most. In this chapter, we examine how the Japanese actually have both monochronic *and* polychronic time (at the same time, to pardon a pun). Although North Americans might be categorized as monochronic, viewing time serially, the Japanese are both monochronic and polychronic, for they adhere to serial deadlines but mix personal and professional times in a truly polychronic fashion.

In this way, time is a great example of Japan's context dependence, because it is impossible to understand the Japanese without understanding their conception of time. One of the easiest ways to see how Japanese people view time is again through their unique separation of public and private arenas. In public spaces, the Japanese like to see time as a finite point with fixed departure, arrival, and meeting points. However, behind closed doors—whether at home, school, or work—in *amae*-laden private spaces where love, loyalty, and interdependence run strong, time is as fluid and plentiful as Japan's sea waters. Nowhere is this more apparent than in the networking twilight hours, when junior employees spend their free time relaxing with senior employers at a dinner, bar, or golf course. *Amae* interdependence is hard at work in this nebulous space of after-work hours—time that would most likely be viewed as an infraction on the independent time required by most monochronic North Americans.

In the eighth and final chapter of this book, we provide readers with a vignette as a cultural case study that exemplifies Japanese style. In this vignette, we provide a story based on an actual Japanese–US midsized company, Up in the Clouds, that specializes in writing cloud platform software. The issues that come up in the case study exemplify many of the topics that we present throughout the book.

Following the case itself, we provide the opinions of three North American professionals who work with Japanese and three Japanese professionals who work with North Americans. Each provides their response to what they found significant in the scenario. These executives give their own views, providing another level of understanding of US–Japanese realities. Following the executive commentary, we ask questions for further consideration and finally furnish our own recommendations.

North Americans have been interacting with the Japanese since Commodore Matthew Perry opened up Japan in the mid–nineteenth century. Since then, the global forces on either side of the Pacific Ocean have engaged in international trade, wars, and trade wars, and have weathered domestic economic and social crises, some of which are still being actively fought. As North Americans and Japanese have negotiated our ups and downs together and apart, we have grown in our mutual perceptions and have developed our skills in intercultural communication. Thus, the next time you are on a golf course with a Japanese business partner or are sharing a bite to eat with local colleagues at an *izakaya* bar, we hope this book provides you with the seven keys to unlock your growing aptitude in understanding intercultural communication with the Japanese.

THE JAPANESE
Language
One Language, One Country

Language is central to communication, and this significance becomes even more key when we consider its role in intercultural communication. Here, in our first key for North Americans communicating with the Japanese, we take a selective look at the important aspects of the Japanese language as well as examining the impact of English as a global language on the Japanese.

Although Japanese is the ninth-most-widely-spoken language in the world, with roughly 125 million mother-tongue speakers, virtually all these speakers live in Japan. This is unique among the world's top ten largest languages, and an important consideration, because, when you choose to learn Japanese, it can mean that you have a real interest in Japan. This is not a given with other languages. If you learn Spanish, for instance, you may be interested in Spain or Mexico or any of the twenty countries where Spanish is a first language.

No significant population of people exists who speak Japanese as a minority language. There is no network of minority speakers in any other country, as there is with Russian and the nations of the former USSR. There is no far-flung diaspora of Japanese speakers the way there is for speakers of Hindi and Chinese.

Moreover, because Japan is an isolated set of self-contained islands, there is not even a shared border of nations among Japanese speakers, as there is for the great Indian regional languages such as Bengali (split between India and Bangladesh) and Punjabi (split between India and Pakistan). In short, the only country where Japanese is official or even widely known is Japan; and because of this, when you learn Japanese, you automatically show yourself as someone interested in Japan and only Japan. People anywhere like it when you are interested in their country in particular, and in this way, learning Japanese shows this clearly to the Japanese people.

The significance of this interest in Japanese as a language takes on even more importance when we consider how many nations still hold resentments against Japan over World War II. Although presumably this has diminished somewhat with the passage of time, large numbers of people in China, South Korea, Southeast Asia, Oceania, and elsewhere continue to hold prejudices against Japan. The Japanese themselves are understandably sensitive to this issue. It is important, then, to note that when we choose to learn Japanese, we demonstrate that we do not share in these historical prejudices. As a result, speaking even a little Japanese carries an extra positive symbolic message that, say, learning Portuguese would not carry in Brazil.

JAPANESE AS A NEAR-ORPHAN LANGUAGE

Japanese is essentially unrelated to any major language group. Most other languages belong to linguistic families, which have evolved from a common ancestor. For example, the Romance languages evolved from ancient Latin to become modern Spanish, Portuguese, French, Italian, Catalan, and Romanian. Because of this, they share many grammatical features and related vocabularies. Similar relationships exist among the members of the Slavic, Semitic, Germanic, and Turkic families, and so on.

In fact, until the twentieth century, Japanese was considered a language isolate (i.e., as having no related languages at all). Today, most linguists agree that spoken Japanese is related to the Ryukyuan languages. These eleven tiny languages are limited to a small number of speakers on Okinawa and its surrounding island chain, with a combined total of roughly 1.25 million speakers. For all intents and purposes, then, we can see Japanese as an orphan language.

The fact that Japanese is essentially unrelated to any other language is more than just an interesting piece of trivia (although it *is* that, too). Rather, this means that Japanese is difficult to learn because its structure and vocabulary have little in common with other languages. Likewise, it is difficult for Japanese speakers to learn other languages for the same reason—particularly English, with all its irregularities from having absorbed the vocabularies and grammatical structures of different languages in different periods.

ENGLISH IN JAPAN

The Japanese accept the idea that English is the lingua franca for communication outside Japan, and they are largely receptive to the idea that English is the language in which most scientific, business, and scholarly work is published. English also influences Japanese popular culture through the entertainment industry of gaming, television, movies, and music, as well as the fashion industry. Advertising frequently includes English words or phrases (which at times are comically misused) to add a cachet of brand, trend, worldliness, or even otherworldliness.

More important, for the Japanese, English is not just a means of speaking with nationals from the United States, Canada, the United Kingdom, Ireland, or Australia whose native language is English. Rather, except for Mandarin Chinese with native Mandarin Chinese speakers, English is the main means for reaching most foreigners. Whether Japanese people speak with Germans, Brazilians, or Thai people, they will tend to use English as the lingua franca.

English as a Technical Skill

Japanese generally view English as a technical skill. This is especially the case in business, government, education, and other areas where communicating with foreigners is required. As a result, the ability to speak English is a job requirement for many Japanese. English is as much of a technical skill as, say, the ability to read a spreadsheet or balance sales figures. In short, an educated person is expected to be proficient in English.

The Prestige of English Proficiency and Face-Saving

From the Japanese point of view, because English language skills are evaluated on par with other technical skills, English proficiency is not just about communication ability and clarity but also about how well qualified a person appears to be in his or her job. In short, to maintain a good profile within a company, it is important for a Japanese employee to at least appear as if he or she speaks English well, because the contrary could have negative repercussions and even hurt an employee's prospects for future promotion.

The upshot of this is that many Japanese employees become skilled at seeming as if they understand more English than they do. This subskill is encouraged by the fact that the Japanese language favors interpretation and positive *I'm listening* feedback, which we explore in further detail in chapter 4, which discusses contexting. Briefly here, head nods and vocals like *mhm* may make it seem as if the Japanese listener understands everything we are saying.

Awareness of the Japanese sensitivity to English fluency brings up another issue in a native speaker's interaction with them: No matter how poor that, say, an Anglophone Canadian engineer or auditor might be at any other technical aspect of his or her job, the one technical skill at which that Canadian *has* undisputed expertise is the technical skill of communicating in English, merely by growing up as a first-language speaker of English. This advantage can be a devastating reality for a senior Japanese professional with a lower standard of English proficiency. It is our strong recommendation that as native speakers of English, we take the prestige factor of the English language in

Japan seriously. With this new key, we can note that a seemingly amusing ice-breaker—such as "So I guess we're not going to be speaking that much English," followed by a laugh—may not be very funny to our Japanese counterpart, and could have the same impact as looking at someone's poorly drafted spreadsheet and saying, "Well, I guess not everyone is a quant." It would only produce a laugh if we knew the other person well. Most English speakers, however, are oblivious to this sort of thing.

Problems of English Proficiency

Because English is seen as vital to communicating with those outside Japan, English is a mandatory subject for all Japanese schoolchildren. Starting in the first year of junior high school, all Japanese students take six years of English. Moreover, roughly 30 percent of Japanese students actually begin studying English in grade school.

Despite this, by the time they are finishing high school, Japanese students generally have a comparatively weak control of English, especially spoken English. This is apparent through numerous surveys. For instance, among those taking the TOEIC (Test of English for International Communication), Japan ranked thirty-ninth out of forty-six countries, with a mean score of only 513 out of 990, considerably lower than neighboring South Korea (which ranked eighteenth, with a mean of 670) or China (twenty-fourth, with a mean of 632).[1]

The TOEIC is taken largely by people who are already considered somewhat proficient, for those seeking a job largely take the test. The TOEFL (Test of English as a Foreign Language), by contrast, is largely administered by schools to track English-level proficiency. But here, too, Japan consistently performs very poorly.

The TOEFL scores in Japan were consistently so bad that in 2009 the Japanese government instituted a program to address this by requiring all schools to use the TOEFL and to raise their test scores. The TOEFL scores in 2009 that led to this action ranked Japan twenty-ninth out of thirty Asian countries, with a mean score of 67 on the 120-point test, far below neighbors China, at seventy-sixth, and South Korea, at eighty-first.[2]

In the summer of 2014, after six years of concerted efforts to improve the level of English in schools, the Japanese government carried out a test at 480 randomly chosen schools among third-year high school students, the equivalent of twelfth grade in North America. The results continued to be disappointing. Using the Eiken Test in Practical English Proficiency, the survey showed poor English in all areas. The results made national news. These remarks from the *Japan Times* in March 2015, for example, were typical:

> The test . . . found that third-year high school students' English skills in listening, speaking, reading and writing were far below government targets. In each section, a majority of students scored at or below the equivalent of Grade 3 on the Eiken Test in Practical English Proficiency. The results were much lower than the government's hope of having 50 percent of high school graduates scoring at Eiken Grade 2 or pre-2, the levels above Grade 3.
>
> Students' English proficiency was especially low on the more active, productive skills of speaking and writing. On the exam, 29.2 percent of students scored zero on the writing section and 13.3 percent also scored zero on the speaking portion. That is even more disappointing considering that only 20 percent of students even took the speaking portion at all. It is doubtful that the other 80 percent of students would have performed any better.[3]

There are many theories as to why performance is so poor. One reason is that Japanese learners do not always learn from native English speakers. One of our coauthors, Haru Yamada, had an exchange student staying with her, and she asked him if British English was more difficult given that his English teacher in Japan was American. He said that the easiest English to understand was that spoken by the Japanese teacher, who also taught the program for exams, and with whom the students spent more time.

Other theories as to why the Japanese continue to have low proficiency in English include a fear of speaking based on face-saving concerns, teaching with the explicit goal of passing standardized tests, and group-based teaching, in which teachers ask questions and the class answers as a group. Whatever the cause, the reality is that the lack of English proficiency is a concern in Japan.

English Proficiency by Region

English proficiency correlates with where you are in Japan. It only makes sense that the more exposure a student has to foreigners, expatriates, and places using English, the greater his or her English ability. This has been confirmed by various studies. For instance, EF Education First, a widely respected, Swedish based language education company, found considerable variation in its 2016 EF English Proficiency Index (EF EPI) survey of English usage in Japan. On the EF EPI survey, "moderate" English proficiency is between 52.0 and 58.0, a category which Japan did not make, at 51.69. That said, English proficiency was much higher than the national average in the Kanto region, at 53.45, with the highest score in Tokyo at 54.81. By contrast, several regions of Japan fell firmly into the "low" English proficiency category—between 50.0 and 52.0. Thus Japanese in the Chugoku region scored 51.34; and in Tohoku, 50.21; and lowest of all was on the island of Hokkaido, at 49.46. In summary, though nowhere in Japan has widespread high proficiency in English, where you find yourself in the country is likely to have a considerable effect on the level of English you will encounter.[4]

JAPANESE NAMES

Japanese names follow the reverse order of names in English. Thus, one of the coauthors of this book, Haru Yamada, is actually Yamada Haru in Japanese. Yamada is her family name, and Haru is her personal name.

Almost everyone in Japan has a Japanese name, because Japan is a relatively homogeneous nation with little immigration. This means that there are many fewer family names in use than in the United States or Canada. In fact, though there are more than 1 million surnames in use in North America, Japan has only 100,000 family names. This has important implications for communicating in Japan. Because most names in Japan are much more common than *Smith* is in English, it is necessary to remember each person's complete name.

Among themselves, however, the Japanese typically distinguish between two Yamadas by referencing a relevant group that would differentiate each Yamada. There may be the Yamada of one bank or another, or one or another department within the bank. This referencing has to do with the way the Japanese manage their inside and outside groups—a categorization of social structure we discuss further in chapter 3.

Returning to the issue of the difference of frequency of family names used in North America versus Japan, to put this in perspective, let us compare the two most common family names in the United States and in Japan. Hands down, *Smith* is the most common US surname, with about 2.38 million people, or roughly 8.8 Smiths for every 1,000 people in the United States. There is a big drop to the next most common US surname, *Johnson*, with only 1.8 million or roughly, 6.88 per 1,000.[5]

Now let us look at the two most common family names in Japan, *Satō* and *Suzuki*, both with 1.99 million people, or just under 16 per 1,000 Japanese each. This means that there is almost twice the frequency of Satōs and Suzukis in Japan as of Smiths in the United States. In fact, six of the top ten family names in Japan have a higher frequency than Smith does in the United States, and all ten have a greater frequency than Johnson does:

The top ten Japanese family names

Name	Number (millions)	Frequency (per 1,000)
1. Satō (佐藤)	1.99	15.7
2. Suzuki (鈴木)	1.90	15.0
3. Takahashi (高橋)	1.47	11.6
4. Tanaka (田中)	1.34	10.6
5. Watanabe (渡辺)	1.20	9.5
6. Itō (伊藤)	1.15	9.1

7. Nakamura (中村)	1.08	8.5
8. Kobayashi (小林)	1.06	8.4
9. Yamamoto (山本)	1.02	8.1
10. Katō (加藤)	0.92	7.3

The upside of this is that even if you are unfamiliar with Japanese names, it is fairly easy to guess which name is the family name, because well over 10 percent of Japanese have one of these ten names. The downside is that it is usually inadequate to just know someone's family name. In any given meeting, there could easily be several unrelated people named Suzuki, Takahashi, or the like.

Most Japanese family names are made up of two kanji. Usually, the names are related to geographical references or nature. *Yamada* (山田), for instance, is made up of the kanji *for mountain* 山 and *rice paddy* 田.

In Japanese, as in English, personal name endings can indicate that someone is female. For example, we can usually tell an English personal name is feminine if it ends with *-elle* (as with Danielle or Gabrielle) or in *-a* (as with Carla or Roberta). In the same way, we can usually tell a personal Japanese name is feminine if it ends in *-ko*, as with Yoko; *-mi*, as with Akemi; or *-e*, as with Fumie. This last name is also a great example of a name with two vowels that follow one another in Japanese, with each one being pronounced. Fumie, then, is pronounced Fu-mi-e, and not Fumey.

In English, masculine forms of personal names are usually the stem forms of the feminine alternate, but lacking the female name's ending (e.g., Daniel vs. Danielle, or Robert vs. Roberta). Japanese men's personal names, conversely, often have their own ending. Some of the more common masculine name endings are *-rō*, as in Tarō, where Yamada Taro is the Japanese equivalent of John Doe; *-shi*, as in Tsuyoshi; *-o*, as in Hayao; and *-to*, as in Masato—as well as *-ko*, *-hiko*, as in Kazuhiko, whose male ending is easily mistakable for the female one because it contains the most typical female ending.

Although most Japanese names are associated with one gender or the other, several are not. This is the same as for names such as Kim and Leslie in English. Our coauthor's name is one such unisex name, as Haru can be a man's or woman's name. One-kanji names are unusual and are typically unisex by sound. Other common unisex names in Japanese include Kazu and Shigeru.

Japanese also has names that sound alike but are written differently. Just as the English names Shawn, Sean, and Shaun are all pronounced the same but spelled differently, so are some Japanese names. The difference here, however, is that this affects more than just pronunciation because Japanese names generally mean something. In other words, the actual meaning of the name changes when the kanji characters change. In this way, the names differ more in the way that the homonyms "bear" and "bare" change in meaning (as opposed to, say, Megan and Meaghan). Haru is one of these kinds of names. It actually has three different meanings, with three different kanji. This book's coauthor, Haru, has the kanji 晴, which means *sunny*. When Haru is written 春, it means *spring*, and when Haru is written 陽, it means *sun*. All three are unisex, but could be made female, by adding -*ko*; or made male, by adding -*o*. Thus, Haruko is a woman, and Haruo is a man.

Finally, partly because family names are common, many parents name their children with common names but personalize kanji characters to "force" them to be read in a certain way. For example, we can use the characters beautiful child 美子 and have it read Haruko.

Japanese often use characters in names, especially unusual ones, as ice-breakers in conversations. If someone asks, "How do you write your name?" the other person would show how it is written on the palm of his or her hand or reference the word in a sentence. When the kanji is disambiguated, the other person would likewise ask to reciprocate. "Oh, that's interesting, how do you write yours?"

Using Japanese Names

Although North Americans prefer to call each other by their first names, Japanese people rarely address one another by their personal names. It is extremely rare to do so in a business setting. Using your personal name in Japan is generally something you only do with your closest friends and family. In fact, it is common to be friends with people and still rarely use their personal names.

Even in a family, personal names are usually only used by older members when speaking with younger ones. Younger members typically refer to the more senior person by role. We have some examples of this in English as well. For instance, North Americans may refer to their mother as "Mom," their father as "Dad," their grandmother as "Grandma," and their grandfather as "Grandpa," rather than by their first names.

The Japanese extend calling family members by their role names to other senior family members. Thus the common practice is to call younger siblings by their given names, and older ones by their role; "older brother" is usually the diminutive, *onīchan*, for example, and likewise, "older sister" in its diminutive form is *onēchan*. In a public setting, however, everyone is referred to by role, and each family member has a deferential role name that is used in outsider interactions. For example, an older brother you would call *onīchan* at home is referred to as *ani* outside the home and as *onīsan* by a third person referring to him. An older sister, whom you call *onēchan* at home is called *ane* outside the home, and *onēsan* by a third person referring to her. In chapter 3, on social organization, we further discuss this critical insider/outsider differentiator on which Japanese base their communication.

In general, in a public setting, the use of personal names is almost entirely absent. Instead, the Japanese normally refer to others by their family name, followed by a title or honorific. For instance, the use of the honorific *-san* attaches to the end of the person's family name (e.g., Tanaka-*san*).

Many Japanese people know that North Americans feel uncomfortable using surnames and sometimes make a compromise by attaching titles and honorifics to the English first name. So if you are Japanese and have a Canadian coworker named George, you might call him George-*san*. This may be foreign in a Canadian or northern US setting, but is recognizable in the US Southeast, where you might show similar respect by referring to older women in this way, as in the title of the movie *Driving Miss Daisy*.

This is complemented by the fact that many Japanese adopt an English "first name" for use when speaking with North Americans. For example, if a man's family name is Tanaka and his personal name is Kichirō, it would appear as Tanaka Kichirō (in kanji, 田中吉郎) on the Japanese side of his business card, while on the English side of the card, it might read Kichirō "Kris" Tanaka. Kichirō has no real attachment to his English personal name, Kris. In an English-language setting in Japan itself, Kichirō's North American coworker George would call him Kris-*san*, just as he might call the American George-*san*.

In the spirit of "do as the Romans do," it would be all right for the North American to drop the honorifics altogether in an English-language setting in North America, although Kichirō might very well be unable to reciprocate, particularly if the North American counterpart is more senior. For a Japanese person, calling someone by their first name alone can sometimes have the same feel as calling a young North American man, "boy." It is for this reason that calling professors by their first names does not come easily for many Japanese.

Titles and honorifics are very important in any Japanese setting, and -*san* is just one of these. The discussion here is just to give you a taste of how they are used with names. In chapter 5, on authority conception, we discuss these in greater detail.

CHARACTERISTICS OF THE JAPANESE WRITING SYSTEM

Japanese has arguably one of the most complicated writing systems of any language anywhere. This is because Japanese uses three systems of writing at the same time. These are called *kanji*, *hiragana*, and *katakana*. To add to this, Japanese has an additional system of writing called *rōmaji* (literally Roman writing) that uses Latin letters. As a result, we can write any word in Japanese in four different ways.

Which Way Do You Read This?

To add to the complexity of Japanese, the language is not even written in the same direction consistently. There are two different directions in which Japanese can be read.

Traditionally, Japanese people read in vertical columns, going from top to bottom. These columns begin at the upper right corner of the page and are read top down from right to left. This kind of writing is called *tategaki*. For English speakers, *tategaki*, like Hebrew or Arabic, seems to go backward, especially when turning pages in print media such as in reading books, newspapers, and magazines, where the binding is on the right and the open pages are on the left.

In modern times, a second way of reading Japanese has become common. This is called *yokogaki*, which reads like English in horizontal rows that go from left to right. Although there is no hard and fast rule as to which way to write what, some types of things tend to be written vertically but others tend to be written horizontally.

Vertical writing (*tategaki*) is still the most common direction for printed material such as literature (including *manga* comics). Perhaps because vertical writing is so much older, there is a sense that using vertical writing is more traditional, formal, or literary. For this reason, most formal writing—including addressing envelopes—uses *tategaki*.

Horizontal writing (*yokogaki*), conversely, has long been used for scientific and mathematical writing because equations and formulas are customarily read horizontally. *Yokogaki* has become particularly more widespread with the advent of the computer and the internet. This is because many computer systems and languages, such as HTML, do not fully support vertical writing systems. As a result, most online writing and texting is done horizontally.

Finally, many written media combine both directions of writing. For example, newspaper headlines are usually read horizontally, while the texts of the articles are commonly read vertically. Similarly, business cards are often printed vertically on the Japanese side and horizontally on the English (or other foreign language) side. Typically, in print media such as newspapers, where there are both forms, however, the writing will still

1.1 Public Service Notice
The ad uses *yokogaki* to give it a smart, modern feel.

be read as if it went up and down—that is, with open pages on the left. When there is a choice in Japanese, it is often because *tategaki* columns can give a text an intellectual feel, whereas *yokogaki* rows can give a text a modern tone. Businesses and public service providers market their products and services with these print prestige factors in mind; see photograph 1.1.

Rōmaji: Roman letters

Japanese can be written out using the alphabet to help foreigners who cannot read any of the Japanese writing systems. Although almost all Japanese schoolchildren have been taught *rōmaji*, it is unusual for anyone to actually use the Latin alphabet aside from transliterating signs for foreigners or for inputting words for computer usage. In texts on electronic devices, there are two input modes in Japanese. One mode is the basic *kana* syllabary, which we discuss in detail just below; the other is *rōmaji*. Increasingly, the Japanese input in *rōmaji*, even if the words that are inputted appear on the screen in Japanese script.

Even when using Roman letters, however, things get complicated with Japanese. There are actually three competing systems for writing out *rōmaji*. The most common version, however, is particularly easy for English speakers. Called the Hepburn System, this version was created by a native English speaker for other English speakers, which sometimes makes it problematic for speakers of other languages. For example, a German speaker may pronounce the letter *w* as *v*, as it would be in German. Despite its shortcomings, the Hepburn System is used throughout this book.

Kanji: Japanese Characters

Characters in Japanese are called "kanji." Each kanji represents a graphic symbol of a full word, called an ideogram.

Although a writing system of ideograms may seem very foreign to a native English speaker, we do actually use a lot of ideograms in everyday life. For example, all numerals are ideograms. The numeral "5" does not spell out the word "five"; but when we see it, we know to say "five." Beyond numbers, when we see © or $ or %, we know that these symbols, respectively, mean "copyright," "dollar," and "percent," even though the actual words are not spelled out. Kanji is just like this, except that every word is an ideogram or a combination of ideograms.

The word "kanji" means "Chinese word," or, literally, "Han word," because the characters were brought to Japan in about the sixth century AD from China. The fact that kanji were superimposed on an already-spoken Japanese complicated things, creating at least two readings for each kanji—the Japanese reading, called *kunyomi*; and the Chinese reading, called *onyomi*. So, for example, the word for mountain in Japanese is *yama*, and the kanji 山 can be read as *yama* in the *kunyomi* Japanese reading but can also be read as *san* in the *onyomi* Chinese reading. The Chinese reading is typically used in kanji combinations, such as 富士山 *fujisan*, which is sometimes mistakenly called Fujiyama. Note that the *onyomi* for mountain, *san*, has nothing to do with the honorific *-san* ending that follows the family names described above.

The fact that Chinese words came to Japan in waves, in different eras, and from different regions compounded the basic difficulty that Chinese is an entirely different language family from Japanese. In tonal languages like Chinese, different tones create different words. This is unlike Japanese, which is more like English in this regard—an accent on one syllable rather than another may sound odd but does not change the meaning of the word. *Hello* more or less means hello, whether it is pronounced *HELlo, helLO, hello!* or *Hello?* Likewise, *konnichiwa* means hello in Japanese, regardless of whether the speaker places the accent on the *kon, ni, chi,* or *wa.* (A quick language learning tip: English speakers like to put the accent on the second syllable, *ni.* However, the way to sound more native is to put the accent on the last syllable, *wa.*) What all this means is that when foreigners speak Japanese, they may sound like they have a foreign accent, but they can still make themselves understood more easily in Japanese than they can in Chinese.

Chinese and Japanese were (and still are) entirely different in grammar. Because a spoken form of Japanese already existed, this meant that Chinese characters could not be adopted without modification. Chinese, for example, does not have a formal tense and aspect system (inflection) for verbs or adjectives with markers. Japanese does. To help connect the grammar, Japanese had to develop additions to the Chinese characters, and this is where *hiragana* comes in.

Hiragana and *Katakana*: Japanese Syllabaries

Hiragana and *katakana* are the two other Japanese writing systems, besides kanji. Called syllabaries, each set is like an alphabet, but with each "letter" representing a whole syllable (e.g., *ka, ki,* and *ku*). Both *hiragana* and *katakana* can be sounded out, just as we do with the alphabet in English. In both *hiragana* and *katakana,* there are forty-five possible syllables. These are made up of five possible vowels (a, i, u, e, and o) and ten consonants (although one is unpronounced). Although this actually comes to fifty combinations, three are never used (*yi, ye,* and *wu*), and two (*wi* and *we*) are obsolete. *Hiragana* is used for those parts of speech that the Chinese origins of kanji did not cover. It is also used to spell out Japanese words that either do not exist in kanji or for which the kanji may not be well known.

Finally, because even first-graders who commute to school on their own can read it, *hiragana* is used to "spell out" kanji.

1.2 Train Station Names
You can spot *Rōmaji* spelling in train station names and other signs around Japan.

Called *furigana*, many train station names have *hiragana* written beneath the kanji. Up until the 1980s, this used to be the only spelling. *Rōmaji* at train stations have made Japan more visitor friendly, but outside urban areas there are still some *hiragana*-only stations; see photograph 1.2.

    Katakana is used to spell out foreign words. In this way, *katakana* acts much the same way that writing in italics does in English. For example, the word for "ice cream" in Japanese is borrowed straight from the English—it is *aisu kuriimu* in *rōmaji*—and so is written in *katakana* (アイスクリーム).

    Katakana is also used for many company names. For example, Toyota is spelled out in *katakana* (トヨタ). Sometimes, Japanese companies will write out a borrowed word as part of their name. Thus, in Japanese, Sony Group is spelled out in *katakana* as ソニー・グループ(or, in *Rōmaji*, as Sonī Gurūpu). *Katakana* is used for newly coined words. For example, *karaoke* (カラオケ) is written in *katakana* because it was a newly invented word meaning empty (*kara*) and short for orchestra (*oke*).

    Finally, *katakana* is also used for onomatopoeia—like bang! splash sounds, animal cries, or any other phonetically described sounds. Interestingly, however, many adjectives and adverbs that might be considered onomatopoeic in English are not in Japanese. For example, *shitoshito*, the sound of a light rain, would be written in *hiragana*, rather than *katakana*, as it is seen as a grammatical part of the Japanese language.

One Last Note

Although kanji, *hiragana*, and *katakana* tend to follow the usages just described, it is often the case that all three are used in the same sentences. For instance, you use all three writing systems when you write, "I went to the karaoke":

カラオケ	に	行	きました。	
Katakana	*Hiragana*	Kanji	*Hiragana*	
Karaoke	*ni*	*i*	*kimashita.*	*Rōmaji*
Karaoke	to	go	(past tense)	English

PECULIARITIES OF JAPANESE

The Japanese sentence given above and its literal English translation give a sense of just how different the mechanics of the Japanese and English languages can be. A difference in word structures between two languages is important, because language learners often use native grammar in intercultural communication in a common language like English, and these can become the sources of many misunderstandings between communicators. Although we cannot cover all the peculiarities of the Japanese language here, we discuss four central features: word order, formality, ambiguity of meaning, and concrete conception of abstract thought.

Word Order

English word order goes subject–verb–object, and English is therefore called an SVO language. Japanese word order typically goes topic/subject–object–verb, and Japanese is therefore called an SOV language. So, in English, we would say:

The employee	*completed*	*the report.*
subject	verb	object

However, in Japanese we would say something like this:

The employee	*the report*	*completed*
topic/subject	object	verb

At first, this does not seem very significant. What is the big deal if the verb comes at the end? The difference, however, can be significant. In English, all the action is in the middle of the sentence. Indeed, after the first three words, we already know what happened. In Japanese, we have to wait until the end of the sentence to figure out the full content of the sentence. We do not know whether the employee *completed* the report or, for that matter, anything else until we have heard the very end of the sentence.

This is even more noticeable when we have a longer sentence. Consider the contrast of these two forms of the same sentence, but with one having the verb come at the end of the sentence:

Standard English SVO
The employee completed the low priority report even though he had other pressing assignments.

versus

Japanese SOV
The employee though he had other pressing assignments the low priority report **completed**.

What this means is that—unlike with native speakers of English—when speaking with native Japanese speakers, we need to listen to their entire sentences to find out whether an action has taken place. This grammatical difference is interesting in light of the fact that native English speakers often interrupt to agree or sometimes to show that they are listening. They also interrupt when they disagree and want to cut off the direction of someone else's argument. Native English speakers interrupt when they are paying close attention to show that they are following so closely that they can even finish what the other person was saying. Native English speakers interrupt for many other reasons, too, and this is because they can.

In Japanese, people do not interrupt in the same way, in part because the Japanese language does not let them. When a Japanese listener does interject a comment before the end of the sentence, it is because the speaker has intentionally paused and is inviting the listener to take a turn (we talk more about this in chapter 4, on contexting, where we discuss listener talk). We do this sometimes in English, but only in special situations. For instance, consider this exchange:

> Ann: So, in your opinion, you would say that you . . .
> [pause] . . . umm . . . [pause] . . .
> Bob: . . . disagree. That's right. In my opinion, we shouldn't do it.

In this exchange, when Ann pauses and says, "umm," she would usually nonverbally signal to Bob through hand and head movements that she expects him to jump in and finish the sentence. This is not really the typical North American spontaneous interruption. Rather, this is a guided interruption, in which Ann is more or less requesting Bob to finish her sentence. And this is exactly what the Japanese are accustomed to doing.

This difference in how we interrupt goes far beyond just the grammatical differences between Japanese and English. Indeed, it has implications even when Japanese people are speaking English. Because the Japanese are not accustomed to interrupting in their own language, it does not come naturally to them in English either. Even when Japanese people are fluent in English, interrupting seems impulsive and somewhat rude. At the same time, North Americans are likely to interpret the Japanese failure to interrupt as indicating that they are unengaged, as they have nothing to add to the conversation.

Formality

Japanese has many levels of formality. English has none. Many foreign languages that North Americans learn have *two forms* of formality. For example, in Spanish we have the "tu" (informal) and "Usted" (formal) forms. In French, these are "tu" (informal) and "vous" (formal); in German, "du" (informal) and "Sie" (formal); and so on. Japanese has *four forms* of formality. Unlike other European languages, however, these gradations in formality are not conjugations but rather a type of honorific language directed by the listener of the conversation. In Japanese, these forms are divided into a plain language, *kudaketa*; a standard polite language, *teineigo*; and a deferential language, *keigo*. *Keigo* itself is further divided into a "respectful language," *sonkeigo*; and a "humble or modest language," *kenjōgo*.

Deferential talk is based on relative rank, and is especially important in the workplace, precisely because what form to use depends on the relative rank of one person to another. Japanese people generally use standard polite language (*teineigo*) for most talk at work when dealing with those of about equal status. *Teineigo* can be used to talk about yourself or other people. By contrast, respectful language (*sonkeigo*) can only be used to talk about other people and is used to show deference to those of higher rank than you (e.g., your client, your boss, a police officer who has pulled you over while driving). You cannot use *sonkeigo* to refer to yourself. Instead, when speaking about yourself to higher-rank people, you would use *kenjōgo*, or humble language. The use of *kenjōgo* shows that whatever action you or your group has performed has been (humbly) done with the intention of serving the person with whom you are talking.

If you were a seller, for instance, you would use respectful language (*sonkeigo*) with your customer. Your customer, in turn, would usually use the somewhat-less-formal standard polite language (*teineigo*) when speaking with you. When speaking about something you did for your customer, you would use humble language (*kenjōgo*). The understood meaning is that it was your honor to get the product delivered to her on time. In this way, just through the particular language used, you as the seller can show greater respect for your customer, and your customer can acknowledge this respect in the way she answers back.

In summary, who uses what form for whom is governed by a relative rank determined by differences in age, gender, type of profession, and so on. Students use more deferential *keigo* language with their teachers, inflecting verbs that refer to the teacher with respectful *sonkeigo* and humbling verbs to refer to themselves. Likewise, *keigo* is used by younger members of any group with older members, by subordinates in a company with superiors, and by company representatives with clients. Rarely do children today use *keigo* with their parents, as they used to, and this tradition appears to be disappearing.

The Japanese use of *keigo* reflects the private language of insiders versus the public language of outsiders, which we discuss further in the remaining chapters of the book. Although the English language may have lost its honorific inflections in verbs, different ways of referencing private and public faces still remain in some nouns. For example, when speaking about our fathers, we have several words with differing levels of respect. When speaking to a formal group, you might call your own father "my father," while you might call him "my dad" when speaking to a group of friends. If you were telling a story and wanted a chatty or somewhat patronizing tone, you could even call him "my old man." In Japanese, we also have gradations of respect—from "my old man" to "my dad" and "my father," too—but these go far beyond the ways we reference our fathers in English. When a Japanese person is thinking in English, it can seem like almost everything is on the casual level of the phrase "my dad."

The Concrete Conception of Abstract Thought

By its nature, writing with characters is more concrete than writing with letters. The Japanese (like the Chinese) must show concepts through images. These images, in turn, try to capture abstract ideas in concrete terms.

First, let us define what we mean by *concrete* and *abstract*. We call *concrete* those things that we can explain through the five senses of sight, sound, touch, feel, and smell. Likewise, we call *abstract* those things that we cannot describe with the five senses.

In other words, an idea, a state of mind, or a general quality is abstract; in contrast, a book, a house, or a person is concrete.

In Japanese, it is easy to see that things that are concrete would have a character to illustrate it. For example, the kanji for tree is 木. Although it is highly stylized, we can still see the central vertical line as the tree trunk and the three lines coming off the trunk as its branches and roots. Once we know 木 is the kanji for tree, we can make sense of it in other words. For example, the Japanese for a small grove shows two trees: 林 (*hayashi*). The Japanese for a forest is three trees: 森 (*mori*). Knowing the first kanji for *ki* (tree), there is a certain logic to figure out the other two kanji, even though we may not be able to pronounce the words as *hayashi* (grove or woods) or *mori* (forest). In other words, kanji all interrelate in some way, so that we can *see* in concrete terms the relationship between the tree, the grove, and the forest in a way we cannot with English words.

This becomes even more significant when we start to look at which kanji illustrate abstract ideas in Japanese. Let us look at the kanji for the abstract idea of *thinking*.

The Japanese for (*I*) *think* is 思う *omou*. The kanji, 思, is made up of the kanji for rice paddy, 田 *ta*, and the kanji for heart, 心 *kokoro*, beneath it. The Japanese say, ". . . *to omou*," to mean, "I personally think that," which also has the sense of "My opinion is that . . ." in English. Even though most Japanese do not think of all the parts of a kanji when they are talking, the kanji they learned as children and wrote hundreds of times to memorize would have made an indelible mark in a Japanese person's latent memory. Thus because of the visual aid a kanji provides, even abstract concepts are potentially illustrated more concretely in Japanese—or at least have more built-in associations—than they are in English.

The pragmatic takeaway here is twofold. First, Japanese speakers are more likely to have specific associations with abstract ideas than English speakers—for example, the idea of thought as a personal opinion rather than an erudite or logical thought form can come from the association of the word in its written character form, a heart and a rice field. We recommend getting to know a few kanji simply to be able to be aware of these associations and to get into the mindset of the Japanese.

Second, the Japanese language probably predisposes its speakers to shared abstract concepts more than the English language does. In other words, the visual representation of kanji in the Japanese language lends itself to sample templates that speakers can conjure up together, so that almost literally, Japanese language users can be sure that they are talking about the same thing. On a larger scale, Japanese speakers use shared imagery in conversation by raising points as examples. In English, we do this by telling stories because a story instantly bonds a group. We can transfer this skill we know in English to intercultural communication with the Japanese in English by telling stories and providing specific examples. Doing so can help us to share in *the same* examples or stories the way Japanese share ideas through ideograms.

Ambiguity of Meaning

The Japanese language is at once capable of being very precise and marvelously unclear. As we have just discussed above, the use of a character-based writing system such as kanji imprints a concrete conceptualization on abstract thought. Moreover, Japan's excellence in engineering, science, and such fields leaves no doubt that the Japanese language has the capacity for clarity. However, one of the frequent complaints from foreigners about Japanese is that the language is ambiguous.

Japanese ambiguity derives from several sources. First, Japanese does not have articles (e.g., *a*, *an*, or *the*). In English, articles change the meaning of nouns. If you say "I am going *to dinner*," it just means that you are about to eat your evening meal. This is a big difference from saying "I am going to *a* dinner." By using the article *a* in this instance, you have indicated that you are going to some sort of event that includes a meal. You add an even more specific meaning by saying, "I am going to *the* dinner." Using the definite article *the* in this instance indicates that this dinner event is a specific event and suggests that the person listening to you already knows about that event.

Articles that communicate very different meanings in English are absent in Japanese. Consequently, we need to interpret those same shades of meaning provided by articles in English in Japanese through other means. For example, a Japanese person might distinguish between going to any old dinner and an event by using the word *event*: I am going to the event. More problematically, however, sometimes when the Japanese are speaking English, early learners often leave off the determiners in English, thus creating the potential for miscommunication.

Second, Japanese does not usually have the same sense of pluralization that English does. Instead, most plurals are like the word "deer" in English (e.g., one deer or two deer). In Japanese, the sentence *Jūgyōin wa kaisha ni konakatta* (従業員は会社に来なかった) can mean any of the following:

- The employees did not come to work.
- The employee did not come to work.
- Employees did not come to work.
- An employee did not come to work.

In intercultural communication, not knowing whether there are one or more employees and whether we are referring to a general employee or a particular one can create a minefield of misunderstandings. Consider, for example, cases where the engineer is completing a project, or a salesperson is contacting potential buyers. Take away the definite article or change the singular person to plural, and we are communicating entirely different scenarios.

Finally, Japanese does not have the same concept as the English language of a complete sentence. This means that you can leave whole words out of a sentence and still be speaking in proper Japanese. Indeed, Japanese regularly leave out subjects in sentences. This is particularly the case with pronouns. Japanese rarely use "I" or "you," even though there are many pronouns for them. Using pronouns often emphasizes the referent, and using *anata* for the pronoun "you" has a generally aggressive ring to it. This is true to a lesser degree with *kare* for the pronoun "he" and *kanojo* for the pronoun "she," which can also be used, respectively, as "boyfriend" and "girlfriend."

There is no common pronoun in Japanese equivalent to the English "it."

To illustrate how this works, let us say that Jon, a North American business colleague of Kenji Watanabe, walks into a conference room expecting to find a signed document for which Kenji was responsible on the table. When it is not there, Jon could ask Kenji where it is. The North American English version might sound something like "Kenji, where's the signed document?" said in a friendly tone. In Japanese word order, this would be something like, "Documents are where, Kenji?"

In Japanese, however, the transliteration "*Shorui wa doko desu ka Watanabe-san*" has a harsh, if slightly accusatory, ring to it. So rather than name him directly, Jon might look toward Kenji, ask "Documents are where?" and drop the subject. But in Japanese, even this question can still sound overly critical; so Jon could take it a notch down by looking at the table, acting surprised, and asking "Ah, Where?" Kenji will surely know what was expected of him. However, if Jon really wanted to act Japanese, he might not even stop here. Perhaps Jon and Kenji have been working together for a long time and would like to carry on having a convivial and professional relationship. If Jon were Japanese, then, he would likely look at the empty table and make a facial expression of surprise and vexation, perhaps vocalizing an accompanying "Ah," with a head-nod. Kenji would still know what Jon meant, even if he had not actually said a single word.

Lacks of plurals, articles, and complete sentences are only some of the ways that the Japanese language can invite interpretation through ambiguity. Later in this book (see chapter 4, on contexting), we discuss this context of nontalk in more detail. For here, however, let us begin with the notion that Japanese speakers use ambiguity to soften the impact and to avoid making others lose face (or to avoid losing face yourself).

RECOMMENDATIONS

As related to language issues in intercultural communication with Japanese people, we offer the following recommendations.

General Strategies for Communication

If you find yourself speaking English with Japanese people, there are a number of things that you can do to facilitate their understanding of the conversation.

First, stay away from slang and try to avoid idioms. Most Japanese will not understand many of these expressions. There are exceptions, however, such as the shared sport of baseball. Whereas most people from outside North America have no concept of baseball, the sport is very popular in Japan. Other sports terms—such as "going the whole nine yards" or calling something a "slam dunk"—will likely draw confused stares. Similarly, references to classic television series and other pop culture references are often difficult for Japanese people to follow.

Second, speak slowly, articulate, and avoid contractions. As native speakers, we do not realize how fast we talk or the number of shortcuts we take when we speak. From textbook and language classroom practice, an average Japanese speaker of English might be expecting to hear, for example, "I do not know. What do you think?" Instead, we are likely to say something along the lines of "I dunno. Whatcha think?" You can make things easier on any second-language speaker if you slow down.

Third, request feedback on what you are saying. Because Japanese in businesses, universities, and many other settings are expected to speak English well, it is rare for someone to volunteer that he or she does not actually follow what you are saying. Asking "Do you understand?" generally will not help because, to save face, the likely response will almost always be a "yes," whether anyone understood or not. Asking a yes/no question will result almost invariably in a yes, which does not give any real insight into the Japanese counterpart's understanding. So instead of asking, "Do you understand how to complete the project," asking "What steps will you take to complete the project?" will likely allow for a stronger verification as to whether what was said had been understood.

Fourth, often rephrase what you are saying. Because Japanese has almost no cognates with English, you never know what vocabulary the individual Japanese person has already acquired when you speak with him or her. So, when you *rephrase* what you are saying *as you speak,* you give your Japanese counter-parts the chance to latch onto a word they *do* understand, even if they missed a word here or there. In short, repeating things by using different ways of saying the same thing is often helpful. Because most Japanese read English better than they speak it, it is also helpful to give written support—which can consist of slides during a presentation or an e-mail of main subjects sent in advance of a meeting.

Japanese Difficulties in English

When listening to Japanese people speaking English, there are also a few things that will help in understanding them. First, avoid phrasal verbs. A phrasal verb is when we combine verbs and prepositions to form a new idiomatic expression, such as "put out," "put off," or "put on." All use the same verb "to put," but the combination of different prepositions make it difficult for many nonnative speakers of English to understand, includ-ing the Japanese. In speaking, the Japanese are likely to use a synonym such as *extinguish* instead of *put out.* However, in some cases, there may be a random use of the second word in a phrasal verb. A Japanese person may well not have the subtleties to dis-tinguish between reading *into, over,* or *through,* or just simply reading an e-mail, and say one when they actually mean another.

Second, the Japanese have no equivalent sound for the "r" sound in English, and consequently they use a sound that sounds closer to that of "dd" (as in "teddy") in English instead. Japanese *hear* the difference when a native English speaker pronounces it; but because the distinction does not exist in Japanese, they have difficulty producing it. Thus, a Japanese person can hear the difference between the names *Larry* and *Raleigh;* but when they try to say them, they come out sounding alike to an English speaker.

Finally, Japanese does not have diphthongs—that is, the two gliding vowel sounds, like the *oy* sound in *boy*—that English has. Instead, it has five single vowel sounds that are each pronounced as one syllable. In the case of repeating the same vowel sound, the Hepburn System romanization used here represents this with a bar over the top of the vowel, such as the ō and ū in Tōkyū.

(Some Japanese names, like Tokyo, are actually pronounced Tōkyō, but we have written it here without the bars over the vowels, as they have become absorbed into the English dictionary.) In Japanese, each vowel sound is a syllable, so even if there are two vowel sounds combined, as in the name Kaori, each syllable is produced separately, pronouncing the name as Ka-o-ri rather than interjecting an English diphthong and producing the name Kayori or Kawori. Likewise, the nine diphthongs present in English but absent in Japanese can also challenge the Japanese person pronouncing English. Because the Japanese speaking English tend to pronounce both vowel sounds with equal emphasis, a word with a diphthong, like *boy*, often ends up coming out sounding like *boh-ee*, which would be written in *rōmaji* as *bōi*.

Our recommendation is that if a person is going to work with the Japanese for any length of time, it is in his or her interest to try to learn to speak Japanese. The insights into Japanese thought that come from an understanding of the language are simply not available to those who never learn it. Despite the fact that English is the language of international business throughout much of Japan, your Japanese language skills will also be useful in many contexts that may appear to be outside the workplace but, as we discuss in later chapters, will echo back into your professional relationships, far beyond what you may have initially imagined.

SUMMARY OF THE JAPANESE LANGUAGE

What We Know about the Japanese Language

- Japanese is spoken only in Japan, making the language and the culture more closely aligned than languages such as English, Spanish, and French that are spoken across many cultures.
- Japanese people view English as a world language, yet Japanese fluency in English is lower than in many countries with a comparable economic impact.
- Japanese English learning focuses more on reading than on speaking; as a result, many Japanese have difficulty holding a conversation and Japanese accents are often significant barriers, even when the speaker understands English.

Japanese Names and Titles

- Japanese names go in reverse order from English names (i.e., the family name comes first).
- Japanese family names are much less diverse than North American surnames, with much larger numbers of people sharing the same family name.
- There are many more titles in Japanese than in English, and the titles are less likely to be dropped.
- Personal names are used much less in Japan than in North America.
- Titles follow the name in Japanese (the opposite of English).

Written Japanese

- Japanese has four separate writing systems: kanji (characters), *katakana, hiragana,* and *rōmaji* (Latin letters).
- Written Japanese does not follow a consistent direction—it can read in vertical columns, going from top to bottom and right to left; and it can read in horizontal rows, from left to right (like English).

Japanese Language Features

- Four levels of formality exist in Japanese.
- Japanese is a back-loaded language, with verbs coming at the end of the sentence.
- No concept of a complete sentence exists in Japanese, allowing for greater word deletion and indirection than in English.

Recommendations

- Ask for feedback to ensure that communication has taken place.
- Speak slowly rather than loudly.
- Rephrase what you are saying as you speak.
- Expect Japanese people to read English better than they speak it; back up your spoken words with writing.

2

THE JAPANESE
Environment
Ma 間 the Human Translation
of Natural Space

This chapter is about how the environment shapes human spaces in Japan. The Japanese kanji character for *space* is *ma* 間, composed of a natural element, with the kanji character for day or sun, *hi* 日, filtering in through a gate or *mon* 門. The character, 間 *ma*, then, as a gated sun, captures how the Japanese view space as their human translation of the natural environment (see photograph 2.1).

We begin this chapter on the environment with an introduction to Japan's islands and regions. We then take a look at how the natural elements of Japan's mountains, seas, and natural energy sources influence its people, as well as spaces in urban centers. We end by considering what happens to a population in the absence of space, and discuss how the Japanese have risen to this challenge through crowd control and a definition of public manners.

2.1 Gated Sun
It is as if the character *ma* was drawn after seeing the sun stream through this house gate. Photo courtesy of Sandrine Burtschell.

THE JAPANESE ISLANDS

Bigger than it is popularly seen, Japan, at 226,480 square miles, sits at number sixty-three in global country size ranking, notably slightly larger in landmass than Germany, the United Kingdom, and South Korea. However, the 1,864-mile long, crescent-shaped arc of Japan's four main islands (Honshū, Kyūshu, Shikoku, and Hokkaidō) plus 6,852 smaller islands only amounts to a country—as you can see from figure 2.1—roughly the size of the state of California. From a North American perspective then, it is probably fair to call Japan small.

JAPAN'S MAIN REGIONS

As figure 2.2 illustrates, the four main islands of Japan are Honshū, Hokkaidō, Shikoku, and Kyūshū. The largest Japanese

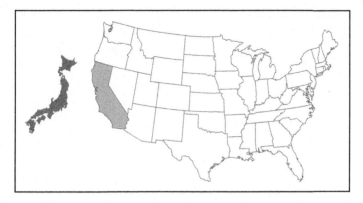

Figure 2.1
Map of Japan in Comparison with the United States

island is Honshū, at the center, with Hokkaidō to its north and the smallest main island, Shikoku, to its southwest. The southernmost island is Kyūshū, which extends to a far-flung string of tiny islands called the Ryūkyūs. Once a separate country, the archipelago ends with Okinawa, its largest member.

Japan is divided into eight main regions where the three islands of Hokkaidō, Shikoku, and Kyūshū count as their own region, and the largest middle island of Honshū is divided into Kantō, Chūbu, Kansai, Tōhoku, and Chūgoku. Here we briefly introduce each region.

Kantō

Kantō, literally translated as "Gate East," lies in the belly of the main Honshū Island. Kantō is the country's most populous and industrial region, serving as both Japan's political and financial capital. Made up of the Tokyo metropolis and six other prefectures, the entire Kantō region has 42.97 million people, of which the greater Tokyo metropolitan area makes up 37.8 million, including the two largest cities, Tokyo and Yokohama, as well as Kawasaki City, Chiba, and Saitama, among others. Not all of the Kantō region falls into this great conurbation, however, as there are 5.17 million people living beyond the Tokyo metropolitan area in such cities as Mito, Maebashi, and Utsunomiya.

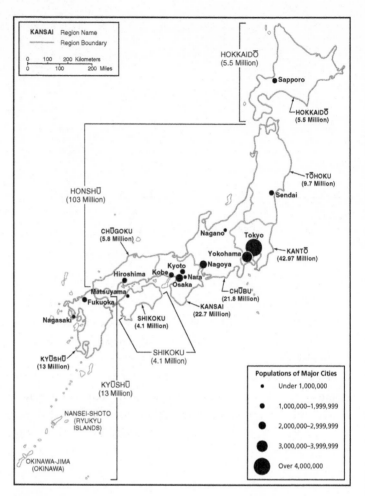

Figure 2.2
Map of Japan's Regions

Kansai

Kansai, literally translated as "Gate West," is often thought of as western Japan, although much of southern Japan lies even farther to its west. The region consists of six prefectures and is the center of Japan's aerospace industry, with considerable economic involvement in pharmaceuticals, electronics, and metal processing.

Tourism is a major industry as well, because Kyoto, in Kansai, was for centuries the traditional capital of Japan during a time when noble court life flourished. This history has forever influenced the city's character. Indeed, with its castles, temples, and shrines, the two kanji characters of Kyoto mean *capital*, making the city a notable example of how humankind can also make a mark on its environment.

Nara, another city in the region, was itself the earliest capital of Japan. Kyoto, along with the other two great Kansai port cities, Osaka and Kōbe, form the Keihanshin metropolitan area. Of Kansai's 22.7 million people, 18.6 million live in the Keihanshin. Other cities include Ōtsu, Wayakama, and Nara.

Chūbu

Located between the Kantō and Kansai regions is the central department of Chūbu. The region is heavily mountainous, with the Japanese Alps dividing what is known as Japan's front in Kantō from its back in Kansai. This divide initiated by the environment is central to understanding Japanese social organization, which we discuss in chapter 3. The Japanese Alps are home to Nagano, made famous by the 1998 Winter Olympics held there.

Chūbu has nine prefectures and 21.8 million people. Of these, 8.75 million live in the Chūkyō metropolitan area centered on Nagoya, the heart of Japan's automotive industry, sometimes referred to as "Japan's Detroit." By Japanese standards, the Chūkyō metropolitan area is a midsized urban center, and it is often overlooked by those in greater Tokyo in the Keihanshin.

By North American standards, however, the Chūkyō metropolitan area is far larger than Toronto, which, at 5.8 million people, is Canada's largest urban area. Likewise, if the Chūkyō metropolitan area were in the United States, it would be its fourth-largest urban area, falling somewhere between Chicago (9.5 million) and Houston (6.3 million). Chūbu's main cities besides Nagoya and Nagano include Niigata, Shizuoka, Toyama, and Kanazawa. Each of these cities has a distinct character that is colored by its proximity to the Japanese Alps, to the eastern region of Kantō, or to the western region of Kansai.

Tōhoku

The northeastern part of Honshu is Tōhoku, which means "Northeast." Tōhoku was the site of the 2011 earthquake and tsunami that devastated the area. There are six prefectures in the region, with 9.7 million people. Sendai, with 1 million people, is the region's largest city.

Hokkaidō

Japan's northernmost region is Hokkaidō. It consists of only one prefecture. Although the island of Hokkaidō is the second largest in Japan, it is sparsely populated by Japanese standards. The entire region has only 5.5 million people. Still, to put this in perspective, this is more than the US state of Minnesota (5.3 million) and far greater than the Canadian province of British Columbia (4.4 million). Hokkaidō's largest city, with 1.9 million people, is Sapporo.

Hokkaidō, unprotected from the jet streams south of the island, is very cold in the winter, a fact made famous by the 1972 Winter Olympics held there. Hokkaidō, unlike much of Japan, has a strong agricultural sector, with economic ties to breweries and tourism, such as the ski resorts we discuss later in this chapter.

Shikoku

Japan's smallest island is also its least populous region, with just 4.1 million people spread over four prefectures. Its largest city, Matsuyama, has just over half a million people. Like Hokkaidō, Shikoku relies heavily on agricultural output, and its economy is based on food processing and tractor equipment. Notably, Shikoku is the only main island of Japan that does not have volcanoes.

Chūgoku

To the southwest of Honshū is the region of Chūgoku. It has 5.8 million people, which is just slightly more than Hokkaido, and spreads over five prefectures. Of these, 1.1 million live in its largest city, Hiroshima. Although the city may have the notoriety as the site of the first atomic bomb attack in World War II, today it is a vibrant and important cultural industrial center. Central to Chūgoku are its automotive, steel, chemical, and electronics manufacturing industries. It is also rich in history, with such famous sites as Okayama Castle and the Shinto Shrine UNESCO World Heritage site, Itsukushima.

In Japanese, Chūgoku 中国 has the same kanji and pronunciation as the country of China, and to avoid confusion, the Japanese often refer to this area as two parts—the Sanyō, or the "sunny" Seto Inland Sea side of the mountain, and the Sanin, the "shaded" side facing the Sea of Japan. The kanji characters *yō* 陽 and *in* 陰 in the names Sanyō 山陽 and Sanin 山陰 represent the "sunny" and "shaded" sides of the region, and are the same kanji characters as the Taoist concept of yin 陰 and yang 陽. Because the kanji character *san* 山 means mountain, Sanyō and Sanin can be transliterated as Sunny Mountain and Shaded Mountain, respectively, providing an excellent example of how the mountainous environment is integrated into the Japanese conception of regions.

Kyūshū

Kyūshū means "nine provinces," although there are actually only seven prefectures, plus Okinawa in the Ryūkyū chain. This southernmost region of Japan has a subtropical climate that is noticeably warmer than most of the rest of the country. The region has more than 13 million people, with only 1.4 million living in the largest city, Fukuoka. Nagasaki is notable as the site of the second and largest atomic bomb attack during World War II. Other major cities include Kumamoto, Kagoshima, Nagasaki, Ōita, and Naha in Okinawa.

The economy of Kyūshū is divided between heavy industries—such as automobiles, porcelain, and chemicals—in the north, and agriculture and tourism in the south. Okinawa is heavily dependent on the US military facilities there, which are often a controversial subject.

JAPAN'S MOUNTAINS

Earlier in the chapter, we talked about Japan's small landmass, and this is exaggerated by the fact that 73 percent of its four main islands are made up of mountains. With a population of more than 127 million and inhabitable space of a mere 20 percent, Japan squeezes roughly 900 people into a square mile.[1] Compared with the United States, which has about ten times fewer people per square mile, or Canada, with even a hundred times fewer people than Japan—Japan can feel packed indeed. This will seem particularly the case for professionals who visit cities, like the two main Japanese hubs of Tokyo in eastern Kantō and Osaka in western Kansai.

If the mountains have played a substantial role in creating the east/west Kantō/Kansai regional divide, they have also inadvertently spurred a rivalry. Although the Tōkaido bullet train that runs between Tokyo and Shin Osaka has transformed the laborious 320-mile trade route that wove around the Japanese Alps' three mountain ranges of Hida (northern), Kiso (central), and Akaishi (southern) into a ride of less than four hours, it has done nothing to take away the fierce pride and prejudices about each region's accents, stereotypes, and customs. For example, Tokyoites will tell you that Osakans are a gregarious and outgoing lot with many comedians, if loud and somewhat overly commercial. Conversely, Osakans will volunteer that Tokyoites can be both mainstream and trendy, but no doubt arrogant and cold, too. And both Osakans and Tokyoites view people from Kyoto as cultured but as sometimes believing themselves to be superior.

The Kantō/Kansai rivalry extends to culinary preferences. Some foods are associated with Kansai, such as udon noodles and *okonomiyaki* omelets; while others, such as soba buckwheat noodles and sushi, are fought over as Kantō foods. As with other culinary battles, however, ultimately it may be the cities that go to the frontlines, such as the Hiroshima/Osaka battle for the best *okonomiyaki*, or the Kyoto/Tokyo battle about subtle flavors (read, imperial court–influenced Kyoto) versus strong, salty gauche tastes (read, downtown *shitamachi* Tokyo).

Today, the mountains that played a role in creating the Kantō/Kansai regional division even influence public transportation etiquette in modern cities. For example, Tokyoites stand on the left of an escalator, and Osakans, on the right. A popular bit of Tokyo folklore is that this difference arose because Kantō samurai wore their swords on their left hip, whereas Osaka merchants kept their money on their right. Viewed as people who do not make anything, merchants were traditionally lowest on the vocational rung in the Edo Period, where samurai came first, farmers next, then artisans, and finally, merchants. We discuss this hierarchical ordering later in chapter 5, on authority conception.

In short, regional identities reflect divides that originated in part from an environmentally inspired separation. We have friends who will say they think of themselves as Osakans before they think of themselves as Japanese. The environment, and notably the mountains, have not only made a deep mark on Japanese national character but also on Japanese regional identities.

The best-known Japanese mountain is the iconic Mount Fuji. Measuring 3,776 meters (12,388 feet), it is also Japan's tallest mountain. It is sacred, as are all mountains in Japan, and many make the pilgrimage to climb it, most often beginning two-thirds of the way up at the fifth station. The mountain is officially open to climbers during the months of July and August, and it receives about half a million climbers every summer. For most Japanese who admire Mount Fuji from Tokyo, the sight of the snow-capped peak on a clear day is like an image of a woodblock print floating in the horizon beyond the building-cluttered city. Since 2013, Mount Fuji has been a UNESCO World Heritage site.

If sacred, mountains in Japan are also common and part of daily life. The sheer number of Japanese family names that contain the character for mountain 山 *yama* show this, for example, Yamamura (mountain village), Yamashita (mountain foothills), and Yamazaki (mountain on a small peninsula). Indeed, for the older Japanese generation, mountains conjure up nostalgic scenes of rice paddies and crows on electricity lines featured and recreated by the likes of the film director Hayao Miyazaki for the younger generation to remember. Mountain resorts like Hakuba and Karuizawa have become holiday and retirement destinations. In stark contrast to overpopulated cities, these resort towns and outlying regions of Japan are sparsely populated, particularly off season. That Japan is crowded requires qualification; it is crowded in the urban centers but only sparingly populated in the outlying regional towns.

The population drain to the urban centers remains a concern in Japan, addressed only by campaigns to take a vacation in nonurban areas. The northern island of Hokkaido has had successful tourism in the boom seasons of spring and winter, using ski resorts like Niseko and Furano to draw international visitors from Australia and China as well as young Japanese professionals and families. Old hot spring spa towns with the alpine snow monkeys of Gunma and Nagano prefectures are making an effort to draw multigenerational families as well. Here vacationers can find new options for dining, shopping, skiing, and playing golf or tennis. Mountains, a permanent fixture in the Japanese environment, have a direct influence on lifestyle, recreation, and the business of active tourism in the twenty-first century.

Yet if mountains are part of the beauty of the Japanese physical environment, they are also the source of natural calamities. For example, 186 miles from Tokyo lies the Boso Triple Junction, the only example of a triple trench junction of tectonic plates on Earth. The Boso Triple Junction is the meeting point of the North American Plate to the north, the Pacific Plate to the east, and the Philippine Sea Plate to the south. Owing to its proximity to extensive urban development, this junction has the highest associated insurance risk in the world.

This brings us to the earthquake that generated the Tohoku Tsunami. Say "earthquake," and for many of us, the live digital feed of the March 11, 2011, tsunami that came pouring through our phones is still a vivid memory. This 9.0 earthquake was generated along the Japan trench to the north of the Boso Triple Junction. With approximately $105 billion (¥11 trillion[2]) in reconstruction costs, the 2011 Tohoku disaster is likely to go down as one of world history's costliest natural disasters.

As a catastrophic consequence of the Tohoku Earthquake and Tsunami, the Level 7 meltdown at the three reactors of the Fukushima Daiichi nuclear complex has led to changes in safety and design standards of nuclear power plants to complement the earthquake-resistant structures that are already in place. Civil engineers in the earthquake-prone areas of the Pacific Ring of Fire between Japan and the West Coast of North America are developing new hydraulic and fluid-based systems to improve earthquake-resistant buildings. The 2011 Tohoku Earthquake is an example of how the environment can destroy human-made constructions but also force innovation for the better.

Japan may not have the tallest mountains, but it does hold the record for seismicity. Sixty of the 200 or so volcanoes in Japan are active. To put this in perspective, only 60 active volcanoes exist in the entire United States, and most of these are in Alaska or Hawaii. Canada has only 21 active volcanoes.

Moreover, though volcanoes in Canada and the United States are for the most part in isolated areas, Japanese volcanoes are often found right near populous towns. Like Pompeii in ancient Rome, villages like Tsumagoimura that were built too close to volcanoes have been covered in lava. When Mount Asama erupted in 2009, the entire neighboring resort town of Karuizawa was blanketed in powder and the ash cloud extended 90 miles to Tokyo.

Despite these natural disasters, the Japanese continue to love and live alongside the volcanoes they call "fire mountains," 火山 kazan. Tsumagoimura is now a tourist spot called Onioshidashi, or "the Place the Demons Pushed Out." Children run around the hardened lava rocks and take pictures alongside statues of mischievous demons that allegedly destroyed the village in 1783. Long featured in Japanese art, poetry, and folklore, an old Japanese saying about things to fear, in order of scariness, perhaps sums up just how integral the environment is in Japanese life: "*Jishin, kaminari, oyaji.*" Earthquake, thunder, then Dad!

WATER BOUNDARIES

Somewhere in the perception that Japan is small is also the view that it is set apart. Japan is set away from mainland China and neighboring South Korea and North Korea on its west coast by the Japan Sea, or what the South Koreans call the East Sea.

The phenomenon of calling the same sea by different names is not unique to East Asian bodies of water. For example, the British call the water that sets the United Kingdom apart from the continent the English Channel, whereas the French call it La Manche (The Sleeve). These different names show how the same body of water represents different things to different people. Today, many water boundaries are contested, illustrating how difficult it is to claim ownership of a body of water. From an environmental perspective, rather than a political one, however, if mountains define boundaries, seas also serve to do so.

Traditional Western history makes a case for how far east Japan can get. The years 1633–1853, before Commodore Matthew Perry opened up Japan, were commonly referred to as *sakoku*—sometimes sensationally translated as "chained country." Contemporary works now acknowledge that the policies in place were maritime prohibitions called *kaikin*, not dissimilar from other nations' isolationist policies. Notably, limited trade did exist during this period on Japan's western coast and outlying western islands. The Japanese traded with the Chinese, Koreans, and, exclusively among non-Asians, the Dutch, on Dejima or Exit Island, an artificial island set up for trade off the coast of Nagasaki. The then–ruling Tokugawa Shogunate, which enforced the maritime policy, was based in Tokyo, then called Edo, and found it challenging to control from the east what went on in western seas.

Owing to the Kantō/Kansai rivalry rooted in these times (which is discussed above), Japan founded its international shipping ports in Tokyo and Yokohama in eastern Kantō, and Osaka and Kōbe in western Kansai. However, accounting for about 10 percent of all Japan's shipping is the country's largest port, Nagoya, which is between Kantō and Kansai in the region called Chūbu or Central (discussed above). The great majority of Toyota's cars leave Japan from Nagoya.

If the sea controls Japan's international water traffic, rivers do so nationally. Linking sea and land, marketplaces grew up around them. The famous fish market, Tsukiji, built on land reclaimed in the eighteenth century from Tokyo's most famous river, the Sumida, is still in operation today (see photograph 2.2).

2.2 Tsukiji Fish Market
Fresh sashimi at Tsukiji Fish Market. Photo courtesy of Sandrine Burtschell.

The Sumida River that runs through Tokyo was made famous by Hokusai's and Hiroshige's woodblock prints and by Bashō's haiku poetry. Once again, this is an example of the environment making its mark not only in trade and commerce but also in the deep collective consciousness of the Japanese.

Before farming came to Japan from China, Japan looked to its rivers and seas for its main food source. In spite of this and its popular image as a sushi-diet nation, Japan is no longer number one in fish consumption, having fallen to fourth, behind Iceland, South Korea, and Malaysia.[3] However, the average Japanese person still eats more than twice as much fish as the average North American, and there is no doubt that the country's seas and connecting waterways have something to do with this.

Unlike the United States and Canada, Japan is not self-sufficient in food. After years of efforts to improve its degree of self-sufficiency, it still remains at 39 percent. This means that without trade, Japan would probably starve.[4] If asked why Japan went to war in World War II, many older-generation Japanese say it was because of the American trade embargo: "We would have starved to death." Because both the United States and Canada produce far more food than they can consume, the idea that trade is necessary just to feed one's citizens can seem foreign from a North American perspective.

Finally, though water can have the destructive force of a tsunami, it can also be an energy source. Dams that produce hydroelectricity are Japan's top provider of renewable energy. Hydroelectricity provided one-third of Japan's energy source until the 1950s, when energy demand mushroomed, and the country doubled its energy consumption every five years until the 1990s. Due to its paucity of natural resources, Japan now relies mostly on imported fossil fuels, the next topic of our discussion.

ENVIRONMENTAL RESPONSIBILITY

Japan is the world's leading importer of both exhaustible and renewable natural resources, and one of the largest consumers of fossil fuels. Japan now ranks second globally, after China and before the United States, in net imports of fossil fuels, following the decision to shut down all nuclear reactors after the breakdown of Fukushima Daiichi in 2011 following the great Tohoku Earthquake and Tsunami. Here is an example of how environmental disasters have had direct and costly consequences for Japan.

Oil is Japan's primary source of energy, although recently it has accounted for half of what it did in the 1970s in total share of energy consumption. Crude oil is imported from the Middle East, and suppliers of natural gas and coal come from closer neighbors in Southeast Asia.

Japan drew one-third of its electric production from nuclear power plants; however, most of this was shifted to coal after the nuclear accident at the Fukushima Daiichi power plant and the closure of all Japanese nuclear plants. Despite protests against nuclear energy, with few alternatives, the public generally accepts the idea of reopening the plants, provided they adhere to more stringent safety regulations.

Nuclear energy as a power source can help Japan reduce its carbon footprint. Currently, Japan produces just 10 percent of its energy from renewable sources. The country hopes to double this proportion by 2020. Indeed, Japan is among the top three producers of photovoltaic or converted solar energy (together with China and Germany), and it outranks the United States and Australia.

Japan, however, is also the world's fifth-largest emitter of greenhouse gases. Adding to energy waste, Japan burns close to two-thirds of its waste in municipal and industrial incinerators. However, with new parks—such as Sea Forest, or Umi no Mori, which is transforming a landfill into 1,000 hectares (10 million square meters) of green space and increasing roadside trees by a million—it seems that Japan is committed to improving its energy waste disposal practices and increasing its global environmental responsibility.

In sum, mountains, seas, and rivers are parts of the natural environment that create a way of life and form the heartbeat of Japan. Its lack of natural energy sources has had an effect on Japan's livelihood and business, providing evidence for how the physical environment has shaped the country's trade and commerce, establishing in particular its two-hub economy in Kantō and Kansai. Next, we examine what happens when we take nearly all its working population and place it in the human-made spaces of urban centers.

URBAN SPACES: THE ZEN OF CROWDED LIVING AND WORKING

Like many other nations, Japan, with 127 million people, incentivized its population to live and work in urban centers. This economized infrastructure has resulted in 91 percent of Japan's population living in cities, compared with 82 percent of Canadian and 83 percent of US populations that live in urban areas.

As noted earlier in this chapter, the great megalopolis of the Kantō region centering on Tokyo is the world's largest metropolitan area, with 37.8 million people (of whom 13.3 live within the city limits of Tokyo itself). To put this in perspective, the entire nation of Canada has only 35.2 million people. Likewise, the two

2.3 Crowded Train
Just another day on the train in Tokyo. Photo courtesy of Eikzilla.

largest US metropolitan area populations are greater New York City (20.9 million) and greater Los Angeles (13.3 million), which together have 34.2 million, still 3.2 million less than the Tokyo metropolitan area's population. This great conurbation spreads out from Tokyo across the Kantō region to Yokohama (which, at 3.7 million people, is Japan's second-largest city in its own right), Kawasaki City, Sagamihara, Chiba, and more.

Add the western Kansai cities of Osaka, Nagoya, Kyoto, and Kōbe of some 18.6 million to the Kanto megalopolis's 37.8 million, and this figure reaches 56.4 million.[5] With this in mind, it is easy to see how the Kantō and Kansai regions have disproportionately high concentrations of the Japanese population.

Tokyo is usually the first—and often the only—stop for the majority of North American visitors to Japan. The population density they feel at the iconic Shibuya crossroads featured in films like *Lost in Translation* is an example of just how crowded a Japanese urban center can feel. Subway pushers, long lines to get on bullet trains during the peak summer Obon Festival travel season, and standstill traffic snaking along highways to get out of Tokyo all serve to confirm that Japan's urban centers are very congested (see photograph 2.3).

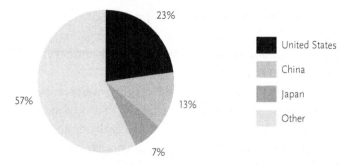

23%

United States

China

Japan

Other

57%

13%

7%

Figure 2.3
The World's Largest Economies, by Nominal Gross Domestic Product, 2015

A limited landmass and a large population create the need for strong and efficient infrastructure and well-orchestrated social organization. Inadequate planning of an overpopulated metropolis has an impact on employment, housing transportation, and safety. Next, we briefly take a look at each of these consequences of urban overpopulation before turning to an exploration of how two aspects of the environment—population density and scarcity—influence Japan's interactions and sense of aesthetics.

DEMOGRAPHIC ENVIRONMENT

As a member of the Group of Seven, Japan is a major economy marked by affluence, and it is generally perceived as having an advanced standard of living. Japan ranks third after the United States and China in nominal gross domestic product, and fourth by purchasing power parity, the instrument designed to create currency equivalencies (figure 2.3).

Employment is a challenge for every overcrowded city. However, despite the economy's notorious lost decades (1991–2010), when funds amounting to twice its gross domestic product were tied up in debt, Japan has been able to keep unemployment relatively low over the years, particularly when compared with other Group of Seven members such as the United States, Italy, and France. Statistics can be deceiving at times, however, and economists have pointed out how low employment may not present

the whole picture of employment in Japanese cities. Social and professional pressure not to quit, and underreporting women job seekers are often stated as the ways in which Japanese unemployment figures are reportedly kept so low.

Still another unwanted outcome of urban overpopulation is homelessness. The homeless are made up mostly of men, and this less-talked-about social issue is reportedly on the rise in Japan. However, in context, there are roughly the same number of homeless people in Mumbai as in all of Japan. São Paolo has twice the number of homeless people as Tokyo; and New York, the world's number one city for homelessness, has twelve times Japan's number, a third of whom are children.[6]

Overpopulation in Japan, may, however, soon become a thing of the past. The current average of births per woman is 1.37, which is below the rate of a stable population. If this current birthrate pattern continues, Japan's population will be reduced by a third by 2040, to about 85 million. Depopulation seems to be under way, with a census showing nearly a million fewer people in 2015 than in 2010—a population the size of San Francisco.[7]

It is possible to see the potential benefits of a decreasing population, such as reduced cost in education, more personal income, and less congested cities. However, in reality, the effects of such a dramatic change in population are unknown, because this phenomenon is unprecedented in the socioeconomic history of a country like Japan. A dwindling workforce might seek other less traditional members for its workforce, such as women and immigrants, through social reform. However, the economist Kathy Matsui reports an estimated 70 percent of women who drop out of the workforce during their childbearing years, and Japanese women who do work do not have children.[8] We discuss the paucity of women in the workforce again in chapter 3, on social organization.

Without a real incentive for women to work, perhaps immigrants could help alleviate the decline in the workforce. Roughly 1.5–2 percent of the Japanese population is currently reported as foreign. This figure, which includes current South Korean and Chinese permanent residents, represents at most just

Figure 2.4
Canadian, US, and Japanese Immigrant Populations

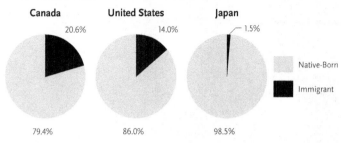

Canada   United States   Japan

20.6%   14.0%   1.5%

Native-Born

Immigrant

79.4%   86.0%   98.5%

Sources: For the data on Canada, see Statistics Canada, "Immigration and Ethnocultural Diversity in Canada," www12.statcan.gc.ca/nhs-enm/2011/as-sa/99-010-x/99-010-x2011001 -eng.cfm. For the US data, see Pew Research Center, "Modern Immigration Wave Brings 59 Million to US, Driving Population Growth through 2065: Views of Immigration's Impact on US Society Mixed," September 28, 2015, www.pewhispanic.org/2015/09/28/modern -immigration-wave-brings-59-million-to-u-s-driving-population-growth-and-change-through -2065/. For the data on Japan, see Richard Smart, "Japan's Population Declines for First Time since 1920s: Official Census," *The Guardian*, February 26, 2016, www.theguardian.com/world /2016/feb/26/japan-population-declines-first-time-since-1920s-official-census.

2.5 million people out of a population of 127 million. By contrast, the United States in 2015 had 59 million foreign-born residents out of a population of 320 million, or 14 percent. Canada in 2011, the last year available from the census, had 6.8 million out of a population of 35.9 million, or 20.6 percent. This means that more than one in every five Canadians is foreign born.[9]

The largest foreign groups in Japan, composed of both workers and students, in descending order, are Chinese, South Korean, Filipino, US, British, and Brazilian (figure 2.4). This immigrant population creates an interesting contrast to the demographic landscape of 1889, when the largest foreign group in Tokyo was the British, with 209 residents, followed by American nationals, with 182.

CITY BUILDINGS AND UPWARD SPACES

As with other urban centers that lack space, Japan has constructed upward to accommodate its population. At 2,080 feet, the Tokyo Skytree has been added to the other forty-two skyscrapers that are taller than 607 feet (see photograph 2.4). Still

2.4 The Tokyo Skytree
To add more space, build taller. Photo courtesy of Sandrine Burtschell.

another effective use of upward space is the automatic car park system that rotates cars on a mechanical setup, stacking cars in a limited amount of space (see photograph 2.5).

More surprising may be the use of precious space in urban Japan for the dead. Above-ground crypts—such as the six-story Buddhist mausoleum where visitors use a swipe card to visit their ancestors, whose cremated urns are brought out on conveyor belts—are becoming more commonplace as other parts of the urban infrastructure, such as transportation, compete for underground space. As in other space-restricted countries, the lack of space can make death an expensive business.

As a result of World War II bombings and earthquakes, such as the 1923 Great Kantō Earthquake, the urban landscapes of many Japanese cities consist mainly of modern and contemporary architecture. Tokyo features many internationally famous forms of modern architecture, including the Tokyo International Forum, Mode Gakuen Cocoon Tower, NTT Docomo Yoyogi Building, Rainbow Bridge, Tokyo Tower, and Asahi Beer Hall (see photograph 2.6).

Tokyo is the largest city in the world, with a population larger than that of Canada as a whole. It is a city of twenty-three special

2.5 Automated Parking System
To maximize space, park your car vertically! Photo courtesy of Sandrine Burtschell.

wards, twenty-six cities, five towns, and eight villages; each has a local government that is headed by a publicly elected governor and metropolitan assembly. Lying northwest of Tokyo Bay, the sprawling city measures about 56 miles east to west and 16 miles north to south. The postbubble recession has sent down prices on commercial property and opened up possibilities for the negotiation of office space that many large foreign companies were able to leverage.

Ironically, however, the absolute availability of office space for the Japanese workforce has not always translated into bigger, more convenient, or more central locations. Historically, Japanese landlords have had the upper hand, and many older landlords, still holding out for a rebound in rental prices, do not negotiate. In practice, then, many Japanese office workers have been forced to occupy even more cramped quarters as ghost office space remains empty. Still, as Japan keeps many urban workers employed within its confined parameters, many workers are resigned to a spot of prime real estate in a bullpen-style office.

The upside of a shrinking workforce is more space for urban living. Still, most North Americans find living spaces in Japan

2.6 Asahi Beer Hall
This is one of the most recognized Japanese buildings. Photo courtesy of Sandrine Burtschell.

smaller than what they can find at home. Typically, Japanese apartment sizes range from bay-sized rooms of capsule hotels to larger ones that resemble small to medium-sized apartments in the United States.

Apartments in Japan have a Western-style layout, typically advertised with abbreviations such as 1DK and 2LDK, where the first number indicates the number of bedrooms, followed by (L)iving, (D)ining, and (K)itchen areas. By contrast, the Japanese have maintained old measuring standards by using the number of tatami mats to indicate size, called *jō*, which is a very rough 3-by-6-feet because tatami mat sizes vary. A 6-*jo* room or a 10–15-*jō* apartment is standard, but a North American might be lucky enough to get an apartment that is 20 *jō*, which will certainly feel more comfortable.

A room in a traditional Japanese house is laid out differently than its Western counterpart, because no particular room has a specific function. For example, a room can be a living room (*ima*, with the kanji characters, 居間 for living + space) or a bedroom, where, traditionally, no locks were used on sliding doors, and everyone slept together. Typically, this was in the characteristic 川 *kawa* river style, where a child slept in between a mother and father. Centuries of living in close quarters have resulted in a certain comfort with crowded living among the Japanese. Ironically, even when there is space, many choose to spend their nights as a cozy family unit.

TRANSPORTATION: SPACE FOR MOVING PEOPLE AND THINGS

Although old trade routes traditionally connected eastern Kantō with western Kansai, today Japanese travel routes are notable largely for their energy efficiency and high cost. Per person consumption of energy in Japan is kept low because of Japan's short travel distances, dense and expansive public transportation system, and high tolls and taxes on roads (although this comes and goes, depending on whether a socialist-leaning government is in place). While it may come as a surprise to the foreign visitor, roads are still the main means of passenger and freight transportation. Cars are particularly useful for exploring outside urban centers, where public transportation becomes sparse. (The visiting driver can see the section of recommendations at the end of this chapter for tips on traveling outside cities.)

However necessary cars are to investigate Japan's regions, public transportation, in the form of trains, is often the best way of getting from one city to the next, and certainly around Japan's urban centers. Japan's first response to its overcrowded metropolitan areas was trains. Though still subsidized with low-interest construction loans and protected with price controls and rolling stocks, the Japanese National Railways (JNR)—including JR East, JR Central, and JR West—have been privatized since 1987, and this has helped recharge JNR from the stagnation that it was previously experiencing.

Many visitors have experienced outcomes that are nothing short of success for JNR. Today, JNR is a world-renowned rail service known for its punctuality and safety. In 2007 its average departure delay was a mere 18 seconds along its 320-mile route; and in the last half century, JNR has not had a single derailment or collision.[10]

2.7 The Tokyo Monorail
Haneda International Airport to Tokyo in 25 minutes. Photo courtesy of Jon.

In the case of transportation, the Japanese have once again built both up and down. Below ground level is a subway network that is interconnected on a mind-boggling five different stories. Monorails make use of the space above roads at ground level. The Tokyo monorail, which has a station at the International Haneda Airport, is the world's busiest monorail, carrying about 100 million people annually (see photograph 2.7).

CROWD AND SOCIAL ETIQUETTE MANAGEMENT

Part of managing an overpopulated city is crowd control, which Japan has made both a science and an art form. For a vivid demonstration of efficient crowd control, see the YouTube clip of "Time Lapse of Crowd Control in Tokyo Japan for Comic Market." Here, more than half a million visitors are moved from the lines outside through the stalls in a day.

A further Japanese strategy for managing crowds in public spaces has been to promote rule conformity. Subway stations, buses, and train cars are wallpapered with public service posters, such as the request to use "manner mode" on cell phones, thus telling passengers not to talk while in transit on public transportation. Although foreigners may not literally have a "manner mode," as they do the international "airplane mode" on their cell phones, this Japanese public behavior control—even if unfamiliar in their home countries—is relatively easy to accept. Manner mode seems justifiable on the basis that hearing a loud conversation next to your ear in a confined space can be a nuisance for everyone, just as it can be for you.

For the Japanese, public behavior control is a requirement that is not enforced by imposing fines or in any other formal way but rather by exerting social pressure. For all these posters to have any impact, everyone must take part in the plan in which the unwritten goal is twofold: (1) to sacrifice individual freedom for the benefit of group endorsement; and (2) to avoid the hostile reception you will receive if you do not!

Although some public manners have been relatively easily accepted, thereby facilitating enforcement, others have proven to be more challenging. Women-only cars, introduced in the early 2000s to combat groping on commuter trains at crowded times, are one example. The Tokyo Metropolitan Police and the East Railway Company reported that two-thirds of women in their twenties and thirties were groped on trains, and poster campaigning failed to reverse the incidences. An article titled "Women-Only Cars: If Men Get On It, It's Legally OK," captures the irony of the ¥10 fine instituted in 1900 that is still theoretically in place but is unenforced.[11] Still, many women prefer riding women-only cars during the specified crowded times, and some men have endorsed it, saying that it saves them from being falsely accused.[12]

However, despite reports of continued inappropriateness on the part of some men in public places, visitors often think of Japan as a country with one of the lowest crime rates in the world. Noticeable aspects of safety in Japan are children who walk home alone; homes and cars that are left unlocked, particularly outside cities; vending machines that sell everything, and from which nothing ever seems to be stolen; and the frequent use of cash for payment. In short, Japan is relatively safe, has been successful in creating a clean and punctual transportation service, and has begun to address its housing and unemployment challenges.

HUMAN-MADE NATURAL SPACES

The image of a crowded Japanese city is an important one because of the contrast it presents with human-made natural places, many of which are respites in urban areas. Tokyo has numerous gardens, such as the famous Chinsan-sō, or House of Camellia, founded in 1877. The haiku poet Bashō allegedly lived in a hut overlooking this property for four years in the seventeenth century. The garden houses a three-thousand-year-old pagoda that is said to have been built by the Chikurin-ji temple monks without using a single nail, as well as the Shiratama Inari Shrine from Kyoto, a pond, waterfall, natural spring, and the famous five-hundred-year-old sacred tree.

An ideal Japanese garden is neither a manicured French Versailles nor a natural English garden. Japanese aesthetics seeks the beauty of nature reflected in human-made things. A Buddhist Zen rock garden is perhaps the symbol of the impression the environment has left on the islands of Japan, where the sense of aesthetics uses nature to shape human spaces to turn the limited resource of 間 *ma* space into a Zen asset where less is more.

CLIMATIC AESTHETICS

In true Japanese reasoning, we have come full circle, returning to the natural environment and its impact on aesthetics. Japan has a temperate marine climate with four seasons, with average annual temperatures ranging from 50–68°F (10–20°C). Note that these averages mask the hot and humid summers and the cold and biting winters, which make temperatures feel much more extreme. Furthermore, the Japanese Alps once again play a hand in creating different climatic zones between the Japanese seaboard and the Pacific Ocean, with humid monsoon winters for the former and a drier front for the latter. Japan has two rainy seasons, one in early summer and the other in early autumn. At these times, cyclones and typhoons are commonplace and often result in flooding damage.

On the upside, rain has resulted in an advanced umbrella culture in Japan. Many hotels are equipped with free umbrellas to borrow. Indeed, the umbrellas that the concierge offers are sturdy, large, and automatic. To play their part and prevent accidents caused by slippery floors, umbrella users are expected to use either the umbrella stand or the tubular plastic bags offered at the entrances to public spaces. If you walk into an office building wet and without an umbrella, you might get a few giggles—a Japanese stereotype of foreigners is that they never use umbrellas.

The Japanese seasons have played a great role in influencing everything from their aesthetic orientation to nature to literature, music, art, and folklore. Spring is marked by the famous cherry blossom viewing, where friends, family, and lovers gather under cherry trees and drink sake. A visiting friend remarked that she was amazed how the normally by-the-book Japanese seemed to cancel everything just to have a moment to experience the favorite national pastime. A Japanese spring is the start of the school year, as well as the fiscal year, and symbolically marks new beginnings.

Summer is highlighted by the Obon Festival, a Buddhist celebration that takes place to honor a family's ancestors. This season is as important in Japan as is Thanksgiving in the United States or Christmas in Western Europe. The exchange of midsummer *ochūgen* gifts among families and companies shows the formal and public side of Obon. However, for many Japanese, Obon is a time to reaffirm ties with nature and with the family. To this end, a child's private Obon might conjure up a time of catching fireflies, telling ghost stories, and testing bravery in misty graveyards. Dressed in cotton *yukata*, hometown families gather together to share food and dance against the backdrop of

chochin-lit stalls, firework filled skies, and the haunting beat of the *taiko* drums at the Obon *matsuri* festival.

The autumn is marked by *momijigari* (red maple tree hunting). Like Japanese cherry blossoms, the Japanese esteem crimson *momiji* leaves, splashing designs across kimonos or screen doors in old houses. Mention *momiji*, and many Japanese people can instantly hear the sound of water-filled bamboo tipping and tapping the edge of an overflowing stone water well in a Japanese garden.

Winter is marked by what nature brings in with the cold. From ice carvings to chattering alpine monkeys with snow crowns in *rotenburo onsen* outdoor hot springs, winter plays a role in the Japanese appreciation of starkness, of which *wabi-sabi* aesthetics are a part (see photograph 2.8). Bare tree branches and imperfect stones are admired as nature's art, and are replicated in daily household items such as tea bowls and ikebana vases.

Since the Japanese talk about life in terms of the four seasons, we leave this chapter on the environment with an old Japanese expression that gives courage to those in a real or symbolic winter: "There has never been a winter that has not been followed by a spring." And so the seasonal environment is present in the thoughts of everyday Japanese life, and an old day is new again.

In travels, going from small to big sometimes makes you feel lost. Conversely, going from big to small—as with North Americans coming to Japan—can make you feel confined. Here are a few ways to deal with this:

1. Option 1: Do as the Japanese do, and *embrace* the smallness, the plainness, the clutter, and the imperfections. Many old timers say that learning to appreciate Japanese aesthetics allowed them to see Japan from a native's point of view. Equally, as many visitors say that small spaces felt less constraining over time. Not only do we get used to many things, but learning to expect them means that we can enjoy minimal spaces the way Japanese do.

2. Option 2: Get some breathing space in a city park, such as Tokyo's Ueno Park, Nagoya's Heiwa Park, or Osaka's Castle Park. Even outside the cherry blossom viewing season in the spring, the park is an oasis. Ueno also has a few museums. The Tokyo National Museum, the Museum of Nature and Science, Shitamachi (Downtown) Museum, and the Museum for Western Art are all worth a look.

3. Option 3 is our favorite: Head out if you have a day or two. You will not have to go far to end up in a village that can roll you back a good five decades and make you feel like Chihiro in Hayao Miyazaki's film *Spirited Away*.

4. If you take option 3, consider renting a car to get to all the hidden gems. Even though the roads are narrow, in general the Japanese drive slowly, though some say painfully so. Take care to remember that driving is on the left side of the road, and the driver sits on the right-hand side. If you take this option, make sure you get a global positioning system tool called car *navi*, and pronounced, *nabi*. The easiest way to find your destination is by entering the phone number. Houses are not numbered chronologically, because historically they were numbered in the order in which they were built.

5. If you know you have a few days to travel, consider purchasing a JNR rail pass. It used to be that you would need to buy these before you leave. Check before you leave. If you make more than one roundtrip on a bullet train, it is well worth the price.

6. Also, if you have more than a day and like the outdoors, try hiking Japan's gorgeous mountains. Because 73 percent of Japan is mountainous, unless you explore the mountains, you cannot really say you have explored Japan. Most mountain hikes are suitable for all ages and fitness levels. For the mountaineer, search the mountains listed in Kyuya Fukuda's *100 Famous Mountains* (Nihon Hyaku-meizan), made famous by the avid hiker and mountain enthusiast Crown Prince Naruhito, who allegedly lists the book as one of his favorites.[13]

7. For urbanites at lunch, remember to look upward, because there are as many restaurants on upper floors as there are on the ground. At ground level, there is often a directory of restaurants for the entire building.

8. Finally, a couple of safety tips: During an earthquake, stay calm, turn off any open gas fires, open doors and windows, and then brace beneath a table to protect yourself from falling objects. Learn gathering areas in high-risk tsunami areas, listen to warnings, and run to elevated areas. If you are in a train, stay calm and listen to the emergency announcements. An automatic signal triggered the emergency brakes of thirty-three bullet trains 15 seconds before the 2011 earthquake. As a result, there were no deaths and no notable casualties. If you are in a train and an earthquake occurs, Japanese cities are where you want to be.

SUMMARY OF THE JAPANESE ENVIRONMENT

The Japanese Islands and Regions

- Japan is larger than the United Kingdom but smaller than the state of California.
- Japan has four main islands: Honshū, Hokkaidō, Shikoku, and Kyūshū.

- Japan has eight main regions: Hokkaidō, Shikoku, Kyūshū, Kantō, Chūbu, Kansai, Tōhoku, and Chūgoku.

Physical Impact

- A total of 72 percent mountainous land makes actual livable land smaller.
- No land borders makes Japan feel set apart.
- The Japanese Alps cut central Honshu Island in half, creating the Kantō/Kansai, east/west two-hub economy and national rivalry.
- Earthquakes, volcanoes, and tsunamis create natural disasters with huge economic consequences.
- The 2011 Tohoku Earthquake and Tsunami are the costliest disaster ever recorded in history.

Environmental Responsibility

- Japan lacks natural resources.
- The country is dependent on imported fossil fuels.

Population and Density

- A population of 172 million.
- A total of 91 percent of the population live in urban areas.
- A sparse rural population.
- A declining workforce.
- Low unemployment and homelessness.
- Very safe.

Urban Spaces

- Upward and downward use of building spaces and transportation.
- Skyscrapers, parking lots, and above-ground crypts.

Transportation

- Efficient.
- The urban subway network extends five stories below ground.

Recommendations

- For a great day out of a city, drive into the country and take a global positioning system *nabi* or purchase a JNR rail pass.
- Learn earthquake and tsunami safety tips and safety for gathering areas.

3

J A P A N E S E

Social Organization

Inside and Outside Faces

This chapter examines the social organization that structures personal and professional interactions in Japan. We broadly define "social organization" as the common institutions and collective activities that members of a culture share. The influence of these institutions and collective activities shape the behavior of people in all aspects of life, from business to education to raising their families. Many of the variables that we examine elsewhere in this book operate without our even being aware of them. In the case of social organization, we generally *are* aware of the differences with other cultures but often are *not* aware of their implications.

We begin this chapter by showing how Japan's social structure is one that focuses on others, whereas the North American social structure focuses on the individual. We then show how the differences between these two platforms set the stage for different relationships and interactions in Japan and North America. We then investigate the Japanese concept of inside and outside faces that applies across all domains,

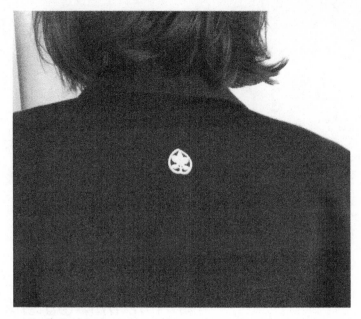

3.1 Family Crest
Family crests appear on traditional clothing, furniture, and stationery. Photo courtesy of Sandrine Burtschell.

at home, at school, and at work. We also look at the ideology of *ikka ichimon* 一家一門, which translates as *one house, one crest*, that still persists in contemporary Japan (see photograph 3.1). This symbolic image of a house united as a clan is replicated and played out in daily interaction in all areas of Japanese organization, such as the ones we examine in this chapter. Finally, we conclude with a brief discussion of three social groups that are underrepresented in the workforce in Japan: women, immigrants, and robots.

AFTER YOU: THE INDIVIDUAL AND THE OTHER

Japanese social organization begins and ends with the other person. If this feels somehow backward, it is possible you are from an organizational structure that starts and ends with you, as an individual. Your culture might be one that promotes initative, leadership, and standing out with a unique profile and set of skills. In such a culture, someone who does not act for himself of herself is likely to be seen as weak.

In a culture such as those of North America, where the *individual* is the starting point, "after you" is an individual's decision to allow someone else to go first, which means that he or she is powerful enough to relinquish this power and offer an "after you." In this context, such an act is more likely seen as a gesture of kindness, empathy, or generosity. At the same time, too many "after you" expressions in North American culture can appear silly or even dangerously patronizing—for example, in some interactions between men and women.

This is also why, when North Americans experience the bowing and "*dōzo, dōzo*" (after you, after you) outside elevators and doorways in Japan, it feels excessive—almost embarrassing—because it looks like groveling. This is reason enough to politely categorize the Japanese as "polite." To a native of a culture with an individual focus, like North America, the Japanese "after you" behavior is politeness gone overboard.

However, for those from an *others*-centered focus, "after you" is a social expectation. In lowering his palm upward and gesturing for others to go first, the Japanese businessman who insists on entering the elevator after his colleagues is not being any politer than his North American counterpart who pushes the "door open" button when he sees someone approaching the elevator. Conversely, not signaling "after you" for a Japanese person is more or less the same as a North American letting the elevator door slide shut while pretending they did not see the approaching person. The likely thing to do for *individual* decision-oriented social organizers who have stepped inside the elevator first is to let him in, just as the likely thing to do for *others*-oriented social organizers outside the elevator is to let others go first.

At this point you might be thinking that if someone is running for an elevator, of course a Japanese person would do the same and let him or her in. You might be right if the Japanese person inside the elevator was its only occupant, and that could become an act of individual kindness. However, if the person facing the elevator door was standing in an elevator full of people, his or her likely reaction to the person running toward them would be to bow apologetically and let the door slide shut. Additionally, the person running toward the elevator would understand this—and not, for example, run up and rapidly press the outside elevator button to try to get in. He would have done the same if in the inside person's position, thinking on behalf of the *others* in the elevator.

This comparative elevator scenario is a simple example of how North Americans and Japanese differ in terms of whom they represent. Whereas the North American *individual* decides to press the "door open" button on his or her own behalf, regardless of who else is in the elevator, to be nice to the individual approaching, a Japanese person makes his or her decision relative to *all the others* in the elevator. This view that a man's or a woman's decision is a part of a whole group's decision, and not a single unit's or an individual's, is a defining feature of Japanese *others*-centered social organization.

Etymology can sometimes help illuminate our understanding, and the written character *bun*, which literally means *part* or *fraction*, is a prime example. Although the Chinese *onyomi* "sound" reading of the character reads the kanji character 分 as *bun*, the Japanese *kunyomi* of 分 used in the verb reads *wakeru* 分ける, which means *to divide*. Demonstrably, the kanji character at the center of *bun* 分 is *katana* 刀—a sword that divides the whole—thereby conjuring up the kind of visual representation that characters can provide, as discussed in chapter 1, on language. Thus, the dividing line in the elevator scenario is between those on the inside and those on the outside; and for the duration of the elevator ride, the person at the front of the elevator near the door button is part of the inside group, and acts on its behalf.

The idea that an individual is always a member of a group permeates Japanese social situations, in the elevator and beyond. Perhaps nowhere is this illustrated more clearly than in how we address an envelope. A US or Canadian postal address locates the individual in a place by writing the name of the addressee first before the address. It is just the opposite in Japan. A Japanese postal address does the contrary, putting first the place where the individual resides. These different emphases on the *individual*

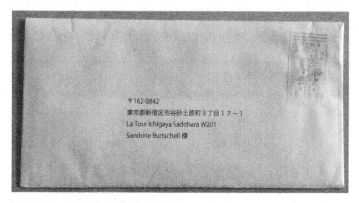

3.2 American and Japanese Envelopes
In Japanese addresses, place comes first and name comes last. Photo courtesy of Sandrine Burtschell.

and the *others* is highlighted in international mail, where the country, the biggest group identifier, goes last in a US or Canadian address but first in a Japanese one; see photograph 3.2.

A professional example of the contrast between these focuses on the *individual* and *others* can be found in American and Japanese styles of introduction. Whereas Sachiko Suzuki introduces herself in Japanese as "Mitsubishi UFJ's Suzuki Sachiko," presenting the largest organizational group first and her individual personal name last, Tim Breer introduces himself in English as "Tim Breer, vice president of corporate relations, Bank of America," placing his personal name first and the company last. Tim highlights the smaller, lesser-known, added-value factor in his initial encounter, and assumes company representation. By contrast, Sachiko assumes smaller representational aspects such as similarity in rank, and reaffirms her ambassadorship for the company, the largest and most important group in the Japanese social context.

INSIDE AND OUTSIDE FACES

The Japanese group is a whole, and its members are fractions. Because of this, an *others* player's key role is to collaborate with the members inside and to represent this group to members outside. The Japanese manage this representation through *uchi-soto-kankei*, or insider–outsider group relations. In *uchi* insider relations, a fractional member can bare his or her face and reveal his or her true *honne* feelings. In *soto* outsider interrelations, conversely, a player must wear a public mask and display carefully crafted and publicly endorsed *tatemae*—literally, *scaffolded* feelings.

Once again, Japanese kanji characters can cast light on the way Japanese organize inside–outside relations. *Honne*, or real feelings, is written with the characters *hon* 本 and *ne* 音, which together literally mean *original sound*. Like music, *honne* can be compared with the melody and *tatemae* with the chords. A whole person has both in his or her repertoire, but may be called to emphasize different parts of the composition at different times.

Here is another analogy that might help in thinking about inside and outside faces. If you live in a centrally heated home, you typically put on a coat to go out in the winter and take it off when you come back inside. Although based on the weather, the decision of whether to wear a coat is usually yours. However, deciding to put on a coat inside the house and taking it off outside is different from deciding to wear a suit to work then coming home and changing to jeans. In the second, there is a socially coded rule for what to wear professionally—and this switch in inside/outside behavior permeates all parts of Japanese social organization. Having an outside face to put on in public is not a custom peculiar to Japan, but there are a lot of them, and like the business suit, each outside face is clearly defined and encoded by the group, and its members adhere to them pretty much unanimously. By contrast, many North American inside and outside faces are an individual's decision, like wearing a coat when you think it is cold outside.

For North Americans, another potentially confusing aspect of Japanese inside and outside interfaces is that many are only exposed to the Japanese outside public faces. When Tim Breer meets Sachiko Suzuki for the first time, he is really only interacting with the public face of Mitsubishi UFJ. This is because Japanese employees are asked to become *kaisha no kao*, or the face of the company, when they join. For as long as they stay with the company—and this can still be a lifetime—they are expected to wear the company face in interactions with people outside the company.

Likewise, in Japan, students are expected to represent their schools with *gakkō no kao*, or school faces; similarly, members of a family wear their family's face. For example, a mother was forbidden to enter a movie theater with her teenage son and was told that children were not allowed in after 11:00 pm. The fact that the movie was rated G, for a general audience, illustrates that the rule imposed was not about moral content but rather was a social rule imposed upon the family's public face.

That even families have an outside face to uphold in Japan is surprising to many visitors, who consider family affairs "personal." For members of *individual*-focused societies, a social rule like the movie curfew mentioned just above flies in the face of individual freedom; literally, it is no one else's business outside the home. However, in Japan, the inside/outside faces apply in every domain, including work, school, and home. Outside social rules are prescriptive and are practiced in public, sometimes equaling or surpassing the law.

Behind closed doors, however, a Japanese family is free to act with all its idiosyncrasies. So whereas a Japanese mother may comply with the not-after-11:00-pm movie curfew at the public theater, at home, she may allow her children to stay up long past 11:00 pm. Whereas North American parents typically apply individual parental rules unilaterally whether they are at home or at a movie theater, saying, "These are our children and we discipline them for their bedtime the way we see fit," the Japanese accept that when in public, their children are members of the public, and therefore are subject to public social rules.

In sum, North Americans typically divide inside–outside interactions to coincide with the split between personal or home versus professional worlds, whereas the Japanese divide every social encounter into two inside/outside faces. Moreover, when in public, encoded rules are always shared, allowing Japanese society to strengthen the largest nucleus of the group, which is the country of Japan itself.

One last challenge pointed out by an American professor was that it is difficult to return to public relations once the line has been crossed from public to personal. Perhaps a way to see how Japanese manage personal and public relationships is to compare them with professional athletes at play. A soccer player on Japan's women's team might be a personal friend with one of her teammates, but she will still uphold her team's strategies and tactics on the pitch. She is not going to pass a ball to her friend just because she is her friend. She will behave as a professional soccer player on the pitch and pass the ball to the player by position and according to a strategy.

The fact that the Japanese rigorously adhere to social rules also has a dark side. Arguably, nothing better exemplifies this than the media representation and subsequent public reaction to the two Japanese people that the Islamic State took hostage at the start of 2015. US and Japanese media both featured the tearful mother of the second hostage pleading for the life of her son. However, the contrast between the two nations' interpretations was striking.

US media cast the hostages as two different individuals—the first hostage, Yukawa Haruna, as arguably guilty; and the second one, Goto Kenji, as a hero. Yukawa was easy to set up as the fall guy. He was a psychologically fragile and disenfranchised individual with right-wing tendencies, and the English-speaking media told its viewers his backstory, of a man who had lost his wife to cancer and failed at business, and then became involved in helping foreign businesses defend themselves militarily. Although Yukawa was meddling in arms and went into the danger zone despite having been warned to stay away, Goto was a journalist who returned to Syria for a second time to rescue Yukawa. In the eyes of English-speaking broadcasters, Goto was a hero more than a martyr, the good guy whose life was worth saving—even at the expense of Yukawa's.

The Japanese news media, however, told a completely different story. Following the teary broadcast of Goto's mother, Ishido Junko, Japanese media televised the clip in which Ishido is seen not only begging the Islamic State for her son's life but also asking for the Japanese public's forgiveness on behalf of her son for having represented Japan as potentially anti-Islam, and thereby endangering citizen lives. In the Japanese broadcast, there is hardly a difference between the two hostages. Although Yukawa is cast as a lunatic, Goto is seen as the journalist who brought global media attention to the issue, and therefore perhaps even more guilty of committing an unforgivable social evil. The line here falls between the Japanese people and the two who created the crisis. The hostages, Yukawa and Goto, stepped outside the group and divided it. They had stepped outside the creed of *one house, one crest*, and they were drawing unwanted attention.

Feeding the growing resentment toward both hostages, the Japanese media quoted Goto's mother Ishido as condemning her son for leaving his own infant son to go to Syria to save Yukawa. Goto's fate was sealed. Even after both men were beheaded, Japanese social media responded with unanimous support, not for the hostages as individuals but for Japan: *Goto's and Yukawa's actions were selfish. Each put his interest above the good of the group. Now every Japanese traveler has to worry. Two lone individuals have endangered us all.*

In a clear example of how social organization biases our reading of an event, an *individual* focus allows us to differentiate Yukawa from Goto, making one the fall guy and one the hero. Conversely, a focus on *others* and the need to wear a public face allows us to defend a nation in entirety as we make Yukawa and Goto both liable for putting the terrorist spotlight on travelers. In an *individual*-focused society, a single person's intentions or actions are what count, but in an *others*-focused society, defending group loyalty is more important.

HOUSE AS CLAN: LOVE AND LOYALTY IN *AMAE*

The clansman's feel to the exterior face of an *others*-oriented society owes itself in part to the feudal social structure of the house put in place by the ruling Tokugawa shogun at the beginning of the seventeenth century. Although a shogun's territory included prefectures, unlike European feudal lords, a shogun was not a landowner, but rather, a military leader whose government was reinforced by the loyalty of his officials and subordinates. Both the shogun and the collective members of his house were not appointed or entitled to their roles but had to compete for their roles through displays of allegiance.

This hierarchical, mutual loyalty, which is based on that between shogunate superiors and subordinates, still plays a powerful role in Japanese group dynamics today. In chapter 5, on the Japanese conceptualization of authority, we examine how the general–subordinate hierarchical relationship plays out in the workplace, in sports, and at home. Critically, what is important is the insistence on the other from both sides. In other words, not only is the subordinate under a manager's care, but the subordinate also must demonstrate his or her loyalty time and time again.

Called *amae*, this somewhat conditional love and loyalty—which is further discussed in chapter 5, on authority conception—can and does occur in both personal and professional contexts in Japan. Though it is sometimes confusing for North Americans that the shared love of a parent and child can recur in a context between a boss and his or her subordinate, this feeling of *amae* is not dissimilar from the kind of mutual appreciation an athlete and coach or student and teacher feel for one another in many North American clubs and schools.

Likewise, although conditional love is a less popular notion than its romantic variant of unconditional love, it does occur in many instances in North American families, too. For example, conditional love is practiced in parenting through incidences of "tough love." Moreover, stories of testing love have a long history, even in the English-speaking world; *King Lear* is such a story, where the daughters of the king must prove their love to him.

Perhaps the easiest way to think about *amae* love and loyalty in Japanese business is to think about how North Americans see family businesses, where, as with the shogun, the administrative center is headquartered in the house. Indeed, the word for "family," *kazoku* 家族, is made up of two characters, *ka* 家, or "house," and *zoku* 族, which means "clan" or "tribe," the topic of our next discussion.[1]

The ideal traditional Japanese family structure—particularly at the nuclear level, with a father, a mother, and children—does not appear too different from the North American one. However, this is where the similarity ends. Here, we talk about some of the ways in which the Japanese family differs from its North American counterpart, notably in the application of inside/outside faces and the practices of marriage and divorce.

A culture's vocabulary often reflects its hidden social structure, and how family members address each other in Japanese is a great example. As we discussed in chapter 1, on language, in both North American and Japanese families, children address their parents by their kinship roles of mom and dad, or *okāsan* and *otōsan*. We also discussed how in Japan, the practice of referring to family members by using their role names extends to older siblings. Rather than address an older brother by name, he is *onīchan*, and an older sister is *onēchan*. Critically, in terms of inside/outside references, different terms of address are used at home and in public. Outside the home, one's own mother is referred to as *haha*; one's own father, as *chichi*; one's own older brother, as *ani*; and one's own older sister, as *ane*. Once again, this shows how the Japanese refer to the same person differently, depending on whether the *others* with whom they are talking are inside or outside members.

The traditional Japanese marriage was more a clan alliance than a man and a woman joined in romantic love. To some extent, marriage in Japan is still seen this way. This does not mean that Japanese men and women do not fall in love, or that there is no affection in Japanese marriages; but a Japanese marriage is initially a deliberate outsiders' union, with one house joining an *other* house clan, rather than a marriage between two *individuals* based on random choice.

In contemporary Japan, house clan prospects can meet either through an arranged meeting managed and volunteered informally by family friends and relatives or formally through a paid go-between. Although the tendency is to think of arranged

3.3 Japanese Wedding
A Shinto Japanese wedding can be expensive. Photo courtesy of Sandrine Burtschell.

marriages as forced betrothals, 見合い *miai* has kanji that literally say *see fit*, making *miai* a series of meetings set to discover whether the other person "fits" with you. The term *miai* is used in the game of Go to refer to two neutral moves; and like this, contemporary *miai* can be seen as meeting opportunities where either side can agree or disagree to continued meetings. *Miai* is, then, perhaps not that different from the kind of online dating that sets up meetings based on best-fit profiles found in the West today.

However, despite the continued use of *miai* set-up marriages, alliances that occur through *renai* random meetings are more commonplace in contemporary Japan. *Renai* roughly corresponds to the Western variety of marriage that is not set up but occurs via happenstance. Today, Christian-style weddings in churches, complete with wedding gowns and long trains, have a popular appeal.[2] Some three-quarters of the weddings in Japan are reportedly Western, Christian-style ones, because fewer contemporary couples opt to take on the expense of a white kimono and *tsunokakushi* (which still has the folkloric name, horn hiding) box hat used in Shinto weddings. Although this

3.4 Western-Style Wedding
Western-style weddings are popular in Japan. Photo courtesy of Sandrine Burtschell.

may seem an odd occurrence in a country that is only slightly more than 1 percent Christian, from the Japanese point of view, young couples often see a wedding gown and Christian iconography as a fashion statement rather than a religious practice; see photographs 3.3 and 3.4.

While wedding bells toll, the social pressure to marry looms large. Compared with a stale Christmas cake, the old deadline for Japanese women to marry at the age of twenty-five years has recently been raised to thirty-one, humoring or shaming women who do not marry before then as past the sell-by date of *toshikoshi soba*, buckwheat noodles eaten on New Year's Eve. Like pasta that is not al dente, in Japan, soggy noodles are frowned upon. Men are also not free from social judgment, because they are also seen as not fully responsible adults if unmarried by sometime in their thirties.

Compared with the United States, there are half as many divorces in Japan; still, divorce in Japan is on the rise, with four times the rate of the 1950s in 2013 and double the rate of the 1970s.[3] Just short of one in three marriages ends in divorce, and this has often been explained in terms of the traditional view of marriage as a family union, and how there is a certain practicality about a divorce in Japan that is not found in the West. For example, it used to be that if the business was not working out for whatever reason, it was a good enough reason for divorce. Because Japan is a non-Christian country, divorce there is discouraged through social shame rather than religious condemnation. As of late, it seems the divorce rate has somewhat tapered off, and this has been explained by the increase in the number of people who do not get married in the first place.

In short, as with many other wealthier economies, single living is on the rise in Japan. Indeed, Japan's lifetime unmarried rate (notice the term "unmarried," rather than "single") at present is roughly ten times higher than it was thirty years ago for men and twice as much for women. The decline in numbers of marriage were said to occur despite a national survey in which 86.3 percent of unmarried men and 89.4 percent of unmarried women responded that they eventually did want to marry. The explanation for the discrepancy between why participants said they wanted to marry but did not do so was that women did not want to marry men who had less than average annual incomes as compared with their peers.[4]

The desire for eligible Japanese men and women to want to be like everyone else is similar to the social pressure that occurs in other parts of the world. The Japanese version of *keeping up with the Joneses* is called *miihaa*, and it is exactly what the thirteenth-century Zen monk Dōgen Zenji warned against when he said, "The foolish person regards himself as another." However, Dōgen Zenji's teaching also called for a wise man to regard others as himself, and this ethics is a way of encouraging *others* to combine with other people in a group in the natural flow of *hitonami*. Rather than being a *Joe Shmo*, then, "a person who regards others as himself" is an unaffected guy who can be himself, or a *sorenari no hito* (just as you are). Because *others*-oriented ethics makes no distinction between the *individual* and *others*, it allows a person to uphold group values.

An interesting traditional feature of Japanese marriage that is still in practice today is *mukoyōshi*, literally meaning *adopted son-in-law*. This use of adult adoption, where a nonblood relation is chosen by the head of the family to become the family successor, began in the latter part of feudal Japan and is still widely in practice today as an effective way of keeping power in a family business intact. Japan has one of the world's highest adoption rates, and more than 90 percent of the 81,000 people adopted in Japan in 2011 were adult males in their twenties and thirties.[5] Said a Mitsui patriarch, "Better to have daughters than sons, for then I can choose my sons."

Still other traditions also continue, such as multigenerational living and children living at home after employment and marriage. The spatial restraints and cramped urban living discussed in chapter 2, on the environment, have validated these practices, as well as the comfort and the practicality of sleeping and eating together. Youth employment challenges and housing expenses have added to the mix in modern times, further solidifying the traditional expectation that the working generation looks after the elderly.

Tiny Monaco aside, Japan has the highest percentage of people sixty-five years and older in the world (and Monaco is mostly retirees who have moved there anyway). Japan's 22.9 percent is approaching a fourth of the nation. Even Germany and Italy (the next two in line) only have about 20 percent. And Japan's 22.9 percent elderly contrast with Canada's 15.9 percent and the United States' 13.1 percent.

Multigenerational living has long helped create the image that the elderly are better looked after in Japan than elsewhere; however, evidence to the contrary is also growing. As Japan's number of dependent elders increases, it has become evident that there is insufficient capacity to accommodate the number of elderly in care, with some 420,000 currently on the waiting list for hospitals for families. With care homes still stigmatized, families that can no longer cope with caring for dependent elderly people are using hospitals as a last resort.[6] Disturbing stories of middle-aged family members abusing confused, aging family members come to the fore each day, mostly through social isolation and financial bullying. These sad factors are a reality in all societies where the elderly population is becoming larger and larger, and perhaps Japan is a forerunner.

3.5 *Kawaii* **Products**
Most everyone is familiar with these "cute" Japanese products.

Possibly because of their increasing rarity, idolization of children or childlikeness is popular. *Kawaii* cute things are found in everything from household decoration to food, clothes, and stationery (photograph 3.5). In fashion, dressing up cute was coined *burikko* (literally, *acting childlike*) back in the 1980s when it began. A cutesy dress is accompanied by a high-pitched voice, elongated vowels, and *burikko*-coded mannerisms. Through anime and cosplay, *kawaii* products have become internationalized. Audi has now even rolled out a special edition Hello Kitty car, not to mention Sanrio's Hello Kitty accessories.

A more traditional use of the term *kawaii* is found in its verb form, *kawaigaru*, which means *to look after* or, literally, *to cute*. Like the love loyalty of *amae* that occurs in both personal and professional circles, parents *kawaigaru* their children, and managers do so with their subordinates. Taking out children or subordinates, buying gifts, or introducing someone such as a future marital partner or employer are all acts of *kawaigaru*. Feeling at once gratitude and indebtedness, those who have been looked after seek opportunities to return the favor and repay their benefactors, often for years to come. For example, the nephew of a childless banker who introduced him to his new employer felt so indebted that he offered to maintain and fund his uncle's grave on his passing. In this way, acts of *kawaigaru* often span lifetimes, pointing to another feature of social organization that defines the Japanese.

Despite its in-built supportive structure, it remains largely true that the stereotype of the Japanese family outside Japan has tended to be the *sararīman* who works himself to death (*karōshi*), a wife that leads a life of domesticity raising children, and children who are subjected to the severe pressures of testing in schools. In the following sections, we address each of these in turn, beginning with children at school, then moving on to the workplace, and finishing with men's and women's places.

SOCIAL ORGANIZATION AT SCHOOL

The house clan's parent–child *oya-ko* relations are replicated symbolically at school between teachers and students and between older students *senpai* and younger ones *kohai*. Just as orphans are generally shunted aside and left in institutions in Japan, not belonging to a group at school is potentially risky socially.[7] Like the masterless disciple in feudal times, the *ronin*—literally, *unretained person*—today refers to the student who has not yet been admitted into university, or is unemployed.

Japanese mandatory education follows the 6–3–3 format of six years of primary school, three years of middle school, and three years of high school. The best research universities are at the national level, and the frequently cited National Seven are Tokyo, Kyoto, Osaka, Nagoya, Hokkaido, Kyushu, and Tohoku. Some 2.8 million students were enrolled in Japan's 778 universities, 597 of which are private.[8] The better-known private universities, such as Keio and Waseda, have exchange programs with English-speaking universities worldwide; and some international universities, such as Sophia University and International Christian University in Tokyo, offer degrees in English. Traditionally designed for women and with an average of 90 percent female enrollment, Japan's two-year *tandai* colleges are typically vocational. There are a few business schools with master's programs, and new graduate law schools that meet government requirements, but graduate school remains relatively rare.

Japanese cram schools are now famous the world over as the model for the East Asian pressure cooker for national university entrance exams. Bearing the weight of family pride, students do their utmost to perform; however, the *ronin* masterless mentioned above are common, and someone who takes a year or even two to be accepted in Tokyo University is possibly less stigmatized than someone who attends a less-branded university. In a country where lateral movement is difficult and group association is important, graduating from a university means a premium brand for life. The four years at a university in Japan is a rite of passage, and the last fling with freedom before adulthood. On graduation and employment, a Japanese person becomes a *shakaijin*, or a society person, and this comes shortly after the year when Japanese are officially considered *seijin* adults at twenty years of age.

In comparison with the United States and Canada, however, university lectures, seminars, and the classroom experience in general are relatively less important, particularly for students in large classes or those who do not have required lab attendance. Moreover, unlike the social transformation that North American families have come to expect from university campuses, Japanese social engineering occurs largely in the primary, middle, and high school years, when mandatory moral education takes up something like 35 hours of a student's class time annually.

In middle school, for example, once a week students open their pages to the textbook *Kokoro no Nōto* (Notes of the Heart).[9] This textbook cites twenty-four keys that will "open doors to the world," and these are divided into four parts: (1) oneself (five keys), (2) orientation to nature and the spiritual (three keys), (3) Relations with others (six keys), and (4) relations with the group and society (ten keys).[10]

In this textbook, there are twice as many keys that promote group relations with *others*, with chapter headings such as "A Collective Society Feels Good to Live In" and "Make Your Own Strength Society's Strength." More interesting still is that even in the keys that appear to be lessons in actualizing the individual, the interpretation reorients the student toward others in the group. For example, the heading, "Take Responsibility for Your Own Action" appears with the subheading "Your Actions

Might Have Bearings on Others," recalling the abolished practice of *rentai sekinin* (group responsibility) where all students were punished for the failing of one.

Once again, we list a few of the main educational differences that regularly surprise North Americans. At number one is always the sight of first-graders commuting to and from school on public transportation alone. Here is an example of how enforced social rules work well in Japan—using public transportation is mandatory.

By world standards, Japan is among the safest countries in the world, and Tokyo and Osaka are often listed in the top ten as the safest cities, especially when compared with America, where the murder rate is 5 per 100,000 population, as opposed to 1 per 100,000 in Japan. The absence of crime and the level of safety often come as a surprise to many families from the United States moving to Japan. Conversely, the level of crime in the United States is a source of anxiety for Japanese visitors to the United States, if not a deterrent.

Another factor that visitors find surprising about public education in Japan is that students clean and eat together as part of group activities. There are often no dining halls, and students bring the lunch into their classrooms and serve their classmates on a roster. The same is true for lunch cleanup as well as cleaning the school in general. Cleaning is considered part of school, and everything is done together. Perhaps, as many say, people are less likely to trash places they must clean up on their own. However, because this is the only educational behavior most students know, cleaning up without professional cleaners feels normal. And because cleaning up and serving food on rotation with a cohort fit in perfectly with the Japanese *others* orientation, school seems like an ideal place to teach and learn the practice of relating to others by putting them first.

SOCIAL ORGANIZATION AT WORK

No one would blame Henry Denton for concluding that he thought business was more or less the same the world over, because cross-cultural business is conducted in the English language for much of global business communication. In chapter 1, on language, we examine how English has accelerated into prominence as a lingua franca in the twenty-first century, and the number of nonnative English speakers learning English for business continues to be on the rise.

Indeed, a growing number of companies based in countries where English is not the native language have embraced the BELF (Business English as a Lingua Franca) movement, and they are even instituting English as their main language of communication. Although this is most evident in Europe, this trend has begun to take root in Japan as well. For example, in Japan in 2010, two major e-commerce firms—Rakuten and Fast Retailing/Uniqlo—adopted English as their official languages. Similarly, in 2012, Honda Motor Company adopted English as its official language for all global meetings.

Since the Meiji Restoration, which began in the latter half of the nineteenth century and continued through the turn of the twentieth century, part of what has fueled the Japanese economy has been the mentality of catching up with the West. Echoes of this view, that Japan was somehow behind, were in part what led to the country's industrialization following its opening, and eventually to more trade and the regeneration after World War II. Even today, Japan still puts great energy and finances into learning things Western.

During Japan's economic bubble, however, it was common to think that Japan had surpassed the West in business management, and in particular, manufacturing. US and Canadian researchers and business professionals alike began to study Japanese business organizations to look for ways to improve their performance, exploring everything from exchanging business cards to quality circles.

This economic "catch up" mentality, combined with the focus on manufacturing quality, produced some uniquely Japanese business strategies that persist today. For example, back then and still today, the *uchi* internal Japanese business style conforms to the general rules of *others* relationships. An informal, consensus-building decision-making process called *nemawashi*, or literally, root-tending, is the default style of interaction among insiders. Intimate *amae* conversations bubble up and prepare the grounds for a proposal-fostering system called *ringi seido*. In the Japanese manner of taking foreign products and concepts and making them Japan's own, *ringi seido* was originally conceived by the US statistician William Edwards Deming but was localized in Japan. We discuss this system, together with the root-tending style of *nemawashi*, in greater detail in chapter 5, on authority conception.

Consensus-building decision making dates back to the organizational style of the *zaibatsu*, a conglomerate, family-controlled company structure that was partially dissolved on the grounds of unfair trade practices following World War II. Regrouped again as associated businesses, the new *keiretsu* structures, frequently translated as "a system of enterprises," literally means *connected columns*. Widely viewed as a forced model shift, the old *honsha-kogaisha* main office–subsidiaries relationships still persist in *keiretsu* structures today.

A typical *keiretsu* has a central organizing bank, a shared board of directors, and cross-shareholding that is sometimes controversially seen as protectionist. Like the *one house, one crest* motto, the *keiretsu* are usually identifiable by a set principles that defines their goal. There are variations of *keiretsu*, such as Toyota, that conform to the traditional vertical type, or the *keiretsu* of merger corporations, such as Mitsubishi UFJ Financial Group, a kind of super-*keiretsu* that has become popular since the Lost Decades.

As far as meetings go, North American business professionals encounter either the initial contact outsiders' meetings (where formally approved and stamped documents are circulated like press releases) or the internal no-decision, no-action style of meetings (where information seems to haphazardly pass up among meeting members). For North American professionals who expect business discussions, actions, and decisions to take place, these meetings are at best confusing, and they have been variously called pointless or go-with-the-flow.[11] Although Japanese corporations now have more professionals who are North American–educated and –trained, the external and internal meeting styles are still common, and are likely to be a mainstay of Japanese businesses. We further discuss this contexted style of communication in chapter 4, on contexting, and again in chapter 5, on the authority conception.

THE SOCIAL ORGANIZATION OF SPORTS

It seems fitting to begin a discussion of Japanese sports with a traditional one like sumo (see photograph 3.6). The original martial art is the only one that is truly competitive, in the sense that sumo wrestlers can be promoted and demoted in each tournament. Called *rikishi*, or strong samurai, sumo wrestlers today fight like the samurai did, in that they must constantly win their place in the house clan. Sumo, written 相撲, is frequently translated as "striking one another." However, though the second character, 撲 *mo*, means attack, rush, or push, the first character, 相 *su*, means *other*, illustrating how attacking opponents means using the force of the *other* against himself, like many other Eastern martial arts such as judo. Sumo therefore not only exemplifies the Japanese *others* orientation but also demonstrates how defending and receptivity in sport can be competitive. Sumo is appreciated by many, and has recently become more globalized, extending initially to Pacific islanders, then to East Asians and Eastern Europeans.[12]

A nontraditional sport that the Japanese love to play and watch is baseball, which was introduced by an English teacher who came to Japan in 1872. Because baseball was originally only played in the United States, when the sport came to Japan it became a symbolic pact between the two countries. Interestingly, in Japanese the word "baseball" is 野球 *yakyū*, with the character 野 *ya* meaning *field* and 球 *kyū* meaning *ball*. In short, baseball literally translates into Japanese as "fieldball," turning it into an *others* game.

Like many foreign borrowings, Japanese baseball has taken on a flavor all its own. The size of Japanese fields is smaller, the ball is tighter, and most notably, ties are allowed in scoring, once again showing the colors of an *others* game. High school baseball

3.6 Sumo
In a sumo bout, competitors try to turn their opponent's strength back on each other. Photo courtesy of Sandrine Burtschell.

is huge in Japan, and whole communities support school teams in the spring invitational and summer playoffs. Called Summer Kōshien, the final two-week tournament is the biggest amateur tournament in Japan, which could explain why many professionals with little leisure time spend all their holiday time attending this event.

Also reaching a feverish pitch among Japanese fans is soccer. Though originally begun with a men's team, Japan's women's team won the 2011 FIFA World Cup Final, beating the rival United States. Since then, the Japanese women's soccer team has lost to the United States twice, once at the 2012 Summer Olympics and then again at the 2015 World Cup Final. Ironically, the Japanese women's team is endearingly called 撫子 *Nadeshiko*, which, named after a pink flower, literally means *huggable or caress-able child.* Symbolically, *nadeshiko*, combined with the old name for one of the early Japanese tribes, Yamato, is a term used to symbolize feminine beauty in the ideal Japanese woman. Although somewhat oxymoronic that a rare beauty should win an archetypically male sports event—the FIFA World

Cup—we have come full circle and conclude with a discussion of three other groups in Japanese social organization: women, immigrants, and robots.

WOMEN'S AND MEN'S PLACES

The World Economic Forum's "Global Gender Gap Report" consistently ranks Japan near the bottom.[13] In 2014, Japan ranked 104 out of 142, with a score of 0.06584. Canada, by contrast, ranked 19 out of 142, with a score of 0.7464; and the United States ranked 20 out of 142, with a score of 0.7463. Japan ranked third worst out of all thirty-four members of the Organization for Economic Cooperation and Development, surpassing only South Korea (117th) and Turkey (125th). Moreover, the score has remained more or less unchanged for the last decade (with one positive blip in 2010).[14]

Women were not always so poorly portrayed in economic terms. Folklore tells us of a sun goddess, Amaterasu Ōmikami, who created Japan. In the third century, before Japan had writing, Chinese chronicles recount the story of a female shaman called Himiko who united the hundred warring countries that would become the Japan we know today. Since then, there were eight ruling empresses until the eighth century, one each in the seventeenth and eighteenth centuries of the early Edo Period, when Japan purportedly turned masculine. Heian courts between the mid–tenth and mid–eleventh centuries had aristocratic women who wrote much about life at the time. Women owned property and took lovers, as did their male counterparts. However, perhaps most important, the aristocratic women of the Heian Period invented *hiragana*, the syllabary writing style still used today. The poetry and prose Heian women wrote are cherished and read in classrooms.

Portuguese missionaries in the sixteenth century were alarmed by women's relative sexual freedom, discussing how women married and divorced more freely than at home. As described above, a family marriage was a kind of professional alliance, where *mukoyōshi* groom-in-laws were commonplace.

If the business collaborations failed to prosper, it was acceptable to part ways so as to dissolve the formal house union in favor of something that worked better.

To reach the modern era and the stereotypical Western view of the Japanese woman, who has a lower status compared with men and whose life is relegated to domesticity and child-rearing, we need not go far to find examples of the paucity of women in power. A look at the diet, a corporate meeting room, or an engineering class might similarly support the idea of a scarcity of women in government, workplaces, and university science courses in Japan. Responding to this, the economist Kathy Matsui has advocated increasing the number of women in the workforce to reverse this trend, arguing that making both working and having children doable would help alleviate the issue of a declining birthrate in Japan as more women would opt to work.[15] Then–prime minister Abe Shinzo endorsed the idea of women increasing their share in the labor force in the so-called third arrow of his reform plan. The best outcome for Abe's social reforms or Matsui's so-called womenomics would be for the Japanese to be able to choose the when and how of career and child-rearing involvement, a challenge and a desired outcome for women as well as men.

These Japanese goals are generally similar to North American concerns regarding female gender equality in the workplace. However, unlike corporate North America's merit-driven workplace, many of Japan's large corporations still operate with seniority-based career advancement, where workers, almost exclusively men and known as *sararīman*, lead a life that is consumed by day at the office, and by night and weekends of serial unpaid outings with the boss. Though *karōshi* or *working to death* may be less common than before, many employees still live as *tanshin funin* workers on solo assignments in distant cities away from their family.

It would not be extraordinary to ask why a Japanese woman would want to replace her role at home where often she is valued as a mother with the slow career progression of a *sararīman* employee's life that consumes him. This would be an even bigger thing for which to ask in the traditional family setup, where

3.7 Salaryman After Hours
In Japan, business never sleeps. Photo courtesy of Sandrine Burtschell.

the mother of the house had a hold on the purse strings. The old Japanese salaryman's joke was that he had a hard day's work, only to come home and hand over all his earnings to his wife, the Ministry of Finance, which in turn handed him small spending allowances.

Jokes aside, conversations about increasing the number of women in the workplace will likely remain confused until the current working environment, composed of a male majority, is improved and reformed. Japanese women have little incentive if the trade-off is between being a homemaker, in many cases with control of the household finances, and receiving a ten-day annual holiday plus zero pay for public holidays. In short, in addition to encouraging women to enter the workforce and ensuring that women's professional needs are met in line with men's, men's current working environment must also go through social reform to attract beneficial outcomes for both men and women (see photograph 3.7). For this to happen, there is also a need to define new inside/outside roles that make sense in native Japanese terms.

GAIJIN FOREIGNERS, INSIDERS, AND ROBOTS

We offer a word about *gaijin* in this penultimate section of the chapter on social organization. *Gaijin* is an accepted if pejorative way of referring to foreigners. Short for *gaikokujin*, which literally means *outside country person*, 外人 *gaijin* takes out the word, 国 *koku* or *kuni*, which means *country*, thereby reducing the reference to mean *outsider*. Theoretically, every foreigner is included in this term; but for the most part, the reference is aimed at non-Asians, who may even further be limited to the smaller subset of North Americans. Japanese refer to Europeans as *Yōroppajin* (Europe people), and Asian groups other than the Japanese are called *Ajiajin* or Asian people, which differs from the American use of Asian to generally mean East Asians but not South Asians. The Japanese term for Westerner is literally *seiyōjin*, but more people today use *ōbei*, which has a more commercial ring to it than the former term.

Cities generally have larger numbers of non-Japanese nationals, but Japan still has little immigration. Because of a rapidly aging society and because many nurses and care workers leave during child-rearing years birth, Japan has a shortage of labor power in hospitals. Increasing immigration seems like a plausible way to offset the declining population, especially in the medical sector, where the Ministry of Health, Labor, and Welfare estimates that 2 million nurses will be needed at hospitals and nursing care facilities as well as for home care services in 2025.[16] Nurses from Southeast Asia have trickled in, but the immigration is not without local resistance and complaint. For example, industry members have voiced that immigrants had to be taught the Japanese language from the beginning, not to mention technical and medical Japanese.

Although not without controversy, robots have been proposed as another way to resolve many modern issues, including those in health care. Science fiction aside, planning for robotic help in hospitals is well under way in Japan. Without the religious issues of the application of robotics found in the West, Japan has had an easier time of introducing anthropomorphic robots into society. For example, Robobear lifts patients in and out of bed any number of times without hurting its back.

Other humanoid robots have also begun to make an appearance in the Japanese social panorama. ASIMO, for example, made by Honda, assists at the reception of the Tokyo branch of

Bank of Tokyo–Mitsubishi. Nestle is investing in robots to sell coffeemakers in stores across the country. Robots guide visitors around the capital's National Museum of Emerging Science and Innovation. A fully robot-manned hotel in Nagasaki is apparently in operation.[17]

Japan's love of technology and robots is not without criticism, because the actual benefits of robots have yet to be truly felt. More than once, however, Japan, the country with close to no resources, has innovated futuristic products. Moreover, training immigrants with soft skills and building robots to do tedious work are not two mutually exclusive initiatives for Japan to be able to achieve. Perhaps in the social engineering unique to Japan, it can again pull off enmeshing the traditional with the hypermodern.

RECOMMENDATIONS

The general rule of thumb for behavior in *others* relationships in public is to be average and general: Go with the flow. If this feels like it goes against our value of the individual, it is important to remember that North Americans have a public face, too, although arguably to a lesser degree. Also, in private, Japanese social organization assimilators can be as specific and as oddball as they like—as we have seen among those who like to dress up in cosplay costumes. In the comfort of friends and family, the Japanese feel they can be unique individuals. This, too, is not unlike the unspoken rules of North American social organization.

The difference in relationships between the Japanese and North Americans comes from the way the Japanese view inside and outside faces. For Americans, insider–outsider relationships correlate to personal and professional ones. For the Japanese, however, inside and outside faces exist in each of the personal and professional spheres, from home to school to work. In Japanese professional relationships, there can be a personal and emotional element, particularly if they are long term.

Similarly, North Americans sometimes have formal expectations of personal friends and families. Each of us can probably come up with examples, such as the different expectations for behavior of a kid brother at home and in a library at school. A similar distinction between inside and outside faces is found in North American sports. The different roles played by the same athlete in the locker room versus out on the field are a great example of inside and outside faces.

Japanese films, such as *Soshiki* (Funeral), are full of satires on the expectation of how Japanese friends and family behave— and require others to behave—in public. Such extreme forms of public face maintenance, in what is typically thought of among North Americans as the "personal" realm, are often noticed and negatively judged. The misunderstood Japanese in these circumstances are often cast as formal or cold. Our recommendation is to try to interpret Japanese social organization in Japanese terms, namely, by understanding that *others* are the primary focus in relationships, and that each relationship is approached with inside and outside faces. Such an awareness can go a long way toward understanding how Japanese people relate to one another, both personally and professionally.

SUMMARY OF JAPANESE SOCIAL ORGANIZATION

Inside and Outside Faces

- Japanese interaction starts and ends with the other person.
- The other has origins in Zen Buddhism and Taoism.
- Identify with a group—biggest to smallest.
- True feelings are for those within the group, and a face is for those outside the group.
- A binary inside/outside face is in operation.

Family as a Tribe

- 一家一門 *ikka ichimon*. One house, one gate; *one family, one crest.*
- All parts of society replicate themselves in the family.
- The ranks and roles of siblings are important.
- It is common for adopted sons-in-law to be heirs of a family business.

Education

- Education is modeled on the family.
- Group ethics is taught at school.

Business

- Business is family.

Sports

- Traditional and contemporary sports like sumo, baseball, and soccer illustrate "others" games.

Gender Roles

- Both women and men have power roles in different social settings.
- Gender equality in the workplace has been recognized as an important area to improve.
- To encourage more women to enter the workforce, the current work life dominated by men could be improved.

Robots

- Robots have long been admired in Japan.
- Humanoid robots are being designed to occupy service and health care positions.

Recommendations

- In public, go with the flow.
- In private, be as eccentric as you like.
- Learn to distinguish and eventually use insider/outsider relationships and interactions in both personal and professional circles.

4

J A P A N E S E

Contexting

Listener Talk 101

Although we may not have superpowers, each of us has something that comes close. It is the glance at the family table that gets someone to pass us the salt, or the smile and nod that get us what we like as regulars at our favorite restaurant. This background knowledge and feeling that we get from knowing each other's habits and characteristics so well that we can practically take them for granted is what we call context.

Interactions in contexts we know can feel so ordinary that we do not even think about what we are doing or saying in them. As when we ask someone to pass the salt at the dinner table, sometimes we do not even have to say anything because talking when we do not need to can be overkill or even take on a different meaning. For example, if the salt does not come your way after several glances and even an extra gesture, you might look directly at the family member who did not get that you had asked for it several moments ago, and say somewhat emphatically, "Could you please pass the salt." The same request for salt would take on a completely different tone if you were asking for salt from a business professional you did not know well. Knowing when and where and to whom to say something and when not to—these also come from our knowledge of multiple contexts, the intuitive experiences of different situations that we share both within and across groups.

The kind of highly coded "in-language" we use in groups with which we have much shared context goes far beyond a request at a family table for salt, a meal in a favorite restaurant, or words in business or technology jargon. People who have shared contexts have entire conversations that are reduced to shorthand. Here is an example.

Chris has worked in the same company as Connie for years, and he knows that she likes to have lunch on her own at Bonnie's Kitchen close to the office, but like many other company executives, prefers to take her clients to Spago, especially if they are important. Given this context, if Chris asks, "What did you do for lunch today?" and Connie replies, "Spago," Chris might assume that Connie probably had an eventful lunch with a client. Chris might then ask, "And?" after which Connie will likely tell him how the meeting with the important client went. If you were eavesdropping on conversation 4.1, it would sound like this:

Conversation 4.1
CHRIS: What did you do for lunch today?
CONNIE: Spago.
CHRIS: And?

An eavesdropper who did not have the background information the two company colleagues had about preferred restaurants would not be able to understand the meaning of "And?" let alone give the answer for which Chris is looking in his question. As the only *content* available in the conversation, "And?" is based in the history or *context* of the colleagues.

Communication is, then, often as much about a kind of contexting literacy as it is about content literacy, or what we sometimes like to call "facts"—the words listed in dictionaries, and the grammar we tend to teach and learn in language classrooms.

A focus on spoken or written words at the expense of context, however, provides insufficient information for a full understanding of a conversation. This chapter first compares the principles of North American and Japanese contexting, and it then explores the strategies each group uses to talk with members within a familiar group and also across groups in intercultural communication. By pointing out some misunderstandings that can arise when we cannot or do not know how to read a native context in intercultural communication, we hope to help build and expand your internal contexting dictionaries.

THE YIN AND YANG OF CONTEXT AND CONTENT

Context and content are often inversely correlated, which means that while everyone uses and needs both in communication, there are cultures that rely more heavily on one than the other. An easy way to illustrate this is through a yin and yang sign, where we can imagine content as the light half and context as the dark, with a little bit of each mixed in each of the opposing sides. Extending this to communication, we can think about the light content as visible text or audible talk, and the dark context as the hidden sociocultural assumptions that lead to leaving out talk or text. Although content and context are both important, context receives considerably less attention because it is unexposed. This chapter gives context the consideration that it deserves and needs.

The anthropologist and communication expert Edward T. Hall was the first to coin the term "contexting," to gauge a group's inclination to rely on shared knowledge to communicate. Calling those who relied on much shared experience a "high-context culture," Hall differentiated people from high-context cultures from those from low-context cultures who relied more heavily on content. In this model, Hall referred to the Japanese as archetypically high-context, distinguishing them from more North American cultural norms, where people were more likely to depend on explicit content to get their meaning across. In his seminal book *The Silent Language*, Hall describes context as the silent language that allows us to monitor and evaluate our conversations, while all the while helping us to know what to say and when to say it.[1]

Because context is relative, it is often discussed in comparative terms. Going back to the example given above, Spago might be more formal, dressy, and pricey compared with Bonnie's Kitchen and therefore more client appropriate. However, Chris and Connie might know even more expensive and classier places than Spago. Similarly, a Canadian or US professional who uses explicit language to manage the company and execute regulations may seem low context to a Japanese but high context to a German.

Somewhere between Chris and Connie's interpersonal microcontext and the larger group assumptions of countries lies contexting knowledge, which varies across other social factors such as region and occupation within a country. In the United States, the Northeastern states—and notably the area of greater New York City, New Jersey, and eastern Pennsylvania—are markedly lower contexted than people in the Midwestern states. People in the Midwestern states, in turn, are notably lower contexted than people in the Southern states. There are similar variations in contexting among Canadians, whereby Anglophone Canadians (the Maritimes in particular) can be categorized as higher contexted than Francophone Canadians or Canadians in the Prairie Provinces. Despite these North American variations, it would probably be fair to say that the highest-contexted Alabaman is still lower than the lowest-contexted Japanese.

Similar to regional differences are ethnic group differences. For example, many of Canada's and the United States' First Nations, as well as Inuit cultures in both countries, are among the most highly contexted cultures anywhere. Salish, Navajo, Lakota, and Inuit groups, for instance, are as highly or higher contexted than most Japanese.

Considerable variability in contexting is evident in other North American ethnic groups as well, especially when those involved live in ethnic communities. In such cases, the people living there would tend to be more closely aligned in contexting with the norms of their country of ethnic origin, even if they are many generations removed from when their ancestors first moved to the Canada or the United States. This is particularly the case in the Chinatowns, Little Saigons, Little Indias, Korea-towns, Little Italies, Little Havanas, and Little Manilas (among others) sprinkled across many cities in North America. In other words, Canadians from the heavily Chinese area of Richmond, British Columbia, are more likely to be characterized by high contexting norms than others in the Vancouver metropolitan area. Likewise, the Arab Americans heavily concentrated in Dearborn, Michigan, are more likely to be characterized by high contexting norms than others in the Detroit metropolitan area.

Variations in regional contexting do exist in Japan, if to a lesser degree than in the United States. Because one of the variables in contexting is shared history, it follows that the greater the degree of shared history among a people, the higher the use of contexting. Similarly, the more mobile a people, the higher the use of content clarity. For example, urban Tokyo, in the eastern Kantō region, has a population with great mobility that makes it relatively mixed. It is therefore not surprising that people from Tokyo are slightly less context dependent than a less mobile group of people from, say, Kyoto, in western Kansai, who can make many assumptions about in-group behavior and language.

For example, in Japan there is an unwritten social rule that one should always refuse an invitation to someone's house, and let the other person insist. Between friends, there is often an understanding that, at some point, the invited person will accept the invitation. However, the number of times one should refuse is a delicate point.

Tokyo comedians joke about the awkward social faux pas of accepting a western Kyotoite's invitation too easily. As residents of the ancient capital, Kyotoites are stereotypically cast as the polite ones. So the punch line goes: "The whole town was talking about how rude I was for accepting an invitation I refused twenty-five times."

If the Japanese make social judgments based on regional contexting differences, so do North Americans. We often hear non–New Yorkers say things like, "New Yorkers are rude, but at least you know where you stand." Or how about typecasting Alabamans as polite but somewhat suspicious: "You can't tell if they are putting you down or really mean what they've just said." People who use more content and less context often see themselves as clear and forthright, but they can be stereotyped with negative personal attributes, such as being rude or obnoxious. Conversely, people who use more context and less content see themselves as sensitive and understanding, but they can be typecast as suspicious or fake, which can actually be the negative undertone of calling someone "polite."

Contexting also varies by occupation. For example, engineers, accountants, information systems professionals, and chemists may need to focus on clarity and specificity of content; while lawyers, advertising agents, public relations agents, and human resources managers attending to clients' needs may be required to be more sensitive to context. Still, it is likely that even the lowest-contexted Japanese engineer will be more context sensitive than the highest-contexted US human resources manager. Similar to social networks, the wider the net of users, the stronger the likelihood that its members can depend on context. A start-up might need to provide clear Web content to identify itself relative to a traditional branded company.

SPEAKER CONTENT OR LISTENER CONTEXT: WHO IS IN THE DRIVER'S SEAT?

Since contexting's inception in the late 1950s, linguists, sociologists, and anthropologists have variously studied the contexts of different cultures and their implications for intercultural communication. One of our coauthors, Haru Yamada, completed a study comparing internal and intercultural meetings between North American and Japanese bank managers. In this chapter, we draw many examples from her study.[2] Yamada argues that while low-context North Americans rely heavily on the speakers to deliver the meaning of content in conversations, high-context Japanese depend more on listener interpretations. Yamada called the speaker-led and content-based North American conversational dynamics *speaker talk*, and the listener-led and context-based Japanese style *listener talk*.

The different emphases are particularly important in intercultural business communication because meetings often take place in English. It is easy for native speakers of English to assume that because everyone is using a common language, they are doing so in the same way. Moreover, in general, we have a tendency to think our native understanding is the only correct version; and worse still, most of the time we do not even recognize that this is the bias of our thinking.

We saw earlier in our discussion that we often make judgments about someone based on the regional characteristics they display. This may range from gestures to dialects to regional variations in language and social behavior, but the point here is that even within a country, we tend to negatively evaluate those who do not use context in the same way we do. At the intercultural level, the differences are more pronounced, and this means that not only are we more likely to judge others' behavior negatively but we are also even more likely to misunderstand what they say and what they do because we do not share their context.

For example, a typical speaker-led, content-driven North American might hear the Japanese vocal feedback like "*Nnn*" (uh-huh) as agreement, when Japanese contexting literacy will translate the listener talk "*Nnn*" to mean "I'm following you." Similarly, a context-sensitive Japanese listener might misunderstand a direct North American question like "Do you understand?" as "He thinks I'm too stupid to understand, otherwise he wouldn't ask me such a question."

Here at work again is the *others* orientation discussed in chapter 3, on social organization: For a Japanese person, the context of the relationship is far more important than the clarity of content—so much so that we can leave out an entire sentence, say nothing, and still expect to be understood. This is extreme contexting, the deeply encoded grammar of ambiguity in the Japanese language we talked about in chapter 1.

Returning to the above question "Do you understand?" an *others* orientation toward social interaction would dictate not asking the question at all, or asking the question in the relational terms of listener talk, such as "*Daijōbudesuka?*" which literally means "Are you OK?" but is analogous to the more commonly used phrase in English "Are you OK with this?" This listener talk question is likely to indirectly elicit the answer to the question "Do you understand?" and have the additional benefit of promoting a more successful high-context interaction.

This chapter highlights examples of speaker talk and listener talk to help us be better able to read North American and Japanese contexts. Taking the time to understand what context is and how it is interpreted is important, because we can come to understand that the Japanese are not intentionally deceptive and the North Americans are not knowingly bullies. Rather, both cultures are simply talking and listening using their own cultural content and contexting bandwidths. We begin by looking at North American and Japanese attitudes toward talk and silence to uncover the key difference in the way each approaches communication.

TALKING GUNMEN VERSUS SILENT SWORDSMEN

A basic assumption we bring to every moment of communication is how we view and value talk and silence. A stylized example of the different attitudes between North Americans and Japanese can be demonstrated by comparing the US western film remake *The Magnificent Seven* with the original Japanese *chanbara* (sword fight movie) *The Seven Samurai*. Both popular stories are about seven heroes who protect a helpless farming village from bandit raids, but that is where the similarity ends. In the US movie, talk precedes every confrontation; but in the Japanese movie, swordsmen launch silent attacks that culminate in swordfights.

In *The Magnificent Seven*, the villain, Calvera, sets the stage for a story about a powerful talking bully who dominates the meek and silent villagers: "We'll have to have another discussion very soon. It's always a pleasure to hear the news of my good friend, Sotero. Maybe when I come back, uh?"

By telling Sotero that he might listen to the villagers the next time he returns, Calvera reiterates that he is the one who calls the meeting; Calvera is the one who talks, and the villagers listen. Because the villagers have no voice, for the next "discussion," they hire the Magnificent Seven. At the entrance to the town, the leader of the Magnificent Seven, Chris, meets with Calvera, and the two men jockey for position as if they are about to draw.

"Ride on," says Chris, staking his place to talk up front.

Calvera is infuriated at his lost opportunity to speak first, and responds angrily: "You hear that Sotero? You hear what he said? Ride on! To me! You tell him to ride on before I become angry. Him. And others. Because if I leave here with empty hands, everybody will answer to me when I come back."

By speaking first, Chris implies he is the person in control. By default, Calvera becomes the less powerful person who can only respond. Naturally, Calvera does not like this, and implies that while Sotero may be listening—"You hear that Sotero? You hear what he said?"—he is not. Ultimately, Calvera pouts, saying he will be the speaker in control next time: "Everybody will answer to me."

Although everyday interaction may not be as combative, the view that the powerful speak and the powerless have no voice is reflected in how North Americans talk about talking. On many American platforms, from Ted Talks to boardrooms to classrooms, a speaker is someone who is knowledgeable and bold. In her book *Quiet*, the US attorney and author Susan Cain supports "introverts in a world that can't stop talking." She also pays tribute, however, to speaking out: "There is no one more courageous than the person who speaks with the courage of his convictions."[3]

Talk, for many North Americans, is not just a medium to resolve or work things out, but also a courageous act of self-presentation. Conversely, if the opportunity to speak presents itself and a speaker chooses to remain a silent listener, such a choice carries negative connotations. A silent child might be told "Speak up!" and jeered at if he or she still does not answer: "What's the matter, cat got your tongue?" The child may be deemed unconfident and lacking in self-esteem; or worse, seen as a sullen, arrogant, and defiant child who chooses not to speak.

In classrooms all over the United States, the student who does not participate in class is judged as not paying attention or not trying hard enough. And the very real outcome may be that he or she even gets a lower grade for lack of class participation.

The leadership theorist John Adair says that communication is the sister of leadership, and speaking is its primary component. Without talk, we cannot interpret, and we must resort to second-guessing others. If we follow this logic, silence, or the total absence of talk, is a communication breakdown. A professional characterized as silent is likely to be seen as underperforming, lacking in drive and leadership, or even hiding something. In the context of North American speaker talk, at best, a silent person is judged as passive; at worst, he or she is seen as suspicious.

The hit song "Silence Is Golden" may challenge the idea that English speakers tend to judge silence negatively. However, when we carefully read the lyrics, it becomes evident that the silence in the song is about masking a lie. The song, like the expression *hush money*, alludes to the belief that speaking is the truth and silence is dishonest. Silence, in the North American culture, is thus not golden at all—speech is.

Language learners often say that Japanese is the opposite of English. We talked earlier in this book about how Japanese write up and down, open a book with the spine to the right, read right to left, and use whole conceptual kanji characters rather than an alphabet. We discussed how English grammar generally follows the subject–verb–object word order, while Japanese grammar follows the subject–object–verb format. Here we add that the Japanese language not only back-loads verbs but also back-loads adjectives, adverbs, and negations, in that order. In the Japanese language, then, critical meaning—in the form of assertions and negations—is given at the end of the sentence, if at all. This grammatical content order *is* vastly different from English, which places negations before a verb that occurs in the middle of a sentence.

With such differences in content between English and Japanese, it may come as no surprise that North Americans and

Japanese also approach context much differently, and even have opposing views about talk and silence. For example, if we go back to the fight scenes in *The Magnificent Seven* and *The Seven Samurai*, in all the instances in the US remake where Calvera stops at the entrance to the village to talk, in the original Japanese movie the samurai stalk the invaders and ambush them, and the only vocalizations heard come from the cries of the villagers and the fighters.

Whereas talk had to be added to the US movie remake, the Japanese did not think they needed talk, because in Japan, instead of the expression "The squeaky wheel gets the grease," people say "A bird that sings gets shot" ("*Tori mo nakaneba utaremaji*"). Thus, in Japan, crying out, rather than being perceived as a voice that needs to be heard, is seen as touting oneself— being a braggart. The bilingual NHK news presenter Sumire Matsubara says that when she speaks English, she is often told she talks too much and sounds conceited by the Japanese public and members of the national television community.

Therefore, from a Japanese perspective, instead of talk, silent communication is idealized via *haragei*, or, literally, "belly art," where *ishin denshin* or feelings are expressed through heart-to-heart transmission. Here, *haragei* may be viewed as gut feelings or intuitive communication, which the Japanese often idealize as purer forms of human feelings when compared with thought-up rational speech or critical expressions. Like a silent tête-à-tête, then, the goal for *haragei* silent communicators is to practice *a-un-no-kokyū*, or *a-un breathing*, a kind of scripted dialogue where one person inhales the first sound of a Buddhist incantation, "*a*," and another knows to exhale and respond with the last sound, "*un*." Continuing in iterations of perfect synergy, such a romanticized ancient worldview features people who know each other so well that words are human-made trivia that could even be deceptive and therefore potentially divisive. From the Japanese perspective, silent communication unites.

If we were to combine the skepticism about the value of talk with the Taoist *other*'s point of view we discussed in chapter 3, on social organization, we might find that an individual's own talk becomes even less important for a Japanese person. As the expression *Bigen shin narazu* (beautiful speech does not beget truth) exemplifies, the notion is that beautiful speech lacks sincerity; halting styles are more honest.

The Taoist teacher Lao Tzu once said, "Those who know, do not speak. Those who speak, do not know." Thus, historically, while leading Roman families were sending their sons to Greece to become fluid political and legal orators, the Japanese were sending their sons to temples to meditate and empty their minds with monks.

That great oratory does not have the same stature in Japan as it does in major Western civilizations adds another dimension to understanding why Japanese students participate little in class. The typical rationalization for the "quiet Asian" is that shyness and a lack of English-language proficiency drives them to reticence. However, in the case of the Japanese and also possibly other Asian students, this view overlooks the cultural importance assigned to silence over talk and critical thinking. Part of why Japanese students talk little in class is because they see their primary job as a student is to apply the culturally important task of active listening.

Moreover, the less favorable view toward talk also puts into perspective why Japanese *uchi* insider meetings begin with trivia and small talk, or what business consultants refer to as nontask sounding, which can sometimes even expand to the full length of the *nemawashi* meeting (which is mentioned in chapter 3, on social organization, and is developed in chapter 5, on authority conception). Devalued talk also underpins *soto* outsider meetings, where formalized, preapproved proposals are passed around for ratification rather than negotiation. In both internal or external Japanese business meetings, the actual content of talk is less important than the relational context. Thus, the primary goal of many Japanese meetings is not to make decisions or solve problems but to have skilled listeners become involved in endorsing a program or proposal. In other words, in high-context and low-content Japanese communication, it is the listener's job to listen actively, using the perceptive listening skill the Japanese call *sasshi*, a concept we explore next.

Sasshi means "to sense," and is another way to describe Japanese active listening. As the listener perceives, listens, and understands from the other's point of view, *sasshi* is the listening component of listener talk. As opposed to only hearing spoken content, a listener practicing *sasshi* also hears the context of what a speaker says from their point of view. Critically, this listener contexting fosters speaking from a listener's point of view. Japanese children learn the receptive art of listening to talk by copying adults in active *sasshi* listening.

Conversation 4.2 is an example of *sasshi*. Here, a mother is talking with her two-and-a-half-year-old son, Kei, from his point of view, and encouraging him to talk back from hers:

Conversation 4.2

MOTHER: *Soo ka. Kei-chan no omeme onaka ga suiteru tte itterune.*
OK. So Kei's eyes are saying, (I'm) hungry.
KEI: *N. Okāsan isogashī.*
Yes. Mom is busy.

MOTHER: (big proud eyes) *Nn. Kei-chan yoku wakatta ne. Okāsan isogashikattakara.* (smiling)
Yes. Kei understands well. Mom was busy.

Instead of just asking, "Kei, are you hungry?" Kei's mother uses *sasshi* to guess and vocalize what she thinks Kei is feeling by reading his eyes: "OK. So Kei's eyes are saying, (I'm) hungry." Similarly, instead of saying, "Is it lunch yet?" Kei copies his mother's use of seeing things from her point of view, and tells her he knows she has not gotten around to preparing him a meal because she has been busy: "Yes. Mom is busy." Kei is then rewarded with praise for playing by the rules of listener talk and seeing things from his mother's point of view: "Yes. Kei understands well. Mom was busy."

In this way, adults encourage children to practice speaking from the other's point of view at every turn of the conversation.

Indeed, children's listener talk provides explicit support for the other's viewpoint, because it allows children to address themselves by name or in the third person. By the time they are adults and fluent speakers of listener talk, they not only drop the third-person self-reference but also omit larger chunks of communication that are assumed to be stored alongside a content language dictionary in their context dictionary.

In this sense, a good communicator in Japan is a good context listener rather than a good content speaker, something that might also describe self-conscious young adults in Japan. In fact, *sasshi* communication became a nationwide trend in about 2007, when a phenomenon called KY hit the streets. Young texters used this *rōmaji* acronym for *Kūki Yomenai*, or *cannot read the air*, to describe someone who could not feel out a situation and made gaffes in social communication.[4] Examples from a young informant of KY are people who turn a light meeting in a café into a heavy academic conversation or a young woman who keeps talking about her boyfriend at lunch in a women's get-together.[5] People who commit such KY faux pas appear to have barged into a group and spoken whatever was on their mind without considering the connection of the group. A skilled user of listener talk, conversely, is someone who is context-literate enough to sense the conversation and be able to contribute talk with all the listeners in mind.

In short, using *sasshi* to feel out the context and then contributing to the conversation with listener talk is useful not just for young Kei at home but also for anyone in social and professional communication with the Japanese. Because of this, in the following section, we present five common ways in which the Japanese practice listener talk. These are by no means the only ones, however; we encourage you to explore these listener talk strategies and perhaps try some out, as you might the contents of a phrasebook.

LISTENER TALK 1: *AIZUCHI* LISTENER FEEDBACK

A good way to start learning listener talk is by using the active listening feedback the Japanese call *aizuchi*. Referred to as

4.1 Mochi Hammerers
Aizuchi literally means "mutual hammering." Photo courtesy of David Pursehouse.

back-channel cues in linguistics, *aizuchi* are the short "uhuh, uhuhs" listeners use to show they are following the conversation. Literally meaning *mutual hammering* in Japanese, the word *aizuchi* is likely to have originated from bladesmiths crafting swords. If you have ever been lucky enough to experience the traditional art form of rice cake pounding, where rice cakes are made by pounding *mochi* rice with a giant wooden mallet in a kind of large wooden mortar, *aizuchi* is like the kneader who folds in time with the pounder (see photograph 4.1). For a fun version of this, see *Dramatic Ricecake Pounding* on YouTube.[6] *Aizuchi*, then, are active "I'm listening" signals that can be a visual head-nod or an auditory "I'm following you" vocalization, like "*N*," "*sō*," and "*hūn*."

Just like *sasshi* training, Japanese parents teach their children to nod and vocalize feedback *aizuchi* by pausing at the ends of phrases, and waiting for the baby to punctuate these pauses with *aizuchi*. A YouTube video example of this is a father reading a bedtime story to his son from a picture book. Every time the dad finishes a sentence, he pauses, and he waits for his son to say "*hai*." "*Hai*" literally means "yes," in response to a question; but as listener feedback, it means "I'm following you" or "Go on."

In the video clip, where the baby listener is the star, both the baby's mother and father loudly laud him every time he delivers *aizuchi* feedback that vocalizes his listenership. At the end of the story, the mother encourages the boy to give his ultimate feedback by applauding the dad storyteller, and reprimands her son when he does not comply: "You're not going to applaud?"

Adult Japanese speakers expect *aizuchi* from their listeners, and listeners use them liberally without hesitation. Like the smile, bowing is introductory feedback that the Japanese send, even when the other person cannot see them. In Yamada's study of internal US and Japanese intercultural meetings, the Japanese gave twice as many listener cues as the Americans.

An interesting feature of the US meetings was that listener feedback was clustered around the beginnings and endings of topics. Once the speaker-in-charge settled into his or her own deal, he or she supported the key idea in the introduction with more talk, and had full reign in presenting it until it was concluded. During the body of the talk, the other bankers listened in virtual silence.

For many North American professionals, sending back-channel cues once a speaker is rolling out a topic can feel invasive. Indeed, the Canadian vlogger Micaela Braithwaite, who vlogs about her experiences living in Japan, claims that she still finds this one of the most annoying features of Japanese, despite her fluency in the language. However, in intercultural communication, back-channel cues misunderstood as agreement can be more than a mere annoyance.

Conversation 4.3, which took place between a Japanese industrial engineer and an agent of the Federal Bureau of Investigation posing as a US company representative, illustrates such an example. Based on the engineer's listener feedback, the prosecution alleged that the Japanese engineer had agreed to obtaining the plans, and that he knew that what he was doing was illegal:

Conversation 4.3
AGENT: You see, these plans are very hard to get.
ENGINEER: Uh-huh.
AGENT: I'd need to get them at night.
ENGINEER: Uh-huh.

AGENT: It's not done easily.
ENGINEER: Uh-huh.
AGENT: Understand?
ENGINEER: Uh-huh.[7]

Here, the prosecution's case rested on interpreting the Japanese engineer's "uh-huh" to mean "Yes, I understand these plans are illegal and hard to get at night." However, the defense argued that the Japanese defendant was only being agreeable to the agent, and thus was saying "Yes, I'm listening to you."

In intercultural communication, communicators may pronounce foreign words with great fluency and grammatical accuracy, but still operate as if they were in their native communicative contexts. Listener feedback is one example of this, and just as a North American might feel that a Japanese person is insincere because he or she agrees to everything, a Japanese person might feel a North American is inattentive, as shown in the somewhat more comical but frequent occurrence in a phone caller's "*Moshi moshi? Moshi moshi?*" (Hello? Hello?) when the feedback the Japanese is expecting is absent from the North American at the other end of the line. The void a Japanese communicator feels here is equivalent to what a North American would feel if a listener is visibly looking away when a speaker is talking to him or her.

In fact, listener feedback, in the form of *aizuchi*, is so important in Japan that sometimes speakers offer themselves *aizuchi*, in the form of a head-nod or "*hai*" at the end of their own statements. For example, an engineer ended his explanation of how a pump works with "*Sō desu. Hai*" ("That's so. Yes"), even when the interviewer was not asking him a question.

Self-feedback *aizuchi*, where speakers act as if they are their own listeners, also occurs in the form of a particle, *ne?* backloaded at the end of a phrase. Similar to the young North American seeking camaraderie from a friend who says something like "Yeah, right?" Japanese can potentially punctuate every phrase with *ne?* which can once again sometimes end up going to comical or exacerbating lengths for those not used to the listener style.

What is important to note here is that both North American and Japanese self-feedback serve as a reminder that in an interaction, speaker and listener are engaged in a relationship, at least for the duration of the conversation. However fleeting, we send contexted content, showing that we are connected, whether through a North American smile or a Japanese bow. For the Japanese, *aizuchi* is a requirement in a conversation where the context—and therefore the speaker–listener relationship—is as or more important than what is being said.

LISTENER TALK 2: INTERPRETATION AND REINTERPRETATIONS

A common and personal form of (re)interpretation we all know is the family member or friend who knows us well and follows what we say so closely that he or she can finish our sentences. Similar to the constant feedback that vlogger Michaela Braithwaite noted as annoying, Japanese listenership involves active following, even to the point of echoing and voicing what the speaker has just said. Maximizing *aizuchi* feedback can mean full-length sentences that develop into interpretations, reinterpretations, or questions and responses that link to the preceding turn.

In every culture, interpreting daily conversation is our way of checking comprehension. In North American conversations, most of us do this by simply asking "Do you mean . . . ?" when we are trying to clarify our understanding of what the speaker meant to say. If we are right, the speaker will tell us so: "That's exactly what I meant." If we are wrong, the speaker will usually tell us so, too, and to what degree: "Well, the truth is . . ." Either way, listeners seek clarification when they are not sure whether they have understood something.

In addition to this "real" verification, Japanese often interpret what a speaker meant, even when it is obvious that they have completely understood what a speaker was saying. In fact, because a good listener talk speaker also has to have been a good listener, when you say, "So you mean . . ." you expect to hear back *aizuchi* and confirmation that even the interpretation was correct. In this way, the listener talk strategy of interpretation is consistent with seeing the world from the *other's* point of view, and occurs frequently in both private and public Japanese interactions.

Conversation 4.4 is an excerpt from an intercultural example taken from Yamada's study, where a Japanese bank manager, Kamiya, is clarifying his understanding of an American consultant, Megan, whose proposal was about cash incentives to executives to improve the bank's profitability:

Conversation 4.4

MEGAN: You understand what I mean?

KAMIYA: You're saying that we should ignore this year in our calculation.

MEGAN: That's not what I meant here.

KAMIYA: I see.

MEGAN: That's one reason why I wanted to talk.

KAMIYA: So you have this five-year period, to build from a 5.5 to 14. And then you're saying, from achieving from 5.5— even though 14 is just an average, because we're so below market, average, that to get there is extraordinary, right? But your point is, so, therefore people deserve extraordinary payments. High bonuses.

Megan uses a direct question to see whether Kamiya understands what she meant: "You understand what I mean?" When Kamiya, an experienced intercultural communicator, interprets what Megan said with the starter "You're saying that we should ignore this year's calculation," Megan disagrees directly: "That's not what I meant here."

Kamiya is determined to understand what Megan says, so he can accurately represent her when he brings his proposal to senior management. After Megan points out, "That's one reason why I wanted to talk," Kamiya reinterprets his understanding of Megan's proposal for a second time, using verbal checkpoints like, "you have," "you're saying," "right?" "your point is," and "therefore." Kamiya then also changes the pronoun, *you* to *we*, to demonstrate how he will incorporate Megan's proposal and submit an interpreted report to pitch to senior management.

Although different styles can often clash in intercultural communication, here is an example of a synergy created between North American and Japanese styles. In Megan's words, "Kamiya is the guy who can push it (the proposal) through," and so it turns out, in later conversation, that he did. As an experienced intercultural communicator, Kamiya was able to use Megan's direct disagreement to reinterpret a pitch he successfully delivered to senior management.

LISTENER TALK 3: CONVERSATIONAL SPACE AND METATALK

People who talk a lot and faster than us often make us feel as if they are interrupting us all the time; we cannot seem to get in a word edgewise. Conversely, those who do not say much and take their time thinking about what to talk about next make us feel as if we must constantly supply topics of conversation. Our impressions about other communicators are in part formed by differences in our conversational pacing.

In Yamada's study of internal US and Japanese bank meetings, conversational pacing was largely determined by how the bankers managed their topics. From the perspective of the US bank managers, each deal is the individual responsibility of the executive, so he or she should bring it up, talk about it, and then close it out. Indeed, in the internal meetings, the officers did just this by opening up a topic by verbally naming the deal, saying something like, "My deal is Morrow." The officers would then also close their own deals with a specific verbal ending, such as, "That's it. It's closed on our books right now."

Whereas the presenting US manager is given the exclusive right to talk about his or her own deal, the Japanese bank managers use pausing before they move on to new topics and then metatalk, or talk about talk, to begin new topics. The result is an altogether slower pace of conversation that can create the effect of a meandering meeting, which is something we often hear about from North American professionals who have been in insider Japanese meetings.

Indeed, meeting conversations can sound pointless or even illogical if we do not understand that the communicator of listener talk is pausing to verify with the other listeners whether it is OK to open a new topic, particularly when the pausing occurs comparatively more frequently and at greater length.

This was the case when Yamada compared internal Japanese meetings with North American ones. The Japanese paused longer than 1.5 seconds 103 times, at a rate of 5.15 seconds per minute, as opposed to the US bankers, who paused 20 times at a rate of 0.74 seconds per minute. The longest silence in the Japanese meeting shown in conversation 4.5 between the end of one topic and the beginning of a new one was 8.2 seconds, nearly twice as long as the American 4.4 seconds:

Conversation 4.5

IKEDA: Because in Japan it's a week at the most.
SHIMIZU: Mhm, it's a week.
   [8.2 second pause]
TANAKA: This talk is completely different but next time there
   is again going to be a regional meeting around August.

Conversation 4.5 illustrates how Shimizu uses listener feedback to repeat Ikeda's comment back to him to interpret and confirm the ending of the topic before the 8.2-second pause expands among the three managers. Tanaka then metatalks about the next topic on an upcoming regional meeting.

In intercultural training role-playing, many North Americans say that 8.2 seconds of silence feels unbearably long for them. Asked what they would do, many professionals said that they would pick up the conversation and continue talking about the current topic because, in the North American view, it had not been closed out. This reaction aggravates an already-confused conversation and adds to the meandering feel that the North Americans have about the Japanese, and the dominating and even pedantic feel that the Japanese have about the North Americans.

In place of the confusion that often ensues when intercultural communicators try to move through topics, we suggest using the kind of metatalk Japanese sales people use to check whether the content of their purchase plans are clear to their clients, because a client needs a clear understanding of the product or service even if he or she is Japanese. Borrowing this sales pitch and comprehension confirmation strategy, intercultural business professionals can ask, "Is it OK?" or "Are you all right with this?" Or, as facilitators whose job it is to manage dialogue between people often do, we can also metatalk by asking, "Shall we move on?" or "Does anyone have anything to add?" A little metatalk can go a long way.

LISTENER TALK 4: NEGATING WITHOUT NEGATING

The Japanese are often caricatured as overly polite—as people who never say "no." In fact, "*īe*" (no) was thought to be so uncommon that books such as the politician Shintaro Ishihara's *The Japan That Can Say "No"* were written in retort.[8] Indeed, the casual form of "no," *unun*, spoken with a rising intonation, is the opposite of the casual "yes," *un*, spoken with a descending accent, which certainly does make it sound as if two yeses equal a "no." *Omoiyari* empathy or *wa* harmony are other common reasons cited for why the Japanese shy away from "no." The implication here might be that the Japanese are nice people who do not want to offend the other person, and that is why they never say "no."

However, another explanation might be that the Japanese rarely say the word *īe*, for the simple reason that "yes" vocalizations—such as "hai," "ē," and "un"—provide *aizuchi* listener feedback, and play by the communicative rules of listener talk by connecting speakers with the listeners.

"No," conversely, does not provide the "I am following you" feedback that "uhuh" and "mhm" do. Instead of being a joiner, "no" distinguishes the individual speaker as he or she speaks out, differs, and disagrees. In short, "no" demarcates a speaker's own view to stand apart from a previous speaker's or other listeners' views.

However, if a direct "no" is rule breaking in most Japanese group encounters, there are still many ways to turn down a proposition or disagree. For example, *sore wa chotto* (that's a little . . .) is one, and this can be made even stronger by adding the qualifier, *muzukashii* (that's going to be a bit difficult). In the following we provide a list of ways to say "no." This, again, is by no means an exhaustive list, but the list does demonstrate that Japanese do disagree, even if they do not actually say the word "no."

List 1: Ways to Say "No"
1. (*Sore wa*) *chotto* (*muzukashii*) ka mo shiremasen (that) might be a little (difficult)
2. *Nnn* Hmm, often accompanied by chin drawn in and nodding
3. *Kentō sasete itadakimasu* (we) will study (it)
4. *Kangaete mimashō* Let (us) think about (it)
5. (*Zenshō*) *doryoku itashimasu* (I) will try my best
6. (*Maemuki ni*) *kangaesaseteitadakimasu* (we) will try to think about (it) positively
7. Silence
8. Stretched talk
9. Intake of breath between the teeth; native English speakers can make a similar sound, followed by "ooh," when they see something painful happen to someone
10. Lowered or closed eyes

Note: ( ) denotes items that can be dropped.

Conversation 4.6 is an actual example taken from Yamada's bank managers' meeting, where the manager, Yamashita, uses numbers 2, 7, and 9 from the list of ways to say "no" to cue that he is disagreeing with the other Japanese bank managers. The translated excerpt begins following Fukuda's suggestion to bring on a Californian broker to collaborate on their project. Yamashita shows his disagreement by sending three common negation cues of (9) sucking in air, (7) a 5-second-long silence, and a very vocal (2) *Nnn (Hmm)*. Until the moment of Fukuda's challenge to Yamashita's disagreement, where he asks "Why?" everyone is playing by the rules of listener talk.

The larger context of the three bank managers is that Yamashita, Fukuda, and Kanda have worked together in the San Francisco office for two years, and have known each other for all of their careers. They have also participated in intercultural development training sessions, and therefore are aware not only of communicative style differences on both sides of the Pacific but also of the possibility that the meeting will likely be used for study. When Fukuda goads Yamashita into clearly articulating his disagreement North American style—by asking the direct question "Why?"—a comedy of negation ensues:

Conversation 4.6

[5 seconds]

YAMASHITA: [Sucks in air}
    Nnn. (Hmm.)

FUKUDA: Why?

YAMASHITA: Well, uhhm, I would not say I wouldn't say
    that it's not that you know, it's definitely out of the ques-
    tion. So in other words, I want to say that it is not that it
    wouldn't happen. I couldn't say that. [laugh]

FUKUDA: What's that? You yourself [3-second pause] are even
    laughing (at your own torturous sentences).

KANDA: [laughing] No way. What? [2-second pause] That's a
    big minus for you, Yamashita-san. It would be really bad if
    you did something like that (in a meeting with Americans).
    [laugh]

Note: ( ) denotes implied.

In tears from laughing by this time, Fukuda and Kanda each tease Yamashita for his reluctance to disagree, laughing not only because they can imagine the trouble he would get himself into in doing so in a meeting with his Californian counterparts, but also because of Yamashita's abuse of the Japanese language, where he grammatically deploys six negatives in two sentences to appear as if he is not disagreeing. As we discussed above,

Yamashita's flamboyant use of multiple negations is engineered in part by Japanese grammar, which places the verb at the end of a sentence and negation at the end of the verb. Unlike English, a Japanese speaker's position in an argument can be stalled and back-loaded at the end of his or her turn, thus endorsing the mechanisms of listener talk, so that speakers can make or undo agreements and disagreements at the end.

Historically, misunderstandings of a Japanese "no" taken for a "yes" are numerous. Among the most notorious is then–president Richard Nixon's interpretation of then–prime minister Eisaku Sato's comment, *"Zenshō itashimasu"* (number 5 in the list of ways to say "no"). The interpreters translated this as "I will do my best," in response to Nixon's question about importing textiles. Nixon understood the translation as a "yes," when Sato had actually meant "no." Taking the promised effort as a positive affirmation, neither Nixon nor his translator knew to look for hedging cues that could imply "not really" but only heard the absence of the definitive word "no."

As humans, we have a great sense for recognizing things once we know what we are looking for. Starting with awareness about the different ways speakers of listener talk say "no," we can eventually listen for the nuanced "not reallys" and the "dot-dot-dots" and look out for more ways in which the Japanese disagree.

LISTENER TALK 5: EXPRESSIONS

So we have said that in Japan, "We will try our best" can simply be a way of saying "no" that conforms to the rules of listener talk. It is an expression—like greetings, apologies, and things we say when we need to be sociable and do not know what to say. Expressions are useful. They help us get in, move on, and patch things up as best we can. We are happy to be able to offer "our deepest condolences," because what else does one say on such an occasion?

List 2 is another nonexhaustive sample of specific listener talk expressions:

List 2: Listener Talk Expressions

Situation	Expression	Literal meaning
Seeing someone you haven't seen for some time	*gobusatashite(ori) masu* "Sorry to have been out of touch"	No news
Calling for someone on entering a store	*gomenkudasai* "Excuse me"	Sorry please
Apologies for starting to eat first	*osakini* "Sorry for having gone first"	(I've) gone first
Entering a house	*ojamashimasu* "Thanks for having me."	(I'm) going to impose myself
Leaving someone	*shitsurei(ita) shimashita* "Good-bye"	Excuse me
Wishing someone who is not well	*odaijini* "Get better soon"	Precious
Wishing someone off	*okiotsukete* "Take care"	Be careful

As language learners, we suggest learning how to use these and other helpful expressions by metatalking about them the way we suggested to move through topics. We might start off by saying "I'm so sorry; I'm not sure what to say in such circumstances. Is it right to say, '*Goshūshoosama*' to extend condolences?" This metatalk can help the language learner apply expressions in live situations and thereby learn them deeply, as well as establish a listener talk bond. As nonnatives, if we make a mistake, the attention given to the context is likely to have our error forgiven and possibly even produce a welcome comical moment.

In sum, we have examined how listener feedback, interpreting, reinterpreting, metatalking about talking and silence, disagreeing without actually saying the word "no," and using set expressions provide strategies within the framework of listener talk, a communicative style that is driven by *others* and listeners and is based on the situation's context. Few things are ever black and white, and this is certainly so when many variables are at play in intercultural communication. However, if it was critical to know our professional competitors during the bubble years, it is perhaps even more important to know our collaborators at a time when global partnerships are the norm. There has never been a better time to observe and acquire an awareness of Japanese contexting as it relates to listener talk.

RECOMMENDATIONS

It might feel like a chicken-and-egg question to ask who starts a conversation—the speaker or the listener? However, this is the crucial point when considering how North Americans and Japanese use context in conversations. For many North Americans, the speaker is the most important person in the conversation. A speaker who does his or her job well not only transmits his or her content clearly but also presents himself or herself well. Such a person is a great speaker who delivers clear message content.

Japanese communicators, conversely, support their conversations through other listeners. In this way, we could say that for the Japanese, the listeners are the most important people. When speakers talk using listener talk, they keep the context of the listeners in mind. A good Japanese communicator is a good *sasshi* listener and interpreter.

In this chapter, we have looked at five strategies for listener talk in Japanese communication and have suggested that learners try them out. An easy approach for North Americans to acquire listener talk is for them to think of where and how it occurs in their own conversations. A good example might be the response to an adult child seeking parental advice. In this role, the parent could go ahead and lecture; but ideally, he or she first needs to be a sounding board before they can offer real advice. In such situations, one intuitively knows that active listening fosters better advice and possibly learning. If one can apply this approach to all conversations—business and professional, as well as personal—this is listener talk.

Three recommendations that can be applied to the principles of listener talk and Japanese contexting acquisition are:

1. *Use plenty of listener feedback, and check your comprehension with metatalk.* It is difficult to emphasize how much listener feedback there is in Japanese conversations. For North American learners of Japanese, we suggest going overboard to earnestly show that you are listening. It is nearly impossible for a new learner to overdo this. For a Japanese person, it is difficult to have too much *aizuchi*. So it is OK to splurge. Check your comprehension, and talk out loud about the conversation and your interpretations. Do this particularly when verifying the discussion on a topic is complete. Metatalk your way through conversations. In short, we recommend talking about the talk and talking about the silence. It is a great tool in intercultural communication, especially with the Japanese, with whom it is OK.

2. *Allow for plenty of pausing and conversational spacing.* Stretch your ability to listen by getting more comfortable with pausing. Look for additional cues about this with the nonverbal cues—such as closed eyes or sucking in air—that could signal disagreement. We further discuss interpreting the meanings of visual communication in chapter 6, on nonverbal communication.

3. *Do not assume that listener feedback means the listener is agreeing.* Learn and reap the benefits of co-creating a conversation that is smooth and whole.

It is important in Japanese conversation to appear as if you are listening. It creates an agreeable situational atmosphere and the likelihood of a smoother and more convivial conversation. Japanese communicators, and perhaps communicators in general, are more likely to divulge information and share it with those who appear more accommodating.

Contexting Defined

- Communication that depends on content or actual words that are spoken (or written) is thought of as low context.
- Communication that depends on experience or previously obtained information (i.e., context) is thought of as high context.

Japanese and North American Contexting

- Typical Japanese communication is more high context than typical North American communication.
- The value Americans place on *talk* and the *individual* creates a preference for a style of communication that is called speaker talk.
- The value Japanese place on *silence* and *others* creates a preference for a style of communication that is called listener talk.
- Speaker talk: The key American communicator is the speaker.
- Listener talk: The key Japanese communicators are the listeners.

Listener Talk 1: Feedback

- Listener talk users punctuate their conversations with many visuals and vocalizations that show they are listening.
- *Aizuchi* listener feedback occurs more frequently and regularly in Japanese conversations than in American ones.

Listener Talk 2: (Re)Interpretation

- Listener talk users frequently interpret, reinterpret, and ask questions to check comprehension, even if they think they have understood well.

Listener Talk 3: Pausing

- Japanese people use pausing to shift topics, as silence distances individual talk and bonds members with others.
- Talk about the silence, and about the emerging talk.
- Metatalk your way through knots in conversations.

Listener Talk 4: Negation

- The Japanese language allows for multiple negations that occur at the end of the sentence.
- There are many ways of saying "no" in Japanese without actually saying the word. See list 1 in the text for examples.

Listener Talk 5: LT Expressions

- There are many listener talk expressions that are useful in set situations. See list 2 in the text for examples.

Recommendations

- The listener is important in listener talk.

- Practice listener talk strategies like listener feedback and interpreting.
- Talk about talk and silence.
- Allow time for slow conversational pacing and spacing.
- Do not assume that listener feedback means agreement, and enjoy influencing listeners through listener talk.

5

THE JAPANESE
Authority
Conception

Playing Chess or Playing Go

We now turn our attention to the fifth key of the LESCANT intercultural approach, which focuses on the role of authority and power in communicating with the Japanese. This topic deals with how we define power and authority, who has power, and how power is shared or exchanged. This category also brings up issues of leadership style, how decisions are made, and how titles are used to show status. Because many of the issues related to authority are culturally based, we examine how authority and power are perceived among the Japanese.

We begin this chapter with a brief look at the Japanese hierarchical authority conception, including its origins both in the influence of Confucian thought and of Japan's old feudal system. Next we discuss the notion of loyalty and the concept of *amae*, which we began discussing in chapter 3, on social organization. After this, we compare and contrast the concepts of power and leadership in Japanese and North American organizations. Next, we discuss how to communicate and achieve a consensus within the framework of the Japanese vertical hierarchical system. Finally, we close with some recommendations for North Americans navigating their way through social and professional organizations in Japan, and point out what to expect regarding the Japanese authority conception.

THE JAPANESE HIERARCHY AND
AUTHORITY CONCEPTION

Japan is a more hierarchically conscious society than North America. We say hierarchically *conscious* because, though the same hierarchies can exist in North America, outside the military, the Japanese tend to generally emphasize and abide by the hierarchical order more than North Americans. Japanese are comfortable with clearly defined roles and responsibilities, whether at work or anywhere else. North Americans dislike feeling limited as to what they can or cannot do.

Both the Japanese and North Americans have a sense of equality within a hierarchy, but their view of this differs. In Japan, the ideal model is that everyone starts out equal but gains authority through their seniority and position over time. In North America, the ideal model is that everyone is not the same but everyone should be given an equal opportunity. In other words, in the North American model, everyone should start out on a level playing field at least in theory, and then advance according to their innate ability and acquired skills.

It may be instructive to compare these two approaches with the games of chess and go. In the game of chess, all pieces start off at the same place at one end of the board. Each chess piece, however, has inherent strengths with significance that is independent of other pieces. The pieces advance to positions of importance based on these individual strengths. In chess, the goal is to attack what already is in place, and in this way reduce any opposition to capitulation until your side wins. Because the same goal is in place in a North American argument or against a competitor, chess can serve as a metaphor for the North

American approach to equality and hierarchy. Like chess pieces, everyone has individual strengths—traits and skills—that they use to advance, even though everyone begins from the same starting point.

In the game of go, there are no pieces on the board at the beginning of the game. Unlike chess, where you tear down what is already there to advance yourself, in go you create something from nothing. In go, unlike chess, you have white and black stones, all of which are of equal value. No stone in go has any inherent or individual strength or quality that sets it off from any other stone. Each piece gains significance only through its position on the board and the attendant relationship of its position with other pieces on the board. In go, the game is won by strategically placing your stones so that your opponent cannot surround and take them but at the same time by collectively arranging your stones so that you can surround and capture any stones your opponent plays inside your own territory. In this way, go can serve as a metaphor for the Japanese approach to equality and hierarchy. Like go stones, no one person has any inherent individual traits or strengths that he or she uses to advance but rather gains significance from a position relative to others. This is in keeping with the view discussed in chapter 3, on social organization, that the Japanese grasp a relationship vis-à-vis the position of others. Seniority is therefore tied to power and authority, not from the individual characteristics of a given person but simply by virtue of having been there first, just as the first stones placed on the go board gain significance from holding the initial position around which other stones are positioned.

SOURCES OF JAPANESE HIERARCHICAL VALUES

Although many influences have contributed to Japan's hierarchical value system, two particularly important influences merit mention here. These are Confucianism and the Japanese feudal system.

Confucian values, which were imported from China, have been a central part of Japanese society since roughly the sixth century, when they were formalized by the so-called Seventeen-Article Constitution (the *jūshichijō kenpō*, or 十七条憲法), which was attributed to Prince Shōtoku, who lived from 573 to 621. The reason for "so-called" here is that this is not really a constitution in a North American sense, but rather the prince listing what he considered to be guidelines for right behavior—which were based on the teachings of Confucius. From Shōtoku's time onward, Confucian principles of the individual's place in society took root and grew into a distinctly Japanese variety that became even more deeply entrenched in time.

Confucius viewed a natural order in the world; and within that, he laid out what he saw as the five central superior–subordinate relationships. The "five bonds" he defined are as follows, with additional interpretations that we believe are generally held to be true:

1. *Ruler–subject bond.* The ruler's obligation is to be benevolent to the subject. The subject's obligation is to be loyal to the ruler. In modern application, this can be extended to the state and the citizen.
2. *Father–son bond.* The son is subordinate to the father. The father's obligation is to be loving to the son. The son's obligation is to be reverential to the father. In modern application, this can be extended to the parent–child bond, regardless of gender.
3. *Older brother–younger brother bond.* The older brother's obligation is to be gentle to the younger brother. The younger brother's obligation is to be respectful to the older brother. In modern application, this is often extended to include mentor–mentee and teacher–student relationships.
4. *Husband–wife bond.* The husband's obligation is to be good to the wife. The wife's obligation is to listen to the husband. This has been extended to include men and women in general. The inherent sexism in this has been challenged in Japan, but arguably only on a large scale in the late twentieth century.
5. *Older friend–younger friend bond.* The older friend's obligation is to be considerate to the younger friend. The younger

friend's obligation is to be deferential to the older friend. In modern application, this can be extended to include senior *senpai* and junior *kōhai* in schools and clubs.

Although pure Confucianism is not literally in practice in Japan (or anywhere else), just as other philosophical teachings, much of its influence is still apparent. The respect for those in authority—whether a teacher, a boss, or a government figure—remains very strong. Likewise, these Confucian principles lay the foundation for the Japanese deference and respect shown to those who are older and the consequent respect for seniority in work and other situations.

The Japanese respect for authority and age, however, is foreign to many North American values. Where Japanese people feel an almost natural trust for those in authority, North Americans in general and people from the United States in particular have a very strong distrust of authority. The US governmental system is based on the separation of powers precisely because of this distrust of authority. In both Canada and the United States, most employees believe that they can (or at least in time could) do a better job than their boss. The goal for many in a North American workplace is to advance beyond one's boss—not, as in Japan, to advance lockstep in seniority tied to the boss's own advancement.

Similarly, whereas the Japanese are imbued with a Confucian respect for age, North Americans are very much a youth culture. There is a tendency to believe that the energy, vitality, and drive of the young are somehow of greater value than those who are old. In Japan, no concept exists of the "wonder child" who advances quickly up the corporate ladder (or any other ladder, for that matter). Far from the North American admiration bestowed on young people who rise rapidly, the feeling in Japan toward this approaches the level of contempt. Advancement is earned only in the Confucian way: with age, wisdom, and experience.

Besides the Confucian system, the other great historical influence on traditional Japanese authority conception comes from the Japanese feudal era. From roughly the 1100s until the Meiji Restoration in the late 1800s, Japan adhered to a strict, four-tier class system. These four tiers in feudal Japan, in descending order of importance, were:

1. *Samurai.* The highest tier in society was the warrior class, the famous samurai. They made up about 10 percent of the population, and they owed loyalty only to their employers, called the *daimyo*, who were the highest level of samurai. These were essentially the equivalent to European high nobility.

2. *Farmers.* The farmers and peasants were admired in Confucian ideals because they produced the food on which everyone else depended to survive. Although they were accorded honor, they were actually poorer financially than many of the artisans and merchants in the classes below them. In fact, even many samurai were poorer than merchants.

3. *Artisans.* The next tier in society was made up of skilled craftspeople. These artisans made the goods on which the Imperial family and the samurai class depended, ranging from artwork to clothing to swords and boats. The fact that they relied on their individual talent, however, was part of what made them lower than the farmer and peasant.

4. *Merchants.* Feudal Japan held considerable disdain for the merchant class. Traveling merchants and shopkeepers alike were viewed as parasites on society who lived off the work of others. Although the samurai acquired land and farmers and artisans produced products, merchants peddled them, and this was what put merchants lower down the nobility rung. The Japanese originally justified their nobility ranking through a product bias rather than through labor or service. Ironically, however, it was the merchant class that over the centuries grew to be the wealthiest, through both products and services. With their wealth, the merchant class was able to buy political influence, which by the end of the feudal period had eliminated most of the restrictions placed on them.

There were also people who were above or below the class system. The Imperial family, the Buddhist and Shinto priests, and the shogun (essentially the chief *daimyo*) were beyond the class system and literally above the rules. At the other end, some people fell below the class system altogether. These included the Ainu (Japan's indigenous but nonethnic Japanese minority) as well as those working in jobs considered taboo in the Japanese Buddhist tradition, such as leather tanners, butchers, slaves, and prostitutes. Worth noting here is that far from being considered a prostitute, *geisha* (originally male performing artists) were classified in the artisan class as the kanji characters for *geisha* 芸者 (literally, art person) denote.

In an ironic inversion of the feudal class system, in modern Japan, the merchants and business leaders are considered the most respected of professions. Artisans can rise to the level of being officially recognized as "living treasures." Farmers have become an increasingly rare profession, given that Japan relies more and more on outside sources of food to feed itself. Possibly because farmers are subsidized by the government, they are now sometimes seen in the way merchants used to be seen— that is to say, as living off the backs of others. Farmers have been caricatured in modern satires. Once, one of our authors overheard a shopper at a local supermarket looking at a daikon (a Japanese white radish) with dirt on it, saying, "Huh, good marketing. As if these really came from one of our natural farms." Farmers are often regarded as being out of touch with modern Japan. Finally, the samurai are long gone, and the warrior class of the twentieth-century Japanese military machine was almost entirely dismantled in the aftermath of World War II.

At first look, then, it may appear that feudal Japan no longer has any influence on modern Japan. This, however, is not exactly the case. In feudal Japan, loyalty was absolute, and each individual's place was rigidly set within his or her own social stratum. That recognition of your own place in society and of having a specific role to play in that society is still very much a factor in the Japanese embrace of a vertical hierarchy in their government, workplace, schools, and families—that is, in almost every walk of life.

Even more to the point, however, is the loyalty imbued in the class system, especially at the samurai level. The loyalty of the samurai to his *daimyo* was absolute, unquestioning, and with full recognition of his authority.

In Japan, you cannot go around those above. You would, for example, bring something to the attention of your boss's boss only by going through your boss. In other words, you would never want to go around your boss to your boss's boss on your own. If you did go around those above, you would need to be ready to bear the consequences of such an action, even under duress or in extreme circumstances. In professional terms, this could mean a demotion or even an expectation that you would resign.

Likewise, in Japan it is important to reach the person at the appropriate level. If you are, say, at level 3 and you need to negotiate with someone at level 2 above you, you would do better to bring someone from your own organization at that same level. This would be the case even if you were the one who would be conducting most of the negotiations yourself. Prior background research to find the right person to contact could only help you.

LOYALTY AND *AMAE*

This loyalty between *daimyo* and samurai—that is, between superiors and subordinates—still plays a powerful role in Japanese group dynamics today. In chapter 3, on social organization, we began a discussion about the concept of *amae* 甘え, which the psychologist Takeo Doi introduced in his book *Amae no Kōzō*. Although the book is translated in its English editions as *The Anatomy of Dependence,* there is more to the meaning of its title than that. *Kōzō* does actually mean "anatomy" or "structure"; but *amae,* which literally means *sweetness,* carries the meaning not only of "dependence" but also of indulgence, loyalty, and love. *Amae* describes the historical relationships between the *daimyo* and samurai in feudal Japan but also the contemporary relationships between a manager and a subordinate and a parent and a child in present-day Japan.

Amae is an important concept to understand in relationships—in Japan, but also the world over. When your baby cries in the middle of the night, you may instinctively respond and tend to your baby without any expectation of reward. In the darkness, you may even check if the baby is frightened, wet, or hungry, and you take care of your child because that is what you feel you should do. Nothing more. When you do this, you are simply responding to a need of the baby as well as your own need to baby the baby, or *amayakasu*, which ranges in meaning from the verb *babying* to *spoiling*. *Amae* here, is insurance.

Perhaps it should be noted here that in Japan, babies commonly sleep in the same room as their parents. However, the North American practice of letting the child cry to sleep to build a more independent child is less common in Japan, because many parents see it as cruel. In the Japanese context, a child's cry is seen as a form of request that the Japanese parent tries to fulfill. Thus, though North Americans try to build a sense of self-sufficiency in their children, Japanese parents try to build a bond with their children based on a mutual dependency that is strengthened by every subsequent *amae* action.

What is significant here is that the exact same term—*amae*—is used to describe a superior's relationship with his or her subordinates and, furthermore, also describes the practice between a boss and his or her managers. If you are the boss, in other words, you look after those who report to you; and if you are the subordinate, you expect your boss to take care of you. In return for a boss's care, a subordinate remains deeply loyal to his or her boss. This is a far cry from the North American disdain for one's boss and desire to do things on one's own.

Amae is in keeping with the relational concept of the Japanese *other* discussed earlier, in chapter 3, on social organization. This is because an act of *amae* begins with the *other*. It is the baby who initiates the cry in the middle of the night, leaving the parent to respond and ascertain if the baby is hungry, wet, or frightened. If you are the parent in Japan, you are skilled, insofar as you are able to perceive your child's needs.

At first glance, this pure and ideal form of parent–infant *amae* may appear similar to the North American notion of unconditional love. However, because Japanese children are socialized into various public worlds, they soon learn the various insider/

outsider codes of conduct attached to each one. At home, though informal behavior and full acceptance within family relationships can continue behind closed doors, constructed displays of *oyako-kankei*, or parent–child relationships, are expected in public. Here is where the loyalty force of *amae*—or at least the appearance of it—must be displayed.

A distinction about how we behave at home and outside is also made in North American families. For example, it is often considered not good practice to wash one's dirty linen in public. However, when we go home, we might argue ceaselessly. From this standpoint, the difference in the expression of emotional relationships among North American and Japanese family members might seem only one of degree.

However, dig deeper, and we soon see that there is more to the difference between the Western notion of giving love and not expecting anything in return and the Japanese one of *amae* sharing. With a worldly realism, the altruistic, romantic, or heavenly ideal of Western love with no strings attached is absent in *amae*. Like the many gods in Japanese folklore, *amae* is seen as imperfect but cherished because it is inherently human. *Amae* can bring both great sadness and joy—a highly different view from the idea that love can conquer all.

In fact, because of *amae*'s intrinsically dual nature, unlike unconditional love, *amae* has no other side. Western conceptualizations of love tend to think of anything other than free, unconditional love as restrictive, domineering, or controlling. An example is Shakespeare's *King Lear*, in which money, land, and power were exchanged for love and loyalty. Overindulgence, or corrupted *amae*, goes on in Japan, as it does world over—except that in Japan, this aspect of *amae* is accepted and sometimes justified as a kind of necessary practical family investment.

In short, the somewhat vocational nuance of *amae* is not incidental. We said earlier that in Japan, a section head can care for the subordinate and the subordinate can depend on the section head in a similar *amae* relationship as that of parent and child. Because North American professionals typically do not think of replicating family love in the workplace, this can be confusing. However, because the Japanese often see the family structure reflected in the workplace (as discussed in chapter 3, on social organization), the loyalty ties of *amae* that bind are often one and the same at work and at home.

Japanese *amae* therefore presents itself in personal relationships between parent and child—but also in professional ones, between boss and subordinate; in scholastic ones, between teacher and pupil; and in sports, between coach and athlete. *Amae* is the sweet glue of belonging, a cocktail of feelings available to everyone who has made the effort to belong to the clan. Championing the collective, *amae* therefore further bolsters the significance of others in Japanese society, and it applies to every Japanese domain—at work, at school, at play, and at home. As *amae* takes root in each of these insider domains, Confucian principles guide outsider presentations.

POWER AND LEADERSHIP IN THE JAPANESE CONTEXT

The understanding of power and leadership relations in Japan flows out of the concept of *amae*. As we have just discussed, *amae* is in keeping with the relational concept of the Japanese *other*. Likewise, the Japanese understanding of what constitutes leadership and how power is demonstrated is also in keeping with this relational *other* concept. In Japan, the leader is essentially parental. We can readily extend the earlier example of the baby crying at night to leadership. In the *amae* relationship at work, it is the subordinate who initiates the action by establishing a need, just as it is the baby who initiates the cry in the middle of the night. If you are the leader in Japan, you are skilled to the extent that you are able to recognize—or, even better, anticipate—your employee's needs. The leader, manager, or other person of authority, then, takes on a position parallel to the parent in Japan. As a leader in Japan, you are skilled insofar as you can recognize your subordinate's needs; just as for a parent in Japan, you are skilled insofar as you are able to perceive your child's needs.

Anticipated need is at the center of the understanding of leadership and power relationships in Japan. The result of *amae*-based leadership is that power is demonstrated by fulfilling anticipated need. This works in both directions. As a good Japanese leader, you anticipate the needs of those you lead. In turn, your employees are expected to anticipate your needs as leaders *before you ask.*

Here we see a major contrast to North American power relationships. Power is demonstrated in North America by giving direct orders and then having them carried out. The more orders you give, the more powerful you appear to be as a leader. In Japan, the opposite is the case. For the Japanese, power is demonstrated by *not* having to give orders. Instead, as a leader, you are seen as powerful to the extent that others anticipate and fulfill your needs *before* you have to ask.

Anticipated need in power relationships is akin to *sasshi* in listener talk, because it requires the ability to sense the context and respond accordingly. Anticipated need is not altogether foreign in North America, although it does develop in situations with shared expectations. On a small scale, for instance, most of us have experienced this. Let us say, for example, that you stay at a North American hotel for an extended period. On the first morning, you go to the hotel restaurant and order a cherry turnover and a cup of coffee with cream. On the second day, you go to the same restaurant and once again order, from the same waiter, a cherry turnover and coffee with cream. On the third day, you make the same order with the same waiter. By the fourth day, when you sit down in this same restaurant, this same waiter may well bring you a cherry turnover and coffee with cream before you even say anything. The waiter anticipates what you want and brings it to you. Without giving an order, you have had your needs met without saying anything. In other words, you have demonstrated power through anticipated need—even in a North American setting.

The difference here is that anticipated need in the United States and Canada is exceptional and depends on particular circumstances, such as the hotel experience just described. In Japan, by contrast, such anticipated need is much more commonplace and is indeed expected. Subordinates learn to read the needs of their superiors. Sellers learn to anticipate the needs of their customers. In both cases, subordinates or sellers then act in accordance with this anticipated need.

Finally, because power in Japan derives from having one's needs anticipated, giving a direct order diminishes one's power. This means that in many cases, the highest-ranking person in, say, a business meeting actually does little once he or she has arrived. The higher-ranking person usually says a few introductory words and then leaves the actual details of the discussion or negotiation in the complete control of the second-highest-ranking person in the room. Indeed, it is common for the highest-ranking person actually to leave the room after the initial interactions, and we have seen the highest-ranking person nod off while the discussion is going on. This may seem insulting in a North American context, but it is not. The main role of the higher-ranking person is to indicate that he or she has full confidence in the lower-ranked members of the team to speak on his or her behalf. Leaving the room or nodding off is the ultimate expression of trust that those speaking will correctly anticipate his or her will.

At this point, it is important to recognize at what level the negotiation will be taking place. In North America, it does not matter if you are negotiating with people at a higher level than you or—as long as they are able to speak for the organization—with people at a lower rank than you are. But this is usually not the case in Japan. In other words, if you are a level 2 rank at your company and come to Japan to negotiate with someone at a level 3 rank, this will be at best unusual, often confusing, and at times unacceptable.

COLLABORATIVE COMMUNICATION AND CONSENSUS IN A VERTICAL HIERARCHY

Japanese communication is at once notably more hierarchical than that in North America, while simultaneously collaborative in decision making and implementation of process. This is by no means a given. In many highly hierarchical societies (e.g., Indonesia or Guatemala), collaboration is minimized as feedback is either unwelcome or too difficult to obtain within the confines of the vertical structures in place. In many cultures that emphasize collaborative decision making (e.g., the Netherlands and Sweden), the dominant organizational structures are horizontal with little hierarchy. Japan, however, manages to be both very vertical in hierarchical structure and highly inclusive in feedback.

Where this collaborative communication and consensus in a vertical hierarchy are most clearly evident is in Japan's larger corporations and government ministries. For this reason, it is probably useful to look at a few business communication systems at play in Japan. To this end, we look at the Japanese business communication practices of *hō-ren-sō*, which is an acronym for *hōkoku*, *renraku*, and *sōdan*, as well as *nemawashi* and *ringiseido*. Collectively, these make up the Japanese strategic policy employment system called *hōshin kanri*.

HŌ-REN-SŌ

Although it may seem as if *hō-ren-sō* (報・連・相), which is a homonym of *hōrensō* (ほうれん草), meaning "spinach," might not have much to do with communication, *hō-ren-sō* is another concept that is key to collaborative communication. In Japanese, *hō-ren-sō* is a combination of the first part of three separate verbs or action words: *hōkoku*, which means "report"; *renraku*, which means "contact"; and *sōdan*, which means "consult." The Japanese *hō-ren-sō* approach is shorthand for a three-part system, whereby people working together on a project continuously report, contact, and consult based on rank.

A significant difference exists in the exchange of information within Japanese institutions and standard North American ones. Whereas in the United States and Canada, many (perhaps most) tasks are self-started as individual initiatives, in Japan, *hōrensō* occur in the context of a hierarchical relationship, such as that between a boss and a subordinate, a buyer and a seller, and a teacher and a student. It is in this context that the *hōrensō* process begins.

The subordinate is expected to report (*hōkoku*) to his or her superior at every step of the way. This may involve reporting from outside the organization to within. When this step is completed without incident, the requested party reports that the task was successfully accomplished. If a problem occurs, the requested party reports that a difficulty came up.

The next step is contacting (*renraku*) the stakeholders in the task or project. This may be just a couple of people within the organization or whole groups outside, such as other companies or alumni. This step is crucial, because it strengthens each stakeholder's relevance and role to play in the project. Each contact goes through his or her own reporting, contacting, and communicating; and once these discussions have settled down, a reporter returns to provide feedback to enter the *sōdan* or consultation step of *hōrensō*. The junior colleague who requested the consultation, then taking the advice of the senior colleague, either goes ahead with the step as planned (if everyone has concurred) or modifies the step according to the suggestions received in the consultation feedback. Whatever the next step (changed or unchanged) that the person proceeds to do, this step is itself once again reported out and discussed in the iterative *hōrensō* circles.

In Japan, *hōrensō* provides the means for constant communication and group input. The result is collective decision making, with the benefits of three main outcomes. First, where everyone's actions are coordinated, all involved head in the same direction toward a common goal. Second, there is a "two heads are better than one" sense to reporting that makes it less likely that whoever does a task has not overlooked anything. Third and finally, there is an implicit buy-in to the actions, because anyone who did not agree would have a chance to provide input—and would be able to do so before anything got too far along.

Hōrensō differs greatly from the North American system. In a nearly exact contrast to the Japanese way, when North Americans are given a request to do something, they generally want to work independently. Reporting out for each step of a process seems a waste of time, particularly when everything has gone as planned. Most North Americans feel there is nothing to report unless either the project is completed or a problem has occurred. Indeed, even when a problem occurs, most North Americans try to fix it first on their own, reporting out only if they cannot do so for some reason. In fact, North Americans receive praise for being "self-starters," acting on their own initiative and fixing problems without supervision—none of which is viewed positively in Japan. In short, in the United States and Canada, Japanese *hōkoku* is usually seen as unneeded micromanagement and disruptively intrusive, whereas the US system in Japan seems too unstructured, overly open to avoidable errors, and nearly wholly lacking in buy-in.

NEMAWASHI

Nemawashi (根回し) is the Japanese term used to describe the informal negotiation process of building a consensus before a final decision is made. *Nemawashi* is a metaphor taken from tree husbandry and bonsai that literally means "root-tending." When you transplant a tree, you need to prepare the tree in advance for the shock of moving it. Without adequate advance preparation, most trees will die after they are transplanted. The shock to the tree's system is generally too great for it to survive unless the roots are carefully tended to. To accomplish this, the tree transplanter must dig around the tree's root system very carefully and often manipulate the roots themselves. In Japanese, this process is called *nemawashi*, from the words for "root"(*ne* 根) and "to turn" or "to revolve"(*mawasu* 回す). In the context of communication, then, *nemawashi* is something along the lines of preparing the ground so that new ideas, objectives, or plans can take root. *Nemawashi*, then, means to have prior consultation with all involved before an action is taken.

Nemawashi is an informal process that often involves casual conversations. These can take place in the workplace itself or in a less formal setting, as in an *izakaya* bar over drinks and snacks after hours. When opposing positions arise, it is common to bargain and compromise to get agreement. Building trust involves growing personal relationships, from which it is then possible to broker alliances and make trade-offs. The success of these personal relationships in one project does not, however, end with the individual project. The relationship and trust built on one project does become transferable to future projects. In short, in tending the roots, the tree continues to grow. That said, in *nemawashi*, the tree will continue to thrive only as long as the roots receive continual attention—the growing trust and understanding resulting from tending these relationships on an ongoing basis.

The small group or one-to-one discussions involved in tending the roots of *nemawashi* are time-consuming, even from a Japanese perspective. By a US or Canadian viewpoint, the time spent in *nemawashi* is nearly insufferable. This is because most North Americans see the hours expended in such discussions as wasted time. But for the Japanese, this time is not wasted at all. In part, North Americans and Japanese differ because they look at different parameters for what is an expected return on investment.

North Americans have a short-term need for a financial return on investment. North American shareholders are primarily interested in a rapid return on *revenues*. The span of time involved is often one or perhaps two quarters before most North American companies need to show results to their shareholders. This makes North Americans value obtaining results or objectives over process.

In Japan, the opposite is true: Process is more heavily emphasized. To ensure that the process runs as planned, for the Japanese, a greater emphasis is placed on the return on investment on *relationships* more than revenues. The span of time involved is often two years (or longer) before companies need to show results to investors. There are reasons involving strategic planning and the nature of stock ownership that contribute to this that we will not go into here. The main point is that North Americans feel pressure to obtain objectives in the short term, while Japanese people feel pressure to show the process involved in a long-term strategic vision. As a result, where North Americans emphasize a return on investment in financial terms, the Japanese emphasize a return on investment in relationship terms— here again, harking back to our earlier discussion of *others*.

Ringiseido (稟議制度) is the system adopted in many larger Japanese organizations to document a consensus. The consensus of *nemawashi* is informal. *Ringiseido* is formalized.

Seido (制度) simply means "system" in Japanese, so *ringiseido* is often simply called the *ringi* system or just plain *ringi*. The word *ringi*, conversely, does not really translate into English very well. *Rin* (稟), in turn, is a cross between something like "report" and "request for approval," and contains elements of the original Chinese meaning of "intrinsic" or "essential." *Gi* (議)—which is made up of the characters for "say," the original Chinese personal pronoun, "I," and "righteousness"—means both "time" (as in time spent deliberating) and "occurrence." *Ringi*, therefore, means providing approval for the essential report and the time needed to deliberate on it.

Ringiseido is an approval system in which everyone involved gives approval to a project. Here is how it works. When you come up with a new idea, you write it up in an official *ringi* document called a *ringisho* (稟議書). You then send the document out to your peers to get their approval. To do this, you must actually print out the *ringisho* on paper (rather than in an electronic format). The first person who reads the document then has the option of making changes and giving it back to you or of approving the document and sending it to the next person.

The way in which your peers show that they have approved the written proposal is by stamping the document with their personal *hanko*. As a quick aside here, a *hanko* (判子) is a seal that Japanese people use as their official signature. If your peer approves, he or she places his or her stamp on the document in the standard vertical *hanko* seal positioning. The document goes through the circle of everyone involved at the same level in a circle of equals. This circle is a "ring," which is a pun between English and Japanese, so that the *ringi* system in English becomes the "ring" system in English—with both meanings intended.

If all your peers approve of the project, you will have a *ringisho*, in which everyone has stamped the document with a vertical seal. Now the entire group sends the document up to the next

5.1 *Ringisho*
Stamping documents symbolizes the review process.

highest level. Your boss then distributes it to the circle of all his or her peers, and the process is repeated. See photograph 5.1.

The process of stamping the document among your peers builds a consensus of its own. For instance, if the next several peers also place their stamps vertically on the *ringisho*, it becomes more difficult for someone further along the approval circle to send the proposal back or rewrite it. As a result, to object to the proposal after, say, seven or eight people have stamped it, you might place your own seal in a way that is less than vertical. If you object fairly strongly, you may refuse to put your stamp on it at all—and then the informal trade-offs of *nemawashi* come back in to play. More likely, however, if there are many stamps already on the document, you will still place your own seal on the proposal, but in a way that lets others know you have reservations regarding it. Thus, when you object, but not enough to reject the proposal outright, you might place your stamp on the *ringisho* off center, sideways, or even upside-down. In doing so, you indicate to the next person reading the document that you have some dissent. After this, it becomes easier for others to place their stamps on the document sideways or the like.

If enough stamps are not vertical when the document returns to the originator of the idea, the group cannot send the document up to the next level. This leads to informal negotiations through *nemawashi* to rewrite the proposal in a way that does achieve a consensus.

HŌSHIN KANRI

Hōshin kanri (方針管理) is the term used to refer to the overall process of consensus-oriented decision making as a strategic policy deployment system within a closed communication loop. The term literally means something along the lines of "compass needle method," but this is really not that central to what the term actually means. A common English substitution for the term is the "catchball method," because this is akin to playing catch. After an idea is articulated, it is thrown to the next stakeholder in the project, who catches it and either throws it to the next stakeholder or (if modifications were needed) throws it back to the originator.

If Japanese organizational communication breaks down into the practices of *hō-ren-sō*, *nemawashi*, and *ringiseido*, they collectively combine in the strategy of *hōshin kanri*.

In the closed circle of communication that is *hōshin kanri*, all actions are circulated throughout the organization for everyone who will be involved. The initial idea can come from any level, from the strategic thinking of a chairperson to a line worker with a way to improve efficiency on some small detail.

Hōshin kanri can be likened to one of those self-circulating decorative waterfalls you might see in a botanical garden or a park. The water flows throughout the closed system. It is unclear where one segment of the water starts or ends, because it is all one system. The water itself flows down to the bottom and is sent back to the top to go through the whole watercourse again; see figure 5.1.

At the top of the waterfall is the executive team. At their tier of the waterfall of ideas, they consider the organization's mission

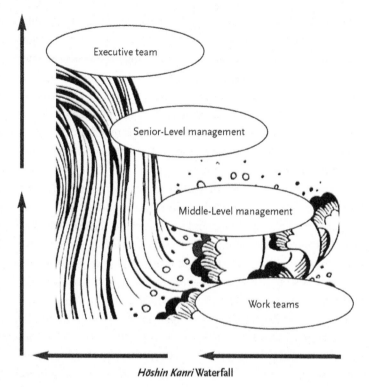

Figure 5.1
Waterfall *Hōshin Kanri*

and strategies to implement it. From there, the water of ideas flows to the next tier—that of senior-level management, who focus on strategies and objectives. At this tier, in other words, they no longer handle the concern for mission, but they share with the executive team the implementation of strategy. They add to this their own concern for laying out objectives. From there, the water of ideas flow to the next lower tier—that of middle-level management, who focus on objectives and goals. At this tier, in other words, they now no longer handle the concern for strategy, but they share with the senior-level management the attention to objectives, adding to it the setting of goals. At the bottom of the waterfall of ideas are the work teams implementing the project. At this bottom tier, they no longer are concerned with setting objectives. They do, however, share with the middle-level managers the attention to goals and add to it specific action items with which to attain the goals. Once the goals are met through the completion of these action items, the whole process is reviewed—to continue with the metaphor, the water is recirculated to the top, where it repeats the process of review and refinement. The communication flows together like water, without a clear beginning or end point, and the communication loop is continuous.

The *hōshin kanri* system works to ensure consensus-oriented communication among all involved at any level, while this still preserves a firm's hierarchical structure. *Hōshin kanri* is, by North American standards, very time-consuming in the short run. Nevertheless, from the Japanese perspective, it allows for continuous checks that are—over the long run—time-saving. This is because *hōshin kanri* ensures that any proposed plan is pragmatically possible at every level of implementation by requiring feedback at every level, including those who will actually be putting the plans into action. By requiring universal involvement from everyone involved, it allows everyone to know exactly what they need to do and how to do it before they actually start. Finally, by involving everyone, this allows the entire group to own the project. There is, in short, buy-in before a project begins.

RECOMMENDATIONS

Given the issues related to authority in communication, we offer the following recommendations:

1. Show respect for authority. Japan is a hierarchically conscious society, and relative rank matters much more than in North America. No one is fully equal to anyone else due to rank, age, position, and more.

2. Build trust. *Amae* is at the heart of Japanese communication. The Japanese return on investment comes through building relationships, through which long-term goals can

be reached. In Japan, you probably should, too, and let go of the idea of the North American short-term, revenue-based return on investment.

3. Do not act on your own. Instead, use *nemawashi* to become part of the decision making. Japanese decision making is done through a consensus-oriented process. The Japanese approach focuses on process more than objectives. If you wish to be part of this consensus-oriented decision making, become part of the network in which this consensus is reached.

SUMMARY OF THE JAPANESE AUTHORITY CONCEPTION

Japanese Hierarchy

- Japan's vertically oriented hierarchy has deep historical roots.
- Confucian philosophy and feudal era social stratifications continue to influence Japanese valuing of a set social order and respect for authority.

Japanese Views of Power

- Japanese power is tied to the fulfillment of anticipated needs, rather than directly giving orders.
- Japanese people do not generally contradict or challenge those of higher rank.

Authority and *Amae*

- *Amae* relationships mean that if you are in charge of others, you take on an almost parental role toward those who report to you.
- *Amae* relationships mean that if you are the subordinate, you expect your boss to take care of you, and in return you show loyalty and deep trust for those in authority above you.

Consensus Communication in Decision Making

- Japanese rely heavily on consensus in decision making, even though it is not acceptable to challenge authority directly.
- Many techniques are formalized, especially in the workplace, to ensure that everyone involved in a project provides input and receives buy-in, including *hōrenso*, *nemawashi*, *ringiseido*, and *hōshinkanri*.

Recommendations

- Show respect for authority. Japan is a hierarchically conscious society, and relative rank matters much more than in North America.

- Build trust. *Amae* is at the heart of Japanese communication.
- Do not act on your own. Instead, use *nemawashi*, and work with those who have academic degrees or positions of power.

6

JAPANESE
Nonverbal Communication

Not Just About a Bow

Nonverbal communication is not a single topic. Rather, when we say nonverbal behavior, we mean everything from how people move and the gestures they make to how close or far apart we stand or sit. Nonverbal behavior deals with eye contact and what we do with our eyes, and it deals with how much we touch—or, in the Japanese case, *do not touch*—each other. Nonverbal behavior also takes into account how we respond passively to the things around us, such as our reactions to the use of certain colors, to the signs and symbols that surround us, or even how we respond to smells and different odors.

One difficulty with discussing nonverbal communication is that—regardless of what culture we belong to—much of it goes on unconsciously. As a result, not only do we fail to recognize that our nonverbal communication is culturally biased, we do not even know that we are doing it or perceiving it. As such, our challenge is to become aware of our own nonverbal communication, and only then can we compare these with the norms of other cultures.

Finally, the difficulty of interpreting nonverbal communication is compounded in Japan because the Japanese rely much more than their North American counterparts on interpreting what is not said. As discussed in chapter 4, on contexting, the Japanese value silence, and pausing is both a vital and positive communication skill. In other words, Japanese people view relying on nonverbal cues and silence as a form of active communication. By contrast, North Americans view reticence (let alone silence) as the absence of communication altogether.

An additional factor is that, relatively speaking, North Americans have a wide range of nonverbal behavior. This is at least in part due to the various ethnic groups that have entered the United States and Canada and the consequent immigration patterns. By contrast, nonverbal behavior in Japan is remarkably homogeneous when compared with that in the United States or Canada. Although regional differences do exist in how Japanese communicate, these are less varied than the ethnic (and regional) differences in North America. Because of Japanese homogeneity, the range of nonverbal variation tends at most to be geographic (e.g., people from Kyoto vs. people from Tokyo) and not geographic plus ethnic. This is much more complicated in the United States.

In this respect, it is arguably easier for North Americans to learn Japanese nonverbal communication than vice versa. Because North American nonverbal behavior is affected by significant differences based on ethnic group and region, the range of nonverbal behavior possible provides a hurdle to Japanese people (or any foreigner). An Alabama handshake is often different from a Michigan one. To add to this, it can be confusing that even in the same state—say, Michigan—the hand gestures in the Arab American community of southeastern Michigan are often much more expansive than in the Finnish American community of Michigan's Upper Peninsula.

Little of this ethnic variation exists in Japan (although we could argue that Okinawans, for instance, use different gestures that are distinctive from those of most other Japanese).

As far as North Americans are concerned, they can expect the same eye contact, bowing behavior, personal space, and the like from someone in Hokkaido in the far north as from someone in Kyushu in the far south.

But homogeneity is where the relative ease of understanding Japanese nonverbal behavior stops. This is because—compared with almost anything done in North America—Japanese nonverbal behavior is at once more subtle and central to communication.

In this chapter, we look at a number of examples of common Japanese nonverbal behavior and compare them with the norms in North American culture. We begin with body movements (or kinesics), including gestures, adaptors (e.g., head-nodding), and the like. Next, we look at dress and appearance. We then deal with physical touching (called haptics) and interpersonal distance (proxemics), and then move on to passive nonverbal communication, including the roles of signs and symbols (semiotics), colors, and even smells. We end the chapter with a few recommendations.

KINESICS

Kinesics refers to the way we use our bodies to communicate without words. Hand gestures are arguably the most obvious and explicit form, but kinesics goes much further. Kinesics includes how we move our legs (as when we cross them), our heads (nodding), our shoulders (shrugging), and our overall posture (stiff, slumped, etc.).

Kinesics exists in both Japan and North America, but how we interpret them on either side of the Pacific may differ significantly. For example, people in both cultures nod their heads when listening to someone speaking with them. If you were holding a conversation with a businesswoman, whether in Tokyo or Toronto, you could rightly expect her to nod her head while you were speaking. In Toronto, however, you might expect that when you were done speaking, your nodding counterpart would say something about how much she agreed with whatever the subject was.

In Tokyo, however, this might *not* actually happen. As we saw earlier, in chapter 4 on contexting, the Japanese nod in such a conversation is merely the listener's understanding of what you were saying, not that he or she had necessarily agreed with what you said. In Japan, head-nodding does not connote more than an encouragement from the listener to you as the speaker that you should continue. The Japanese person *might* agree with you and indicate so when you are done speaking, but he or she just as likely might *not* agree with you. Nodding feedback is unrelated to agreement. In other words, it is equally possible that when you (as the North American) finish speaking, your Japanese counterpart would grimace and even say something along the lines of "this might be difficult"—which, as we saw, is actually a way of saying, "No, I disagree" in a high-context manner.

Head-nodding belongs to the subset of kinesics called *regulators*. These are the nonverbal cues we give others to influence or even control what the speaker is saying. All cultures have a wide range of regulators. In addition to head-nodding, there are a host of cues that allow the listener to interact in this way. The Japanese arguably give more attention to regulators than in most other cultures, for two reasons. First, regulators are at the heart of Japanese listener talk; and second, the *frequency* of regulators in Japanese communication is far greater than that to which most of us are accustomed in the United States or Canada.

The good news is that both in Japan and North America, many of these regulators—unlike head-nodding—are similar. If someone raises their eyebrows or makes a pained expression or grimaces in Japan, it means pretty much the same thing as in the United States or Canada. That said, many Japanese regulators are subtler than the same regulators in North America. In both Toronto and Tokyo, we may cock our head to the side to show that we may be questioning what someone is saying. In Toronto, however, what we would view as a small turning of the head to the side might well appear to be a very large gesture or even an exaggerated one to the Japanese. In turn, the same gesture in Tokyo might well be lost on the North American, as it may be so slight that it is unseen altogether. Indeed, if a

Japanese person were to cock his or her head to the side to the same degree as a Torontonian, the regulator could well take on a different meaning through its emphasis. Thus the head-cocking that in Toronto might suggest "I'll have to think about that," by its greater size might in Tokyo mean something along the lines of "Are you kidding me?" This is in large part because regulators and nonverbal behavior in general are in keeping with North American and Japanese communication principles: North Americans use nonverbal communication as a way of delivering content to convey meaning, while Japanese use nonverbal communication to support the flow of the conversation. Similar to saying *no*, cocking one's head stops this process, and can therefore be seen as aggressive among the Japanese.[1]

EMBLEMS

In Japan, people touch their noses to express in gesture the phrase "Who me?" In North America, people tend to point with one finger to their chests to express the same "Who me?" This type of gesture is known as an *emblem*. We use the word *emblem* for nonverbal messages that act as deliberate signals used in place of a verbal message or accompanied by a verbal equivalent. Many of the most common emblems in North America differ in meaning or have no equivalent in Japan, and vice versa.

Another emblem in Japan is the "come here" gesture, which simply does not exist in the United States or Canada. The "come here" emblem, illustrated in photograph 6.1, involves holding an outstretched hand at shoulder height, palm down and scratching the air with your four fingers closed together. This does not mean anything to a North American counterpart, who would use the gesture of holding the hand in a loose fist palm up and wiggling a bent index finger back and forth. The Japanese can interpret this North American gesture as a somewhat rude, *"get over here"* gesture. The consequence of using our own emblems in other cultures can then result in an unintended *mis*communication.

Table 6.1 provides several gestures with no equivalence between Japan and North America.

6.1 "Come Here"
Gesturing for someone to
"come here" in Japan. Photo
courtesy of Koji Kodana.

Where miscommunication is more likely is when an identi-
cal emblem is used meaning one thing in Japan and something
else in North America. In such a case, the emblems are known
to both cultures but could easily be misinterpreted because their
meanings do not translate. One example of where emblems have
different meanings would be the following. Imagine that you are
on the phone and a colleague standing near your desk begins to
speak with you. On either side of the Pacific, it would be common to use a gesture (rather than words) to say "wait a second"
or "just a moment." The most common emblem gesture for this
in the United States or Canada would be to hold up your index
finger and perhaps nod at your colleague. But in Japan, this
gesture makes little or no sense in this context. Holding up your
index finger has more or less one meaning in Japan, and that is
the number "1." The most common emblem gesture for asking
your colleague to wait a moment in Japan would be to hold the
entire palm up to the other person, with all the fingers straight
up and held together. However, this gesture in a North American

Table 6.1
Nonexistent Emblems in Japan and North America

Meaning	Japanese Emblem	North American Emblem
A. "Me"/"I."	Touch nose with index finger.	Touch chest with index finger, thumb or hand.
B. Let's get back to that another time/let's put this subject to the side for now.	Make a motion to the side with both hands a small distance apart, with palms facing and fingers held together, as if moving a small box from in front of the speaker to the right.	No equivalent.
C. Thank you/I'm really grateful (typically used casually with peers or subordinates).	Hold the right hand thumb up between the eyes about a hand's distance away then shake it out once to a point about a foot in front of the face.	No equivalent, although often a handshake can be used in this context if actually saying thank you out loud.
D. *Osaki ni* gesture: Excuse me for walking in front of you (or between two people).	Bend slightly at the shoulders and, holding the hand thumb up with fingers together, move the hand slightly up and down as if in a stiff handshake while edging forward and while walking partially sideways.	No equivalent in gesture, although the equivalent is done by saying the words, "excuse me" out loud.
E. Denying a compliment, as if saying "I don't deserve such praise" or "that isn't so" or "not me."	Moving the hand quickly back and forth, the hand at about chest height with the open palm facing the other person (as if wiping away the compliment).	No equivalent gesture, and arguably no equivalent concept, as most North Americans readily accept compliments when deserved.

Table 6.2

Emblem Gestures with Differing Meanings in Japan and North America

Emblem Gesture	Japanese Meaning	North American Meaning
A. Covering the mouth.	Done when laughing or smiling. Socially acceptable way to smile, as showing teeth can be seen as vulgar/tacky, like chewing with your mouth open for North Americans.	Done when yawning, gasping, surprised, or as a sign of embarrassment.
B. Moving both hands up and down at about waist height, with palms facing the floor.	Done while saying "maaah . . . maaah" in time with the gesture. Equivalent to saying, "Calm down! Take it easy!"	Done when speaking to a group. Equivalent to saying, "Let's all sit down now" or possibly, if to applause, "that's enough, thank you, but let me go on."
C. Striking the palm of one hand with the fist of another.	I strongly agree.	I'm angry.

context usually means "stay back" or even "watch where you are about to step." Moreover, the "just a moment" hand gesture in Japan would also be accompanied by a bow, even from a sitting position. Without a bow, the hand gesture has the same impact as an adult telling a child, "Not right now." In other words, Japanese and North Americans use the same emblem to carry different meanings. Table 6.2 provides several emblem gestures that are used with different meanings in Japan and North America.

BOWING

The most notable Japanese emblem is the bow. Bowing is used to greet people, to say goodbye to people, to recognize, to thank, to apologize, to thank and apologize (not the same thing as each independently), and to ask a favor of or request something from someone. The Japanese bow is related to head-nods and vocal feedback, in that it is used to recognize the pleasantness of meeting the other person in a similar way to a North American's "Great to see you," but also adds an *others*-oriented validation, "I'm grateful to see you" thanking and apologizing the other person all at once for taking time out to greet the other person. The Japanese bow is so deeply ingrained as kinesic behavior that it is common to see Japanese bowing while speaking on the phone with someone who, of course, cannot even see them.

At this point, it might be worth mentioning that bowing, like the Japanese language, is more or less unique to Japanese culture, and that any variation from the way Japanese bow is felt strongly by its recipients. As an others-centered culture, they absorb the greeting of a bow as physically as a touch—like a handshake or side-to-side kisses. Any amount of awkwardness on the part of another communicator is therefore felt in a similar way to feeling a body tense up when hugging a person from a nonhugging culture, say a Japanese. We share this here not to discourage you from trying to bow, but to enable you to be aware of your Japanese counterparts' feelings and the consequent impressions that you make on them.

In business with North Americans, some Japanese will shake hands; however, most will not be able to resist the engrained bow. From your end, a good deal can be learned from watching Japanese bow to each other, and practicing with your friends, because, contrary to the way that bowing is used in other countries, particularly with royalty, bowing in Japan is not so much showing respect as simply a recognized civil greeting and an interactional reminder that we are others centered.

Men and women bow somewhat differently, as shown in photograph 6.2.

When bowing, men keep their hands at their sides, with the palms pressed against their legs; but women clasp their hands in front of them at their waist. Both men and women, however, keep their feet together and bow in a smooth motion from the hips with their neck and spine aligned. Of particular importance, neither looks up as he or she bows.

6.2 Shallow Bows
The 15-degree bow for people who know each other well. Photo courtesy of Sandrine Burtschell.

How long and how deeply you bow makes a difference. The average bow lasts about three or four seconds. In general, the more deeply and the longer you bow, the more you are seen to be elevating the other person's status. The value here is how you are seen. If you bow longer than the other person, this is seen as showing greater respect. If the other person bows longer than you, then that person will be seen as showing you greater respect. If you find yourself straightening your back up while the other person is still holding his or her bow, and this is socially inappropriate owing to the social relationships described in the chapter on authority, you will bow a second time. However, if you held your bow longer with your second bow than your counterpart, he or she might feel the same way you did, and you might find the cycle starting over again, as the other person may bow again—thereby producing the Japanese "comedy" that is often caricatured when outsiders see Japanese bowing.

The general rule of thumb is that the lower-ranking person bows lower to the higher-ranking person. This follows a modified form of the Confucian Five Bonds listed in chapter 5,

6.3 A Man and a Woman Bowing
A man bowing with hands to the side, and a woman bowing with hands at her lap. Photo courtesy of Sandrine Burtschell.

on authority conception. This works out so that younger people bow lower to older people, women bow lower to men, citizens bow lower to the state, subordinates bow lower to superiors, sellers bow lower to buyers, and students bow lower to teachers. Although there are exceptions, in principle, the greater the difference in authority through position, age, or power, the greater the difference in the bow. Often this is easy to determine. When a junior executive greets a senior executive at a partner company, the junior executive will bow more deeply to the older and higher-ranking executive.

Still, who bows lower is not always that easy to determine. For instance, it is not always clear who should bow lower in a situation, with, say, a younger female buyer with an older male seller. The buyer merits the respect of the seller, requiring the seller to bow lower. The older person merits the respect of the younger one, in this case suggesting that the buyer should bow lower. Traditionally, women bow lower to men, which would suggest the buyer would bow lower. However, the level of respect differs for each of these three relationships: seller–buyer,

6.4 Kaz Hirai Apologizing
SONY's Kaz Hirai apologizing for the Playstation Network security breach.
AP photo/Shizuo Kambayashi.

younger–older, and female–male. First, the respect shown to the buyer is generally stronger than the respect shown to the age or gender difference. Second, the amount of age difference is a factor, with the greater the age gap, the more age matters. In short, who bows lower to whom is not all that easy to determine, even among the Japanese themselves, let alone for foreigners.

Given this complexity of bowing in Japanese culture, we suggest you do not get hung up on bowing too much and simply bow to the extent you consider respectful, and then perhaps comment about your bow if you feel awkward about it. As we said above, the Japanese will generally not expect you to bow the way they do, for they have been practicing bowing since they were born.[2]

In short, how deeply someone bows relative to another person depends on a host of factors. Shallow bows, such as the one shown in figure 6.2, are used to greet a friend or colleague of similar rank. A midlevel bow (shown in figure 6.3) is used to greet customers or people of higher authority. Workers at Japanese stores and restaurants will greet customers. You would return a shallower bow or even a slight nod of the head acknowledging their bow. Again, however, the exact depth of the bow will vary based on relative differences in authority, age, and the like. This is also the usual bow used when entering (or leaving) a conference room for business. You would also use a midlevel bow when thanking someone. Finally, people bow very deeply to express very strong thanks or very deep apologies. If someone did something extraordinary for you or you felt particularly bad about something you had done, you might use this bow. A fairly famous example of such a bow was widely published in the press in 2011, when Sony's (soon-to-be) CEO and president, Kaz Hirai, apologized for the Playstation Network security breach. At a press conference apologizing for leaving 77 million customers open to hackers, Hirai bowed this deep sort of bow; see photograph 6.4.

ILLUSTRATORS

When you tell someone that you own a small dog and hold your hands apart to show the size of the dog, you are using another type of kinesics called an *illustrator*. As you might expect, illustrators show what you are saying by reinforcing, describing, or emphasizing what you are saying. These are common in most cultures, and the good news here is that most people in North America readily understand illustrators in Japan.

The converse, however, is not the case. There are many more variations in illustrators in North America than there are in Japan, in great part because there is greater variation in ethnic and linguistic backgrounds. One of the largest variables in this regard is with illustrators.

AFFECT DISPLAY

One more category of kinesics is known as *affect display*. These are nonverbal messages communicating emotion (affect) through body position (e.g., slumping or leaning forward) and especially facial expressions (e.g., frowning or raising eyebrows).

Although a number of researchers have shown that certain basic affect displays are nearly universal, what varies from culture to culture is the degree to which it is acceptable to show that emotion in various settings (in public, at home, in the workplace, etc.).[3]

It is arguably in the acceptability of displaying emotion through affect display where North American and Japanese most differ. For strong emotions, affect displays in both cultures are very similar, both in nature and size. For lower-intensity emotions, however, the Japanese are much more subtle in their display of emotion; and it does not take a very strong expression to communicate emotion in Japan. This is once again because the Japanese must be good readers and listeners, rather than speakers and displayers of emotion. The result is that—in terms of nonverbal cues—the Japanese may view North American affect displays as showing emotion stronger than is actually felt, whereas North Americans may view Japanese as expressing emotion weaker than is actually felt.[4]

ADAPTORS

When you have an itch, you tend to scratch it. *Adaptors*, the last category of kinesics, are the movements we use to fill some personal need, not only of scratching an itch but also of shifting position while sitting, yawning (or stifling a yawn), clearing a stuffy nose, and so on. As with affect displays, adaptors are fairly universal—when you have an itch, you want to scratch. The thing that shifts across cultures is how much we allow ourselves to fill those needs in front of others. Sometimes the norms governing adaptor acceptability are shared across cultures. In both North America and Japan, for instance, an itch on the back of your neck is more acceptable to scratch than one, say, on your behind. Sometimes, however, the norms governing adaptor acceptability differs across cultures.

For example, regardless of what culture you live in, when your nose is full, you feel the need to clear it. North Americans generally do not have much of a taboo about blowing their nose

6.5 Wearing a Mask
Chestnut vendor wearing
a mask in Kyoto Central
Station.

in public. But most Japanese do. In the United States, if you need to blow your nose, you can use a handkerchief or a tissue, after which you may put this back in your pocket. In Canada, nose-blowing is acceptable if it is done without making noise. In Japan, however, blowing your nose, whether noisily or quietly, is viewed as disgusting. Instead, the Japanese will sniff in a manner that seems annoyingly perpetual to North Americans. For the Japanese, blowing your nose is a usually private matter, best done in a toilet.

Because people get colds and runny noses in Japan just as much as anywhere else, Japanese accommodate this problem by courteously wearing a surgical mask when they have a cold. Photograph 6.5 shows a chestnut vendor at Kyoto Central Station wearing such a mask. This is very common, not only for people handling food as here, but also for people riding the train, walking down the street, or working at an office. By the way, you will notice another emblem in this shot: The woman is holding up her hand in a "v" for the photo. Except in formal photographs, Japanese very frequently make the "v" sign. In an ironic twist, most North Americans find the custom of holding up a "v" odd, even though this sign's origins are in the United States. The "v" sign was derived from "v for victory" and evolved into a peace sign, meaning "victory over war," in the 1960s and 1970s in the United States. The Japanese use of a "v" when posing has nothing to do with "v for victory" as it does in North America, even though that is where the emblem originated. Although the "v" may have come from US soldiers during World War II at one time or the Vietnam Era peace sign, today it is simply the equivalent of smiling for the photo.

The fact that Japanese adults do not touch when greeting and touch little in public often seems to figure into the perception that Japanese people are cold and aloof. To counter this image of an unemotional Japanese, we suggest attending a baseball event and watching the Japanese cheerleaders. Unlike the North American variety typically monopolized by young women, Japanese cheerleaders are mostly boisterous young men with megaphones and headbands shouting loudly in support of their teams. Likewise, children's emotional outbursts are tolerated more in Japan than in North America, as are men's tears when suffering a loss. Frequent bowing also counterbalances the idea that the Japanese have smaller and less frequent gestures, and it may very well be that the gestures are different contributes to a feeling that there are fewer of them.

Nonverbal behavior often takes place independent of language and is learned earlier than our oral language. Babies are able to communicate without words long before they can speak. Nonverbal behavior, in short, is modeled behavior that is very deeply engrained. This is one reason that—in immigrant-based societies such as Canada and the United States—someone's ethnic background so often influences their use of gestures and the like. In short, when someone speaks in a second language, this in no way means that they will somehow naturally replace all of their mother-language nonverbal behavior. In other words, just because your Japanese counterpart is speaking very good English, it would be a mistake to believe that they will automatically use a North American standard of nonverbal behavior.

Closely tied to kinesics is the concept of oculesics, which refers to how people use their eyes to communicate. This entails more than just eye contact, but also includes general eye behavior such as closing one's eyes, looking away from someone, and basically reading emotions in the eyes.

Few cultures have as big a difference in oculesics than do Japan and North America. In Japan, people lower their eyes to show respect. In the United States and Canada, people sustain eye contact to show respect. Far from showing respect, when North Americans lower their eyes it suggests one of several nonverbal messages—but none of those messages is respect. Although there are some exceptions (especially for Native Americans and First Nations), in most cases in the United States and Canada, people lower their eyes because they (1) are lying, (2) lack confidence, or (3) do not consider you worth their interest.

By contrast, the Japanese view sustained, unbroken eye contact as aggressive. Lowered eye contact is an indicator of respect for relative rank and authority. Just as people of lower standing bow more deeply, people of lower standing make less sustained eye contact. The higher the relative position in Japan, in turn, the longer the allowable eye contact.

This difference in oculesics can easily create miscommunication. Photograph 6.6 shows a young Japanese job applicant called in for an in-person interview with an older human resources manager at a US company. It would be natural for the Japanese job applicant to lower his or her eyes. The human resources manager is a person of greater authority, and indeed has the power of deciding whether the Japanese applicant will get the job. The Japanese applicant is, in addition, younger than the interviewer, another reason to lower the eyes to show respect. From the Japanese interviewee's position, lowering the eyes here shows respect and deference. From the US interviewer's perspective, however, the same lowering of the eyes would indicate that the Japanese applicant was lying or lacking in confidence, or perhaps both. In short, in this situation, the same oculesic act could easily result in entirely different interpretations.

6.6 Differing Eye Contact
For Japanese, lowering one's eye gaze is deferential.

In Japan, lowering the eyes (as with bowing) can also be a way to augment an apology and show remorse. This is the exact opposite of eye contact during apologies in the United States or Canada. If a Japanese person lowers his or her eyes often or for a sustained period during an apology, this helps nonverbally to communicate that the apology is heartfelt. But if a North American lowers his or her eyes during an apology, this indicates that the apology is insincere or lacking in respect.

The result of this intercultural difference in how eye contact is understood results in much less eye contact in Japan than in almost any culture in the Americas or Europe. Japanese people maintain their eye contact during intracultural conversation roughly half the time, far less than people of the same age from the United States. Anjanie Kang-Lee, Shoji Itakura, and Darwin Muir indicate that gaze (i.e., eye contact length) differs, depending on whether the person knows how to respond to a question. This study, which was done between Japanese and Canadians, found that Canadians who knew a response made eye contact 64 percent of the time. Japanese who knew a response made eye contact 54 percent of the time. Canadians who did not know a response averted their eyes 53 percent of the time. Japanese who did not know a response averted their eyes 64 percent of the time.[5]

Masuda and colleagues found that although initial direct eye contact for Japanese and US study participants was similar in length during the first second of an interaction, the two groups diverged rapidly in their eye contact after that: "Whereas both the Japanese and Westerners similarly attended to the central figure during the first second, . . . the Japanese started their attentive allocation to the background figures at the next second." From this, Masuda and colleagues concluded that "overall, these results suggest that, at first, both the Japanese and Westerners attend almost exclusively to the central figure, but after 1 [second], Japanese start to show their context sensitivity." This disparity was even more marked when the emotion encountered was sad, happy, or neutral. That said, when faced with someone who was angry, the Japanese maintained eye contact longer than they would otherwise, but still notably less than their US counterparts.[6]

Finally, in Japanese oculesics it is also possible to close one's eyes in several situations where North Americans would not. Closing the eyes for longer than a blink in a North American contact carries pretty much one of two meanings: falling asleep; or totally ignoring those around you. Japanese who have fallen asleep, of course, would also close their eyes, but that is not the only reason for doing so. In fact, one reason the Japanese may close their eyes is the exact opposite of this: They are paying particularly close attention. As Rochelle Kopp writes:

The fact is, when Japanese close their eyes in meetings, most of the time they aren't actually asleep! Often, closed eyes are a sign that a Japanese person is listening intently. Japanese believe that by closing their eyes, they can hear more effectively, because they are screening out the visual stimulus and focusing only on the sound. Because Japanese find it challenging to listen to English conversations for long stretches of time, they are especially likely to use this technique in meetings with Americans.[7]

There are not always clear differences in the ways that North Americans and Japanese dress. However, there is more regional, ethnic, and religious variation in what is considered appropriate professional attire in the United States than in Japan. For example, a Jewish kippah, Muslim hijab, or Sikh turban would be very rare indeed in Japan, and, if worn at all, would be the dress only of foreigners.

Generally speaking, Japanese attire, and especially business attire, tends to be consistently more formal than the norm for North America. The business casual attire popular in much of North America is much less commonly accepted in Japan, and in many situations is openly frowned upon. Indeed, even in formal business attire, the average Japanese businessperson would be more likely to be more formal than the North American counterpart in the same situation, wearing dark-colored suits with attention to styling and detail (e.g., a dress shirt or blouse), with no facial hair for men; see photograph 6.7.

The tendency of conformity of attire is arguably overstated at times. Japan has its share of fashion and costume designers,

6.7 Japanese Business Dress
No matter what your business is, more formal attire is generally the standard in Japan. Photo by Katri Niemi; used with permission.

6.8 Sanitized Slippers
There's clean. And then there's Japan clean.

of which a good part make ready-to-wear designer clothes. In the workplace, however, if everyone wears white shirts and dark ties, and you wear pastel-colored shirts and light ties, you would be making more of a statement doing so in Japan than in Canada or the United States.

One item given much more attention in Japan than in North America is socks. In Japan, you remove your shoes before entering someone's home or dormitory, or (quite often at least) in such public places as restaurants, shrines, and temples. You are expected to take off your shoes in the *genkan*, a recessed foyer in the entrance that typically has a shoe rack, cubbyhole, or cupboard. There are sometimes whole rooms devoted to placing your outside shoes in cubbyholes and putting on your inside slippers. See photograph 6.8 for a pair of very clean slippers.

When you remove your shoes, of course, your socks will be exposed. Most North Americans would care if they had a run or hole in their socks or stockings, but perhaps less so than the Japanese, because at least in the case of socks, the holes are always covered by shoes. In Japan, a hole will be quite embarrassingly apparent.

6.9 House Slippers
House slippers in a clinic *genkan*. Photo courtesy of Sandrine Burtschell.

In someone's home, and often in shrines, temples, clubs, and clinics, you will be provided with a pair of slippers, like those shown in photograph 6.9. You are generally expected to wear these. As most Japanese tend to have smaller feet than most North Americans, these often do not fit well if you are, say, taller than average. But you are still expected to wear these slippers, even if they do not fit.

In addition to house slippers, Japanese use bathroom slippers, such as those shown in photograph 6.10. The bathroom is considered an entirely different part of the house or restaurant than the main areas. You are expected to take off your house slippers outside the bathroom and step into the bathroom slippers as you enter the bathroom. You then reverse the process going out and turn the bathroom slippers the right way around. The house slippers are typically made from fabric, whereas the bathroom ones are usually plastic. Putting on and taking off shoes and slippers are all done for the sake of hygiene. Bathroom slippers often have "toilet" written on them, which is why many Japanese giggle at first-time visitors who forget to change back into the house slippers when they come out!

Very few people today wear traditional Japanese silk kimonos, as shown in photograph 6.11, or the more casual cotton summer *yukatas*. These remain important parts of Japanese culture, however, and are often worn by participants in formal rites, such as a couple in a Japanese wedding (although, as discussed in chapter 3, on social organization, these are becoming less and less common), or by practitioners of traditional Japanese cultural events—ranging, for example, from those taking part in the Japanese tea ceremony to New Year's Day to Seven-Five-Three Day, which celebrates the growth of young children. Kimonos are also worn by entertainers such as geisha and *maiko*. Some people wear kimonos or *yukatas* on a regular basis (especially in Kyoto, the center of "old Japan"), but this is more of a statement than a common practice, somewhat akin to a Texan who wears a cowboy hat and chaps.

Cosplay apparel is another type of uniquely Japanese dress. Cosplay is actually a combination of two English words—costume and play—and that is what it is, "costumed play" or role-playing. Cosplay apparel has grown greatly in popularity as a

6.10 Bathroom Slippers
Don't forget to leave the bathroom slippers in the bathroom! Photo courtesy of Juriaan Simonis.

6.11 Geisha Wearing a Kimono
Rare glance at a geisha wearing a kimono outside Kyoto.

hobby in Japan since the late 1980s, and today represents a multi-million-dollar industry. Cosplay costumes, like the ones shown in photograph 6.12, are often based on video games, manga, anime, and television series. This hobby exists to some extent in North America, with fans of various series such as *Star Trek* or *Star Wars*, as well as superhero comic books, who dress up as associated characters and then meet in conventions and conferences as well as on a small scale in clubs and local organizations. In Japan, however, cosplay is very widespread and covers a much wider range of fandom than just a handful of series. Cosplayers—pronounced *kosupure* (コスプレ) in Japanese—often do more than dress up as the characters they portray, instead trying to embody the character fully through role-playing that often approaches method acting. Cosplay, it should be mentioned, is not limited to Japan, as cosplay movements are growing in popularity in such countries as the Philippines and Singapore, with major Western events as well, such as Comicon in the United States, the Japan Expo in Paris, Anime North in Toronto, Anime Expo in Los Angeles, the Supernova Pop Culture Expo in Australia, and the London MCM Expo. That said, cosplay began in Japan, and to this day Tokyo's twice-yearly Comiket (コミケット) remains the largest such gathering in the world.

6.12 Cosplayers
In districts like Akihabara in Tokyo, there are many cosplayer gathering spots.
Photo courtesy of Sandrine Burtschell.

On a smaller level, Japan has many cosplay restaurants, most famously in Tokyo's Akihabara district (but elsewhere as well).

One last type of dress worthy of mention is the uniform, which the Japanese are inclined to wear much more than people in the United States or Canada. In addition to the expected uniforms for police officers, train station attendants, members of sports teams, nurses, flight attendants, and fast food workers common in North America, the Japanese wear uniforms in many other sectors of society. Although some private North American schools require uniforms, virtually all schoolchildren in Japan wear uniforms, as you can see in photograph 6.13. And though some stores and restaurants may require their staff to wear uniforms or comply with a dress code, far more Japanese stores and restaurants require their staff to wear uniforms. Furthermore, the Japanese wear uniforms for professions for which North Americans rarely if ever require uniforms, such as construction workers and car salespeople. Finally, though some North American companies require uniforms for line workers in manufacturing jobs, this is not the norm. In Japan, such a requirement for

6.13 School Uniforms
Almost all Japanese school-children wear uniforms just like this. Photo courtesy of Sandrine Burtschell.

manufacturing jobs is the norm. Indeed, in many companies, the same uniform is used from the lowest-level entry staff to the highest-level supervisor.

HAPTICS, OR TOUCHING BEHAVIOR

Haptics refers to how people communicate through touching. In the case of haptics, a certain level of touching signals a professional relationship, and a different type of touching signals a social, friendly, or even intimate relationship.

In public, interpersonal communication, Japan is known to be a relatively *ahaptic* society—in other words, its people touch very little, especially in comparison with other cultures like North America. In a case where two North Americans shake hands, as we have discussed, two Japanese bow, without touching. As a result, because many Japanese are unfamiliar with how to shake hands, they often shake weakly. North Americans, in turn, frequently misinterpret this lack of knowing how to shake hands as a lack of interest, or worse, as a lack of personal warmth. Conversely, some North Americans who shake very firmly (as in some regions of the United States, or when showing strong approval) actually end up hurting the hands of their Japanese counterparts who are unfamiliar with shaking hands in the first place. Some Japanese may also say that shaking hurts because they simply do not like to shake hands.

Although North Americans, generally speaking, touch less often than those in North Africa, Central or South America, or Southern Europe, they still have a fairly large range of touching behavior that falls within the norm. Variability in touching behavior is particularly the case in many regional and ethnic subcultures in North America, where some people might give hugs while others give cheek-to-cheek kisses.

In Japan, none of this variation exists. Moreover, the Japanese are not comfortable displaying touching in public, or with being hugged or kissed by people who are relative strangers. That said, compared with the population in general, public displays of affection among teens and young adults are more common. Similarly, for female friends, hand-holding used to be a common occurrence, but it has declined with the influence of what is considered "modern" appropriate Western behaviors.

One of our authors, Orlando Kelm, recalls a time when he was in the exhibition hall of an academic conference. From opposite ends of the hall, two Japanese women recognized each other. In excitement, they ran toward each other, both squealing with delight and clearly anxious to greet an old friend. But at arm's-length distance, both stopped to bow, and then they continued to squeal and laugh and talk. During this entire exchange, touching was minimal, and almost nonexistent. Yet for the Canadian-born Kelm, the encounter left a lasting image of how strong emotions could be expressed with almost no physical touching.

If the Japanese are ahapatic (nontouching) in their public interpersonal reactions, the opposite holds true in public crowds. In a crowded subway station or on a busy street, Japanese people regularly bump into each other, ranging from lightly brushing against someone to a more major jolt. Most Japanese ignore these as unavoidable occurrences in crowded conditions. By contrast, North Americans are extremely offended if someone bumps into them or brushes up against them, even in a very crowded situation. It is necessary to apologize immediately if you bump into someone or—as many Japanese in North America have found out, to their discomfort—you will hear an angry retort from the person you have touched in this way.

At home, Japanese children often sleep and bathe with their parents. This shows how Japanese haptics conform to the insider/outsider relations mentioned previously. Furthermore, although most North Americans may never encounter this, the Japanese can be a haptic culture behind closed doors, where they are not exposed to the social judgment of the public display of emotion.

PROXEMICS, OR PERSONAL SPACE

Proxemics deals with how people use the space around them. One of the most important areas of proxemics is how near or far people stand from each other when talking, sitting, or speaking. Although there is some variation between regions and linguistic or ethnic groups in North America, most people in the United States and Canada stand at about 1.5 feet (just under 46 centimeters) apart from someone of the same gender. Men and women stand slightly farther apart from one another. The Japanese, by contrast, stand about 1.8 feet (56 centimeters) apart. This is nearly a third of a foot (over 9 centimeters) farther apart.

If you are one of two North Americans of the same gender standing across from each other in a normal conversation, you should be able to extend your arm fully and then be able to place your thumb in the other person's ear. If you are one of two Japanese of the same gender standing across from each other, you should be able to extend your arm fully and then be able to swing your open hand to a point just beyond the other person's nose. However, in intercultural communication, the Japanese requirement of a bigger interpersonal distance often results in a situation where the Japanese appear to the North Americans to be literally "distant" or "stand-offish." At the same time, North Americans' smaller interpersonal distance appears to the Japanese to be aggressive and literally "in your face" as they speak.

Public proxemics, by contrast, is just the opposite. The average North American protects his or her bubble of space in all sorts of public settings, ranging from sitting in an office at a table or in a row of seats at a theater to standing in line to board a subway or bus. For a North American, the less you know someone, the more respectful you must be of his or her personal space. For the Japanese, however, the division of space is not defined individually by how well you know someone but organized by social structure. A respectful Japanese person will usually try to abide by this social definition.

Here is an example. In North America and Japan, seats are spaced at pretty much the same distance around a boardroom table, or on a bus or train, or in a theater row. The difference is in how people fill these seats on either side of the Pacific. In Japan, people take the seat directly next to another person, even if other seats are open. In North America, this adjacent seat is reserved only for family and friends (and sometimes not even them). At Disney World Orlando, a staff person must come into a show to tell people to fill up the theater seats and not leave any empty. But at Tokyo Disney, this prompting is not needed; everyone automatically fills in the rows.

This cross-cultural difference in proxemics is particularly evident in forming lines. The Japanese tend to stand at a distance, where the toe of the person behind is just short of touching the heel of the person in front. This is evident in photograph 6.14, which shows Tokyoites lining up to enter an office. This sort of distance in public lines makes many in the United States and Canada feel as if their personal space is being invaded. This is because in North America, people generally leave an entire body-width distance between each other.

In restaurants, during busy hours, it is customary for entering patrons to be seated at a bar or table where people are already eating. This never happens in North American restaurants, where patrons prefer to eat at a table rather than at the bar. Unless they are hosting foreign visitors, the Japanese, by contrast, will choose the counter over a table at a sushi bar if there is space available.

6.14 Lining Up
Lining up is second nature for the Japanese. Photo courtesy of Sandrine Burtschell.

PASSIVE NONVERBAL COMMUNICATION

In addition to the nonverbal communication behaviors that we have discussed so far in this chapter, other nonverbal cues are also called passive, because they are in the environment around us. In other words, these are things to which we respond rather than causing others to respond.

There are three main types of passive communication: (1) colors, (2) numerals and numbers, and (3) symbols. We look at each of these in the rest of this chapter.

Colors

Several colors carry associations. Some of these are fairly personal, ranging from your favorite color to colors that you believe complement your personal appearance (based on skin tone, hair color, etc.). These sorts of associations are individually based, regardless of culture. Still, color associations in general are actually highly subject to cultural variation, and this is true of different views of certain colors among people in Japan, Canada, and the United States. For example, in Japan, the color yellow is associated with courage. But in North America, yellow stands for cowardice, the exact opposite (as with the expression "yellow-bellied coward" or "you're just yellow").

In the United States, if you called someone "true blue," you would mean that he or she was loyal and dependable. For starters, the Japanese language does not even define blue in the same way as English. The Japanese word *ao* (青) more or less covers what in English would be both blue and green. In more modern Japanese, we have the word *midori* (緑), but this is really a subset of the blue-green that is *ao*. In English, by contrast, blue and green are as separate from each other as yellow and green.

Many things that are seen as green in North America are seen as blue in Japan. For the Japanese, some vegetables are called "blue" (*ao-na*), as are traffic lights, even if the Japanese still see them as green. In fact, because the Japanese do not make a distinction between green and blue, there are even instances where the traffic lights actually *are* blue, even using the English definition. This was the subject of a *Japan Times* article:

> "Traffic Safety Guidelines for Pedestrians and Cyclists 歩行者と自転車のための日本における交通安全ガイド,"a recent bilingual publication by the National Police Agency. Here the English text specifies that the "green light" indicates that "pedestrians can proceed to cross the street." In the accompanying Japanese text, by contrast, this very rule applies to 青色の灯火 (the blue-colored light).[8]

By the way, both texts refer to the same illustration, the image of a traffic light in red, yellow, and, well, something that NA might call turquoise.

More important, many Japanese expressions use "blue" where an English speaker would use "green." For example, the expression "you are blue" in Japanese means that you still lack enough experience; a direct translation to English would mean that you are feeling depressed. It would be possible that if a Japanese referred to someone as blue and said so in English, a North

American would misunderstand this as being depressed rather than inexperienced, and vice versa. Even if the Japanese and North American understood both meanings of "you are blue," a problem still exists. The issue in this case would not be that Japanese cannot understand the English translation. They do. Rather, it is that at the word associational level, blue takes on a different feel to someone speaking Japanese versus English. In the back of your mind, if your mother tongue is Japanese, there is an association of blue with immaturity or newness. In the back of your mind, if your first language is English, the association of blue is with loyalty or feeling sad. The Japanese, too, have colors—such as *enji* and *momoiro*—that do not have an equivalent in English, and many cultures categorize colors and the associations they have variously.

Numerals and Numbers

Numbers and numerals have specific meanings, but also cultural interpretations of these meanings. A square has four sides, no matter how lucky or unlucky the number four might be. In Japan, some of these cultural meanings are quite strong. Japan is not alone in this. Throughout China, South Korea, Singapore, Vietnam, Myanmar, and other Asian countries, the attitudes toward lucky and unlucky numbers approach the level of a religious belief in a North American context. In Japan and East Asia in general, numbers affect the day-to-day choices of many (if not most) people. Although everyone does not view this with the same importance, it is so widely believed that you would discount this as unimportant at your peril.

As a result, lucky and unlucky numbers often play a part when Japanese people consider selecting an address to locate an office, a hotel floor on which to stay, or a date on which to meet. The strongest example of this is with the number 4 throughout East Asia. The number 4 is so unlucky because it sounds like the word for death in many languages in the region. In Japanese in particular, the pronunciation for both 4 and death is *shi*. It is an exact homonym.

The aversion to the number 4 in Japan is much stronger than the only even partially comparable aversion to the number 13 in

6.15 The Missing "4"
A homonym for death, "4" is bad luck in Japan, so it is often omitted. Photo courtesy of Holawand.

the Americas. Fear of the number 13 is generally seen as a superstition and rarely affects much beyond that in the West. In Japan, by contrast, the unluckiness of 4 is in an entirely different category. Most Japanese hospitals and many hotels, apartments, and office buildings have no fourth floor. In hotels, the fourth floor is often set off as the mezzanine, and even then many people will not use that floor if given a choice. As shown in photograph 6.15, a parking lot in Shizuoka goes from 3 to 5—with no 4 at all.

This also affects dates. Many Japanese will not plan an important meeting or event on April 4 (4-4). This can affect everything from hotel availability to wedding dates to sales meetings, and extends to any numeral ending in 4 (14, 24, 40, etc.).

The aversion to the number 4 also affects things such as gifts. Four is a rather favored number for boxed sets of gifts in the United States. Four items fit well into a square box, for instance. A box of four chocolates in Toronto is a good thing; but in Tokyo, it is likely to be five. Many of our Japanese friends buy two sets of five dishes, for example, to have an even number when inviting Western couples who have a preference for even

JAPANESE NONVERBAL COMMUNICATION

numbers. The fact that we call odd numbers "odd" makes this point itself.

Although no number is as unlucky as 4, many Japanese view 9 as unlucky, too. The number 9 (九) is pronounced *ku*, which is a homonym for the word for suffering (苦). So though 九 and 苦 are written differently, they are just like the numeral 4 and death. Many Japanese hospitals, as a result, do not have rooms or beds numbered 9. One would be particularly unlucky to end up in Room 49. The combination of 4 (death) and 9 (suffering) would suggest that you would suffer to death in such a room.

Not all number associations in Japan are unlucky, however. There are lucky numbers, too. The Japanese actively seek out lucky numbers (though not anywhere as strongly as they avoid 4). Notable among these is 7, which is often seen as a lucky number in North America as well. In Japan, there is a folklore story *Shichifukujin* (七福神) about the Seven Gods of Luck who travel in their Treasure Ship, the *Takarabune*. The Seven Gods of Luck often decorate New Year's gift envelopes for children, and seven is a favorite number for those at gambling tables or pachinko parlors. The date July 7 (7-7) is generally seen as a propitious one, and many Japanese celebrate the folk holiday Tanabata then as well. It is also worth mentioning here that *shichi* unlucky number 4 *shi* is not pronounced the same as the *shi*-sound in the lucky number 7 because the *i* in the latter is compressed. The fact that *shichi* (七) is one kanji character also reinforces the view mentioned in the language chapter that the Japanese conceptualize their words by kanji characters and not by sound.

One other lucky number is 8, although this one is less deeply felt and probably falls more into the category of superstition than, say, would 4, 7, or 9. The luck associated with 8 rests not with its pronunciation, *hachi*, but with the way the character is written, 八. Because the character spreads out at the bottom, some Japanese interpret it to mean prosperity and growth.

Symbols

Every culture has symbols. Each nation's flag stands for the country itself, often with very strong emotional attachments.

6.16 Chrysanthemum Lantern, Myondō Shinto Shrine, Kyoto Symbol
You will find the chrysanthemum symbol on anything that has to do with the emperor.

The maple leaf stands for Canada, and the bald eagle stands for the United States. The chrysanthemum, as seen on the lantern in photograph 6.16, stands for the Japanese emperor, and you will see it in Japan wherever the emperor is involved, from shrines and palaces to gifts from the emperor.

Probably the most beloved symbol of Japan, however, is the cherry blossom, which is the country's national flower. So important are cherry blossoms that when they first bloom in the spring, people often camp out to be sure to see the first flower appear on the cherry tree. Cherry trees, accordingly, are planted widely across Japan's parks. Photograph 6.17 shows people lining up to view the cherry blossoms in Ueno Park (and, of course, to capture the event on their smartphones).

Many symbols are becoming universal. In the Americas, Europe, or Japan, an airport is 🛬, and a bus is 🚍. That said, many Japanese map symbols simply do not exist outside Japan. For example, in Japan ⊗ stands for a police station, whereas in North America, the symbol is usually 🅿. This can make

6.17 Cherry Blossoms
Catching a first glimpse of
the spring cherry blossoms in
Ueno Park in Tokyo.

Table 6.3
Some Common Japanese Map Symbols

Meaning	Japanese Symbol	Meaning	Japanese Symbol
Courthouse		*Kōban* (small police substation)	
Ferry		Municipal or ward building	
Fire station		Police station (full station, not a *kōban*)	
Government office building		Post office	

6.18 A *maneki-neko*
A "beckoning cat" might greet you as you enter a business in Japan. Photo courtesy of Sandrine Burtschell.

traveling difficult for North Americans in Japan and for Japanese outside their country. Table 6.3 gives some of the most common map symbols that are unique to Japan.

Far beyond map signs and building identifiers, however, Japanese culture is rich with other symbolic objects. Although, quite literally, hundreds of these exist in Japan but not in North America, we look at just a few here to give the idea of what to look for when in Japan.

In many Japanese shops and restaurants, you will see a waving cat greeting you as you enter, like the ones in photograph 6.18. This is called a *maneki-neko* (招き猫), literally meaning a "beckoning cat," who brings good fortune. Although they are often intentionally meant to look like a child's toy, you should take them fairly seriously. They are not, in other words, something that you would let your child play with as you entered a restaurant. By the way, which paw the cat is waving is signficant. The left paw raised brings money or customers. The right paw raised brings good luck.

Omikuji (御御籤) are paper fortunes that Japanese get at temples and shrines. Photograph 6.19 shows a monk writing out an *omikuji*.

These fortunes are *not* like North American fortune cookies in Chinese restaurants (which, by the way, are a US invention). Japanese take these seriously, and *omikuji* are quite expensive. Roughly half are bad fortunes. Good fortunes are usually held

6.19 *Omikuji*
A monk writes out an *omikuji* at the Dabutsuden, Todai-ji in Nara.

6.20 *Omikuji* **Fortunes**
Tie the bad ones on the pine tree. Take home the good ones, or leave them on the pine tree, too. Photo courtesy of chiron3636.

onto for several months, or until the fortune comes true, if earlier. Often, *omikuji* are tied to trees at shrines, as shown in photograph 6.20, to bring greater good fortune.

There is a tendency to make light of fortune-tellers and portents in North America. This is in no way shared by many Japanese. It would be just as cross-culturally insenstive to look

6.21 *Daruma*
Daruma showing the different stages of a wish.

down on Japanese who believe strongly (or even weakly) in such fortunes as it would be to look down on North Americans and their religious practices.

On someone's desk, you may often see a squat doll with one or two eyes painted on it. These are called *daruma* (達磨). These papier-mâché dolls are designed to look like the sixth-century monk Bodhidharma. They are sold without eyes. The buyer then fills in one eye when he or she sets a goal and the other when the goal is met (photograph 6.21).

Japanese business people very often go out to eat and drink with colleagues after work to socialize and to network, and otherwise to build the relations necessary for conducting effective business. One of the most common places to do this is called an *izakya* (居酒屋), which is a small (often extremely small) restaurant with a few tables set up for quiet discussions accompanied by drinks and small food dishes like tapas, such as yakitori or skewered pieces of chicken. Often, a large, red lantern called an *akachōchin* (赤提灯) is hung at or beside the entrance of an *izakaya* to identify the establishment as such. In fact, in informal Japanese, some people simply call such a place an *akachōchin* or a red lantern. The akachōchin in photograph 6.22 is typical.

One of the most recognized symbols of Japan among foreigners are the picturesque *torii* (鳥居). These are the gates between the sacred and profane space in Japanese Shinto. They are made

6.22 An *Akachōchin* at an *Izakaya*
Can you find the *izakaya* on this street in Demachiyanagi, Kyoto?

6.23 *Torii*, Kasuga Taisha Shrine, Nara
Torii gated path from the birthplace of Shinto.

up of two pillars with a kasagi arch, and are either left plain or are painted bright red and black. Although *torii* gates are typical in Shinto shrines, they can appear anywhere at a site that is imbued with spiritual power. The *torii* in photograph 6.23 are on a path leading off from the birthplace of Shinto, the Kasuga

6.24 *Torii*, **Middle of the Road**
A gateway to the gods.

Taisha Shrine in Nara. By contrast, the *torii* in photograph 6.24 are located not at a shrine per se but rather in the middle of a busy road in Kamakura.

The *torii* bring up a concept that is ever-present in Japan but largely lacking in North America. This is that there is a balance between the natural and human-made worlds that is always there for those seeking it. This imbues not only the Japanese appreciation for areas specifically separated off (as with the *torii*) but also for those in almost every aspect of life. It makes up the Japanese highly rarified appreciation for aesthetics through balance and simplicity which we discussed in chapter 2 on environment.

RECOMMENDATIONS

In general, we believe that Japanese people are very accommodating to *gaijin*. They are sincere in their desire to help foreigners and in their attempt to be good hosts to those visiting their country. This is helpful in the area of nonverbal communication because it means that the Japanese are understanding when foreigners do things differently. Still, in a highly homogeneous society, the Japanese are less accustomed to those who do things differently. Thus, even though they may tolerate the different and (to them at least) foreign behavior North Americans do unknowingly, they can become uncomfortable if such nonconformity is done knowingly. This brings up a balancing act of sorts. On one hand, the mere fact that no one but the Japanese is expected to act like the Japanese means that *gaijin* are expected to behave oddly. As a result, foreigners automatically receive more understanding and accommodation. There is no expectation that foreigners will or should act or be Japanese. On the other hand, being tolerated or being cut slack for odd behavior is never really an ideal situation. Thus, it behooves you to try to learn as you go along. The Japanese will not condemn you for your mistakes and will appreciate your efforts to try to conform to Japanese nonverbal behavioral norms as you progress.

One of the challenges related to nonverbal communication is that so much of it goes on unnoticed. We generally do not know what we are communicating nonverbally. There may be times when miscommunications arise, and nobody will know the reason behind them. Almost nobody will tell you that you are standing too close (or far) from him or her—they will just feel uncomfortable. Few people will comment on your eye contact or lack of it—they will, however, react to it without knowing why.

Our recommendation is to be flexible and be forgiving. Your first reactions probably will not be accurate—and that is all right. The only way to never make a mistake when dealing with the Japanese is to never interact with the Japanese at all, and that would be the biggest mistake of all. That said, with careful observation and an open mind, over time the nonverbal cues that differ between North America and Japan will become easier and easier to recognize and accommodate.

SUMMARY OF JAPANESE NONVERBAL COMMUNICATION

Kinesics

- The way people move their body, their gestures, and their posture.
- Japanese people use a number of gestures that are not understood by North Americans: bowing, scratching the air to mean "come here."

Affect Display

- Relates to how much or how little a person displays an emotion. Do not confuse display of emotion with the intensity of the emotion.
- In general, Japanese people display emotions much less openly than North Americans.

Oculesics

- Relates to how people use their eyes.
- Be aware that Japanese people have much less direct eye contact than North Americans and may even close their eyes when listening closely.
- Japanese people lower their eyes to show respect.

Dress

- Japanese people tend to dress more formally in professional settings than North Americans.
- Japanese people wear uniforms more frequently than do North Americans for school and the workplace.

Haptics

- "Haptics" refers to the way that people communicate through touch.
- Japanese people touch much less frequently than North Americans do in public.
- In private quarters, the Japanese sleep, eat, and bathe together, and arguably have more haptic contact than North Americans.

Proxemics

- "Proxemics" refers to the way that people use the space around them. For the Japanese, their proxemics are categorized as insider and outsider relations.
- In interpersonal interaction, Japanese people are likely to stand farther from the person with whom they are talking than North Americans.
- In public situations, Japanese people have much closer personal space, such as standing in lines or sitting on public transportation or in theaters.

Passive Nonverbal Communication

- Those items that are less related to a person's body, and more about the environment around us.
- Japanese and North Americans often differ in their associations with colors, such as yellow, blue, and green.
- Japanese people often feel strongly about numbers being unlucky (4, 9) and lucky (7, 8).
- Japanese public markings are often unique to Japan.

- Japan has many signs and symbols that have no counterpart in North America (and vice versa).

Recommendations

- Be aware, but remember that Japanese people are forgiving of foreigners' missteps, especially when they are seen as trying.
- We frequently are not even aware of our nonverbal communication errors, so remain open to misreadings and be aware that things may not be as they seem.

7

THE JAPANESE
Temporal
Conception

The Right Thing at the Right Time

We use the term "temporal conception" to refer to how people understand and use time. Although we can use a clock or a calendar to arrive at a mutually agreed upon measure of time, our perception of time varies from person to person. In other words, there is often a gap between how we physically measure time and how each of us perceives time in any given situation. Perceptions about the spread of time vary across personal, social, and cultural contexts rather than being universally the same. For example, we may have had the experience of enjoying an activity so intensely that we do not even notice the passing of a period of time. Conversely, we may have also attended meetings that seemed to go on for hours, only to look at the clock and find out that a mere 30 minutes have gone by. In addition to these personal conceptions of time, other approaches to time are culturally based, and North American and Japanese perceptions of time are the focus of this chapter.

The anthropologist and communication expert Edward T. Hall classified cultures as "monochronic" and/or "polychronic." Hall identified "monochronic" cultures as those where activities are coordinated by sequentially doing one thing at a time. In monochronic cultures, events submit to the clock and the calendar, and activities have specific, often rigid, beginning and ending times. Furthermore, monochronic cultures tend to subordinate personal relationships to the clock or calendar, so that scheduling allows you to meet theoretically with anyone, as long as we can get on that person's calendar. Both the United States and Canada are classic monochronic cultures. Likewise, Australia, New Zealand, Singapore, and most of Northwestern Europe are also typically monochronic societies.

In "polychronic" cultures, the opposite is true. Tasks are not sequentially handled, but rather many tasks are handled at the same time. Time seems to stretch depending on the specifics of what is being done and for whom you are doing it. Personal relationships bend the schedule. Beginning and end times are often blurry, as tasks are completed at the expense of preset schedules. Personal relationships trump schedules, and networking allows you to act quickly if you are adequately connected to others. Conversely, it is very hard to get on the schedule or otherwise meet someone unless we already have some common connection. Polychronic approaches to time are evident in much of Southern Europe, Southeast Asia, Latin America, and most of the Middle East and Sub-Saharan Africa.

Japan does not fall into either one of the categories. When it comes to categorizing cultures as either monochronic or polychronic, Japan becomes problematic, because it is actually both. During much of the workday, in public interactions, Japan operates under monochronic time. However, after work and even at work, during in-group interactions, the Japanese follow polychronic time. This includes the informal *uchiawase* meetings after work hours described earlier in the book, when Japanese meet at *izakaya* or otherwise get together to bond socially and discuss issues in a more informal setting.

Until the Meiji Restoration that began Japan's Industrial Revolution in the late 1800s, Japan was a classic polychronic society.

With the emperor's imposition of North European (largely German) work-related values during this time, Japan attempted to refashion its temporal conception within the workplace. The result was a compromise that is fairly unique to Japan. It adopted a public workday monochronic orientation and a polychronic after-work orientation.

For newcomers to Japan, this dual view of time can be frustrating. If by chance we are included in an internal task-sounding *nemawashi* meeting, it may seem never-ending because we do not expect such a polychronic use of our professional time. Likewise, we may be willing to give up a few hours after work for drinks, but not spend an entire evening with the same people we were with during the day. In North America and much of the Western world, we have assigned those precious hours to our families rather than the intimacies of the company. Although initially confusing, this dual view of time fits neatly into the Japanese *uchi-soto* insider/outsider categorization of interactions, and is a perfect example of how awareness of underlying cultural influences can have a positive impact on our intercultural understanding.

During the average workday in Japan, just as in North America, if a meeting is scheduled to go from 8:00 am until 9:00 am, participants are likely to end the meeting at 9:00 am, even if there are agenda items that were not covered during the designated time. Similarly, if a lunch meeting is scheduled from 12:00 noon to 1:30 pm and if 1:30 arrives before dessert is served, it may very well be that the participants skip dessert in order to get activities back on schedule.

In one respect—deadlines—Japan is even *more* monochronic than the United States or Canada. Because the Japanese follow a processive approach to planning and emphasize the need for consensus-oriented decision making, the deadlines they set are usually accurate. As a result, in Japan, deadlines are very firm. By contrast, in North America, though people often use the word "deadline," the actual meaning is something more akin to "target dates." Deadlines are weaker in North America than in Japan largely out of necessity. Because North Americans generally make decisions by setting objectives first and then backing into how to reach those objectives, the time frames that are initially set may not be realistic. Because decisions are made by individuals who attempt to get buy-in among those involved only after the decisions have been made, it is often difficult to anticipate delays based on conflicts of timing or resistance from those same people. As a result, the Japanese tend to view US and Canadian "deadlines" as disturbingly unreliable.

Outside the workplace, however, Japan differs notably from North America. In the United States or Canada, the same mono-chronic adherence to schedule applies even to social events, such as parties and dinners. In Japan, this is definitively *not* the case. In North America, everything has a beginning and ending time. People will literally stop doing an activity that all find pleasant because the designated time for that activity is past. All this implies that North Americans—as members of a monochronic society—can plan their schedules with precision. In Japan, this is only true in the workplace itself. After hours, the country becomes much laxer toward time. A conversation at an *izakaya* or an evening spent at a karaoke bar is often unscheduled, tending instead to occur spontaneously. Moreover, there is no set end time. Things end when they end, not when they are scheduled to end—except, of course, somewhat comically if public time imposes itself, which is the case for many inebriated salarymen boarding the last train home. Even so, polychronic time overrides the missed last train, in part explaining the availability of capsule hotels near train stations.

Indeed, people surmise that one of the positive ramifications of monochronic time is that it enhances efficiency and productivity. Of course, on the flip side, one of the negative repercussions is that people can also become slaves to the clock. Historically, it is not difficult to imagine agrarian lifestyles, when time was dominated by the changing seasons, the hours of sunlight per day, the weather, the amount of land that could be plowed, and the behavior of animals. Thanks in part to the Industrial Revolution, all this changed when society started to define productivity by the number of units on an assembly line that were completed per hour.

Another thing to note here is that the Japanese do not generally share the North American separation of personal time and work time. This is a characteristic shared by most polychronic societies. The workday does not necessarily end at 6:00 pm in Japan, or for that matter at any particular time. The workday generally does not end until the boss goes home (which depends on how much the boss needs to still accomplish rather than on the time on the clock). Even then, the day may not end for you. If there is more work to finish to meet a deadline, it is likely employees will stay at the office in Japan. Likewise, even if the work is done, workers may continue to stay at the office to provide moral support for the rest of the group or wait for others to finish for after-work gatherings. Above all, it is almost unheard of for a subordinate to go home before the boss.

Here, too, is another difference. The after-work gatherings are not officially required, but neither are they really optional. If there is good reason not to join the others (e.g., your child is in a school play performance or you have had a death in the family—and even these may not be sufficient in many places), joining others is not mandatory. That said, it really is not acceptable to regularly choose not to go with others, especially as a junior employee. These are not really just social gatherings with work colleagues. They are a form of *amae* building and social bonding and—more important—the most readily available times for networking and *nemawashi* (described in chapter 5, on authority conception). In short, though never required (unless they involve clients, when they are required), employees are nonetheless expected to participate regularly in these after-hour meetings, just as other role players would be expected to participate in other types of obligatory social gatherings.

THE RIGHT THING AT THE RIGHT TIME

Even during the monochronic public workday, Japanese people apportion time variably, especially when compared with North Americans, for whom, whether in Houston or Hiroshima, the concept of time remains constant and connected to the clock and calendar. In other words, whatever side of the Pacific you are on, for a North American, schedules, meetings, and travel times all happen at specific times. However, rather than simply marking the beginning and ending times of events, as in North America, in Japan, there is also an awareness of scheduling the right thing at the right time. That is to say, rather than simply looking at time sequentially, compared with North America, the Japanese have a greater sense of pulling back, looking at the big picture, prioritizing, and then choosing what activity leads to the best long-term outcome.

Evidence of this is the Japanese-initiated system of just-in-time manufacturing, which builds on more than the mere concept of keeping track of units per hour, but concentrates instead on effectively communicating and instituting key elements in a steady flow to optimize efficiency and maintain a balanced inventory. The result is that Japanese activities do not simply follow sequentially from activity A to B to C, but to all points individually and collectively before a decision is made to act. This is tied closely to the issue of consensus-oriented communication in decision making, which is discussed in chapter 5, on authority conception. Because decisions are made with input from all involved, the Japanese plan out the time needed to gather feedback and adjust actions accordingly. By North American standards (where decisions are largely made by the individual without having reached a consensus in advance), the process of Japanese planned communication seems very slow indeed.

By analogy, consider how people use global positioning system (GPS) navigation. Some people simply turn on the GPS and start driving to their destination, without looking at the route they are taking. They simply get going. Others, by contrast, turn on the GPS, study the routes and alternative roads, and then choose the path to follow. A North American approach to time is similar to the driver who follows the GPS commands without worrying about the overall path. A Japanese approach to time is more similar to the driver who looks at all the paths and then decides which road to take. From a North American perspective, it may seem at times that the Japanese delay in getting going.

From a Japanese perspective, it may seem that the North Americans are charging forward without regard for how each plays into the decision.

At the social level, Japanese-style decision making creates the potential for an inefficient number of choices. Ritual is a handy shortcut when faced with a plethora of choices, and we see an example of this in the way Japanese exchange business cards. North Americans treat business cards as a way to get contact details or recall someone's name and address after you have met. The Japanese use the calling card as an efficient trigger for how to behave vis-à-vis the key information provided or confirmed on the card. Though largely viewed as a waste of time from a North American perspective, the Japanese business card exchange is like a colon in a sentence, in that like many other interaction rituals, it punctuates the relationship with a view toward the future at what is to come.

ENVIRONMENT AND TIME

The physical environment around us affects how we interact with time. For example, the sheer size of the Unites States and Canada results in many different time zones (six in Canada, and four in the United States, plus Alaska and Hawaii). For those who come from countries that fit within one time zone, it is sometimes confusing to think in terms of time zones. In the continental United States, the East Coast is three hours ahead of the West Coast. Sports fans in New York do not think of it as strange to watch a ballgame that starts at 11 at night. A sports fan in Los Angeles may watch a game at 5 in the afternoon. In Japan there is only one time zone (UTC/GMT +9 hours). This does imply that regions in the far northeast, such as Hokkaido, experience very early sunrises at certain times of the year, at about 4 am, but it also means that everyone is on the same time. In addition to the difficulty associated with different time zones, in the United States some states participate in daylight savings time and others do not. For example, there are times of the year when Arizona is an hour ahead of California, and there are times of the year when Arizona and California have the same time. Japan does not participate in daylight savings time.

Population density in urban settings also affects time. For example, New Yorkers and Tokyoites spend a lot of time working and commuting. New Yorkers work an average of 42 hours and 30 minutes per week, and commute for an average of 6 hours and 18 minutes. And those who ride the subway spend almost 8 hours per week on their commute.[1] Similarly, the Japanese Broadcasting Corporation (NHK, Nippon Hōso Kyōkai) releases data every five years from their surveys regarding the Japanese use of time.[2] According to their latest release, business operators and managers spent an average of 9 hours and 29 minutes per day at work, with an additional 2 hours and 43 minutes on Saturday and 1 hour and 8 minutes on Sunday, which is officially less than what it used to be before the bubble years, when the official workweek was five and a half days. Practice is another matter, and 88 percent of those surveyed responded that they worked on weekends. As to commuting times, for those in Tokyo, job-holders spent an average of 1 hour and 37 minutes per work day commuting. The data between the Tokyo and New York workers cannot be directly compared, but they do indicate that both groups spent between 50 to 60 hours per week between work and commuting.

The Judeo-Christian tradition is responsible for the idea that a week should consist of work and rest. Sunday was the original day of rest for Christians and Saturday was the Sabbath, a day to observe restraint from work for religious Jews (and also certain Christians). In the United States, the first five-day workweek was thought to have been followed in a cotton mill in New England to allow Jewish workers to observe the Sabbath.[3]

The NHK surveys also showed that Japanese students (at all levels) spent similar amounts of time in class and in school-related activities, spending an average of 8 hours and 14 minutes per day, and 3 hours and 38 minutes on Saturdays and 2 hours and 52 minutes on Sundays. Until 2002, Japanese schools had a six-day week that was reduced to half days on Saturdays in many schools. In actual practice, 41 percent of the students said they engaged in school activities on Saturdays and 25 percent on Sundays. Students said they spent 1 hour and 25 minutes on their daily commute.

With so much time dedicated to work and commuting, one wonders how much sleep urbanites get. Recent data, which perhaps are less than scientific but nonetheless very interesting, come from a recent study of 2 million users of the Sleep Cycle App from fifty different countries.[4] They report that Japanese ranked second in going to bed late, with an average bedtime of 12:49 am. And the Japanese also ranked fifth in the earliest average wake-up time of 7:09 am, which gave them 6 hours and 19 minutes of sleep. By comparison, the US participants' average bedtime was 11:54 pm and their wake-up time was 7:20 am. The Canadian average bedtime was 11:57 pm and their wake-up time was 7:33 am. Both the Americans and Canadians get more than a full hour of sleep per day more than the Japanese.

Finally, the fact is that Japan and North America are on opposite sides of the globe. In any telephone or videoconference call, someone will be up at an inconvenient time. When it is 5 pm Eastern Standard Time (or 6 pm AST, 4 pm CST, 3 pm MST, or 2 pm PST), it is already 7 am *the next day* in Japan. Incidentally, if you plan to have someone on the phone in the middle of the night, we strongly recommend that the person be the one whose native language is the one being used. If you are speaking Japanese, then feel free to be the one making the 2 pm phone call, and have your Japanese counterpart be up at an odd hour. If you are not speaking Japanese but rather your own native tongue and expecting your Japanese colleagues to understand you, we recommend that you let them be the ones who are more awake.

The pace of life in today's world is fast in all large cities, but in Japan the combination of long work hours, long study hours, long commute hours, and shorter sleep durations cannot help but influence the Japanese concept of time. Those who insist on specific time schedules are likely to be seen as unreasonable, and in the end the insistence may not change anything anyway. Our recommendation is that we not ignore the effects of the environment on how the Japanese divide their time.

The Dutch researcher Geert Hofstede (1991) explored the degree to which societies held long-term versus short-term orientations.[5] Hofstede empirically collected data to rank a wide range of countries on a "long-term-orientation" (LTO) index regarding how much each culture maintained ties to its history while addressing its current and projected future challenges. Societies that favored long-held traditions and felt uncomfortable with social change scored high on the LTO index. Conversely, societies that scored low on the LTO index were less tied to traditions and tended to equate social change as positive.

High-LTO cultures emphasized networking and other connections between people. By contrast, low-LTO cultures tended to view interactions as one-off events without a strong connection to networking or personal connections.

High-LTO cultures also placed great importance on a sense of perseverance, as demonstrated through the determined and consistent effort to attain goals regardless of obstacles faced along the way. The main point in high-LTO culture interactions is to acquire a long-term benefit in which all interactions are seen in a collective overview rather than as one-off events. Low-LTO countries, conversely, tended to favor quick returns and flexibility in the process undertaken to obtain objectives (and even rapidly changing goals). The main point in low-LTO culture interactions is to get an immediate benefit for each event in isolation.

A correlation exists between cultures that have Confucian values (as discussed in chapter 5, on authority conception) and a high-LTO score. In fact, when Hofstede first introduced this dimension (he measured four others before this one), he named it the Confucian Dynamism Index. Not surprisingly, then, Japan, as a Confucian culture (as discussed in chapter 5) ranks high in LTO.

The high-LTO score of Japan correlates with the Japanese understanding of most interpersonal interactions and social networks as part of set of long-term relationships. The Japanese emphasize building and maintaining long-term relationships through what is known as *kankei* (関係). *Kankei* is not a word that translates well into English. Literally translated as *barrier engagers*, the Japanese concept of relationships conjures bridge building or, more poetically, a spider's web of relationships of connections made in the past. Just as a spider can feel something happening at any spot on the web, so too the *kankeisha*, or the maker of the relationship, can focus on any point in his or her *kankei*. Likewise, just as a spider must constantly work to keep its web in good shape, repairing any rip quickly to avoid having the whole web collapse, so too must a person maintain the relationships that make up his or her *kankei* to keep it in good shape and keep it from falling apart.

The LTO ranking between the United States (twenty-sixth) and Canada (thirty-sixth) is not particularly great. Both countries are quite low. Both countries, however, show a vast difference from Japan, which scored eighty-eighth, a very high LTO score indeed. Evidence of this, for example, is seen in how North Americans seek quick returns on investments, while Asian cultures, such as Japan, traditionally wait for slow and sustained results. However, we look at this dichotomy with caution.

TIME PRODUCTS

It is impossible to talk about Japan and time in a single breath and not talk about the Japanese love of speed, particularly in relation to trains. The maximum operating speed of a Japanese bullet train is 320 kilometers an hour (200 miles an hour) (on a 387.5-kilometer section of the Tōhoku Shinkansen); see photograph 7.1.[6] Test runs have reached 443 kilometers an hour (275 miles an hour) for conventional rail in 1996, and up to an April 2015 world's record of 603 kilometers an hour (375 miles an hour) for maglev trains that run on magnetic levitation without touching the ground.[7]

The other product of time is Japanese watchmaking. Japanese watchmakers like Seiko burst onto the scene following what came to be known as the Quartz Crisis in the 1970s and early

7.1 Bullet Train
The iconic *shinkansen*. Photo courtesy of Sandrine Burtschell.

1980s. Although Swiss watchmakers had previously dominated the market, Japanese watchmakers who more readily embraced quartz technology soon replaced their mechanical competitors. Although the Swiss responded with the Swatch, the North American market still continued to buy Japanese digital and hybrid brands such as Casio. To keep in time, Japan also manufactures chronometers and metronomes like Nikko.

PUNCTUALITY

Watches and keeping time bring to mind the notion of punctuality. Once again, Japanese trains are an example of the Japanese obsession to deadline and the feverish pitch with which they keep to the timetable. It is rare for Japanese trains to be late; and if they are, they are announced even if the train is delayed by 1 minute. Transfer times between trains are honored to the tee.

Tardiness at the workplace is frowned upon, and shift workers adhere to their schedules with precision. However, as mentioned above, in closed circles where punctuality is no longer an obligation, segments of time become more lax depending on the degree of intimacy among friends and family. Sam, an American in Japan whom the authors know, noticed this distinction in punctuality between the public and private worlds. He was surprised that his friend was always showing up late. His friend apologized, *"warui ne"* ([my] bad), but he kept on arriving late. He asked us if it was because he was a *gaijin* foreigner or because the Japanese friend felt comfortable enough with him to be late. It is difficult to say without knowing his friend or the full context, but perhaps it was a mixture of both.

DURABILITY AND THE EPHEMERAL

In reference to time perceptions, many sociologists claim that some cultures, such as the North American one, have more of a short-term orientation toward time. Japan, conversely, is seen as a culture that has more of a long-term orientation. Evidence of this, for example, is seen in how North Americans seek quick returns on investments, while Asian cultures, such as Japan, traditionally wait for slow and sustained results. However, we look at this dichotomy with caution.

In a recent media podcast on NPR's *Freakonomics Radio*, Jiro Yoshida of Pennsylvania State University discussed why Japanese homes are disposable.[8] In Japan most homes lose their value within thirty years, and some within fifteen years. The market for used homes is proportionally much smaller in Japan than in North America. In fact, half the homes in Japan are demolished within thirty-eight years and then new homes are rebuilt on the same property. In North America, by comparison, half the homes last more than a hundred years. The result is that in the United States old homes are refurbished, remodeled, and resold, and thus there is a market for old, classic-styled homes. In Japan, by contrast, because homes do not hold their value for resale, owners are more likely to tear down an existing home and put their efforts into a new design, complete with personal idiosyncrasies. Architects are free to create unique designs, and all with the mind-set that the land is more valuable than the structure. Yoshida claims that there are multiple reasons for this tendency. First, after World War II, much of Japan was rebuilt, and not always with high quality. Structures that were built post–World War II were replaced little by little. Second, given the number of potential earthquakes in Japan, people build with less of a sense of permanency. Also related to earthquakes, as earthquake standards rise, homes that used to be within code no longer are. It is just as easy to demolish the home and build to a new standard. And finally, Yoshida mentions that Japanese people value things that are new, clean, or fresh, which is perhaps a modern spin on the Buddhist cyclical notion that all things come and go, for even the beams of the oldest temples and shrines are gradually replaced by new ones.

If Japanese money is on new things, their aesthetic appreciation is on the ephemeral. Unlike a favorite Western image of the strong oak that stand the test of time, Japanese poetry delights in the frailty of the windswept petals of a cherry tree. Japanese time also has this delicate side, which is brought to light with the word 時 *toki*, in the Japanese reading of *a time*, as opposed to the word 時間 *jikan*, or time space, which is also frequently translated as time, but might be better characterized as a time-tabling period of time. Hence *kodomo no toki* (the time when [I] was a child) evokes a different image than *kodomo no jikan* (children's time/hour). Thus, though the Japanese are typically characterized as a people with a strong uncertainty avoidance, perhaps somewhat counterintuitively they can also see time as fleeting with an aesthetics that carries emotive connotations.

The less scheduled and natural view of time is largely owed to Japan's animistic origins practiced before Chinese philosophies were brought to the islands. Time was then divided into seasons, and the passing of one season to the next is still marked and celebrated in the spring and autumn equinox observations. *Setsubun*, for example, is the spring festival celebrated on the first day of spring according to the lunar calendar, and literally means "season divisions." Marked by the ritual of *mamemaki*, or "bean throwing," children throw beans at the *toshiotoko* (eldest male of the house), who plays the role of the *oni*, or "evil spirit," shouting *Oni wa soto! Fuku wa uchi!* "Evil spirits outside! Good

7.2 Oni Public Service Message
Guilty *Setsubun* demon hogging subway seats. Photo courtesy of Sandrine Burtschell.

spirits inside!" Insider/outsider forces are at play here again. Old folklore collides with modern scheduling to produce a concept of time peculiar to Japan (see photograph 7.2).

THE JAPANESE LANGUAGE AND THE REPRESENTATION OF TIME

Language was the first key to understanding intercultural communication, and it seems fitting that we spend the last section of our book discussing how time is represented in language. Unlike English—which divides verbs into three time categories, or tenses, of present, past, and future—or Mandarin, which does not use verb tenses to categorize time, Japanese categorizes verbs into the past and the nonpast, which include the present and the future. Both Japanese and Mandarin segment present, past, and future activities by naming the day or time.

Just as in English, the Japanese define time with descriptions such as 4 pm today, yesterday morning, and after school tomorrow. However, as we saw with the Japanese style of addressing envelopes, bigger times subsume smaller ones, so the Japanese talk about the 4 o'clock of tomorrow, yesterday's morning, and the after-school of tomorrow. In comparison with English, as shown below, Japanese has broader conceptions of periods of time, adding two words further into the future than tomorrow and two words further back than yesterday.

Sakiototoi   Ototoi   Kinō   Kyō   Ashita   Asatte   Shiasatte
(–2 days) (–1 day) Yesterday Today Tomorrow (+1 day) (+2 days)

Not only does Japanese categorize bigger spans of time; it also distinguishes between one's own private future (将来 *shōrai*) and a public distant future that even includes science fiction (未来 *mirai*). These examples illustrate that the Japanese differentiate between the present and the future, even though it is not declined in the verb in the same way it is in English or other European languages.

With such time differentiators, native speakers of Japanese have many ways to check and clarify potential misunderstandings based on time. However, the different encodings of time in English and in Japanese create the likelihood for miscommunication when a language learner is speaking in a second language. For example, a Japanese person might tell his or her host, "I go to the airport," as a way of saying "Don't worry, I can get to the airport by myself." And his or her generous host might respond, "Of course not," and get his keys ready to drive his Japanese colleague to the airport. We have a friend who participated in such an interaction, and because the Japanese friend did not have the heart to tell his host that his flight was not until much later, he ended up waiting at the airport for the entire afternoon. Although there are many linguistic and intercultural factors at play in this single misunderstanding, differences in time perception are a big part of it.

RECOMMENDATIONS

The recommendations we offer come with an initial caution: It is easy for people who have more of a monochronic way of looking at things to believe their way is superior to that of those who follow other ways of looking at time. Monochronic time users tend to see themselves as more efficient and consequently as more productive. Conversely, they may evaluate polychronic time users as time-wasters or procrastinators, or even label them lazy.

Throughout this chapter, we have discussed how there is an insider/outsider face to time. The Japanese adhere to strict punctuality at work but can loosen up in private spheres. The truth is that it takes a long time to get to know the Japanese at an intimate level, so chances are these close-up friendships will not happen early on, except in the after-hour drinking environment. During these times, the Japanese open up and might even become surprisingly frank, to the point of rudeness. For better or for worse, it is an unwritten rule in Japan that whatever happens under the influence is pardoned the following day. Because these rules do not necessarily apply to North American colleagues, we recommend wearing a thick skin when listening to Japanese remarks but personally keeping in check a demeanor that would be considered professionally acceptable in North American circles.

SUMMARY OF THE JAPANESE TEMPORAL CONCEPTION

Japanese Temporal Conceptions

- Japan is monochronic in orientation during the day and polychronic in orientation after work hours.
- Japan has a strong long-term orientation, emphasizing perseverance, with less emphasis on quick results than that of the United States or Canada.
- Japanese networking and *kankei* are the results of the nurturing of long-term relationships built and maintained throughout one's career and life.
- Japan also observes more relaxed, natural pre-Confucian notions of time in folkloric festivals and in insider daily relations.

Recommendations

- Be prepared to join in after-hour meetings and gatherings; relax, with discretion, in after-hours drinking.
- Expect meetings during the day to follow the clock and those after work *not* to follow any set hours.

- Expect Japanese deadlines to be more firm than North American target dates.
- Be aware of the time difference between North America and Japan.
- Be aware that there is only one time zone in Japan rather than multiple time zones as in the United States and Canada.

8

Case Study

Getting Down to Earth with Cloud Computing

Now that we have seen the application of the LESCANT approach to Japanese business communication, in this chapter we present a brief vignette—a cultural case study—that provides a chance to apply what we have learned to a real scenario of a situation that happened in Japan. The names of the company, the location, and the people involved have all been changed, but the events occurred as reported in this vignette. The case deals with a United States–based multinational information technology company that has multiple teams working on projects for worldwide subsidiaries. Their constant challenge is how to deal with and allow for local modifications. In this story, Dallin Bates is the project director of cloud platform software projects. He is the lone North American (located in Albuquerque) in a team that works exclusively in Tokyo. All their work is completed remotely; and in this case, after six years of working together, Dallin makes his first visit to Tokyo to meet face-to-face with the team.

After the case itself, we then provide observations and opinions from three Japanese and three US executives who have experience working in similar situations. These comments represent their actual opinions, and these are the real names of these people, who have graciously offered to share their opinions. As authors, we also offer our comments and observations about the case. In the final section, there are questions and topics to assess the cultural issues about this case, which we hope might inspire you to come up with your own solutions.

Company: Up in the Clouds

Focus: After six years of working together, a North American project leader meets for the first time with his project team in Japan.

Cultural issues: In a role reversal, despite the fact that this team has worked together for six years, now for the first time they are meeting not only in Japan but also on Japanese terms. The project leader does not go to Japan with the specific intent to build better relationships with his team, being focused on the project particulars, but he comes away with a greater sense of how these connections were important, and how it changes the relationships beyond the context of work.

CASE SCENARIO

In an increasingly high-technology world of team projects, it is not unexpected that we work in international teams. Dallin Bates has been with Up in the Clouds for eight years. It is a midsized company that specializes in writing cloud platform software, and is often subcontracted by large information technology companies. End users deploy this software for their own use of the cloud. Dallin is in charge of building and testing the systems, and generally overseeing the entire product release. Although the company's central offices are located in Austin, Dallin works from his home, which is located in Albuquerque.

For the past six years, Dallin has taken the lead on a team that is mainly based in Tokyo. The Tokyo office has more than two hundred engineers and software developers. Dallin works with a team of about thirty, directly interacting with seven section leaders on patterns, images, user interface, serviceability, deployment, business logic, and product code. Dallin himself had only met face-to-face with three of these section leaders. In previous years, when a new product was to be introduced, all the section leaders would meet in Austin for two weeks. It was just easier to get everyone together at the beginning of a project. In general, however, most of the team members interacted virtually.

"We do a lot through e-mail, live chat, and digital documents. Our digital docs work from a template, where we keep track of things in a forum-like conversation. This is the most common way for us to communicate back and forth."

Dallin actually prefers this method because he finds video chats to be much more difficult: "The truth is that I understand the section leaders well, their English is excellent, but some of the other team members are hard to understand sometimes. I don't want to be embarrassed if I make some weird face when I don't understand them. And I don't like it when they feel embarrassed when they know they aren't being understood. So, I actually prefer to use written communication over video." The system generally tracks things well through the forum-like conversations from digital documents, and things work fine.

Recently, Up in the Clouds was about to begin a new project, and rather than bring all the section leaders to Austin for two weeks, it was decided that it would be better to send Dallin to Tokyo. Dallin was more than willing to do so.

"I know how much my relationship changed with the three section leaders that I had met with previously in face-to-face meetings. Now I know them. We talked about families, hobbies, sports, and we went out to bars. It just set the stage for a new level of comfort in working with them." Dallin was anxious to build this same type of relationship with the other section leaders and team members. And to be honest, after six years of working with some of these partners, he was excited to meet them personally.

When Dallin first arrived at the Tokyo offices, everything he had imagined about this office came into full focus.

"I had always thought of the Tokyo office as rather chaotic: no cubical walls, everyone sitting in the same area, spontaneous meetings in the same room, no privacy for phone calls, and so on."

This vision was confirmed. And indeed, the scene was totally unlike his workstation at home, where he has his own private room down the hallway from his bedroom. Dallin is also a self-confessed workaholic, which is actually convenient when working with partners who are hours ahead of you. Because the Tokyo office is full of people and Dallin is by himself, he generally tries to conduct live chats with his team on their time, when they are in the office.

Working in different time zones sounds difficult, but generally it is not. Calls in the evening in Albuquerque come to the Tokyo office team before their lunchtime. And late calls in the evening in Tokyo are the early hours when Dallin starts working in Albuquerque. This only becomes an issue when decisions are time sensitive, and having to wait causes delays. Sometimes there is a message that needs to be answered, or a follow-up item that needs to wait for the team to arrive in the office the next day. All in all, however, Dallin tries to communicate on their schedule.

And after seeing the Tokyo office, Dallin now understands even more why the time lag is useful. It is not that they do not keep long hours, too, because all of them do; but beyond the thirty members of Dallin's team, the Tokyo office also has many others from other departments. Dallin now realizes that by calling his team during their working hours, it helps them to be able to follow up with others from other departments who would also be at the office.

When Dallin arrived, he had expected to simply get right to work with the team. After all, they had known each other and worked together for years. He quickly caught on, however, that his team felt it was important to introduce him to the other managers in the Tokyo office. Some of these introductions were simple professional courtesies. By contrast, other introductions seemed much more formal than he had expected, with clear deference, bowing, and extensive greetings that went way beyond what Dallin was used to. He was also surprised to see the ages of those in the office. Dallin is in his late thirties, as are most of the members of his team. However, the office was full of very-young-looking men and women, and really only a few senior-looking executives who were in their fifties. He also noticed that men significantly outnumbered women. His own team was split between 60 percent men and 40 percent women, but in the Tokyo office the men clearly outnumbered the women by something like 85 percent men to 15 percent women. Most were dressed a bit more formally than he had expected, with most in very similar dark-colored business casual suits, with a few here and there in shirts and ties. Dallin did notice that the section leaders seemed to dress much more formally, and this was especially true of the women who were leads.

Given Dallin's jet lag, initial introductions, tour of the facilities, and many orientation activities, his first day of work was tiring, but it went off OK enough. Indeed, given that Dallin knew everyone from a work context, he ended the day feeling that things were going to go well. That evening, however, was another matter. This was Dallin's first experience in Japan, and it was the Japanese team's first opportunity to expose their North American colleague of six years to all that Tokyo had to offer. There was no doubt that they were ready to take on the challenge.

"I don't know how my Japanese team could keep up with that pace," Dallin related. "It's one thing to be in Japan for the first time; it's another to be in Japan with a whole team of work colleagues who want to show you around."

First up was a pub-like tavern, an *izakaya*—very Japanese looking, with a large red lantern hanging in the entrance with cool doorway curtains. The *izakaya*'s chalkboard menus, its bright colors, and the smells of the food all seemed to expand Dallin's desire to observe everything around him. They started Dallin with *hiyayakko* (a kind of a cold tofu with various toppings), *yakitori*, and *kushiyaki* skewers, *sashimi* of all types, and *yakisoba*, and the foods just kept coming and coming. It was amazing how little servings for a group of twenty people could pile up, and how the increased noise level coincided with the number of dishes—and drinks. Dallin knew about sake, but what was this *shochu*?

"I kept thinking, there is no way I can keep up this pace!" Dallin had always heard of Japanese group dynamics, but here was his first experience seeing it first hand, and even more with him as the center of attention.

And when asked about the major takeaway from this experience, Dallin says, "I think I learned that when I thought the group was laughing 'at' me, that they were really laughing with me. In these situations when you don't know what to eat, how to eat, what sauces to put on the food, the whole chopsticks thing, what combinations are appropriate, etc., they may be laughing, but it really isn't to make fun. It's really more as part of the enjoyment of being together. I enjoyed the interaction, and if it happened at my expense and they enjoyed seeing me experience new things, so be it."

Reportedly, the pace did not keep up every day. However, in the next two weeks Dallin was exposed to many examples of group dynamics in entertainment outings. *Irasshaimase!*—which means Welcome!—quite possibly became the Japanese phrase that he learned best and heard the most.

Dallin is quite a sports fan, so many of his favorite activities outside work were related to sports. The project team took him to a golf driving range. With space at a premium, he enjoyed the setup: the prepaid cards, the automatic tee-up systems, even the cool towel service. It was just a fun activity. Next, baseball. Since then, and forevermore, Dallin would think of the American version as the dull and boring baseball. He felt that the Japanese knew how to turn baseball into a party. The fans were intense, with chants, cheers, towel waving, horns, fireworks, bento boxes (purchased outside the stadium), and the uniformed beer girls with kegs strapped on their backs.

"Are you kidding?" Dallin recalled enthusiastically. "Baseball in Japan. You gotta love it!"

Besides baseball, there was sumo at Ryogoku Kokugihan. The great thing about sumo is that the same event happens over and over again, with different people of course, but after a while Dallin said that he started to catch on to the moves and objectives. He even found the *rikishi* sumo wrestlers parading around at the beginning of a new round to be cool. Although he did not know why he was doing it then, he even joined his team members in throwing his seat cushion to express how upset they were with a wrestler's performance.

Unlike the sporting events he enjoyed, Dallin did not enjoy the Pachinko parlor. It seemed as if his team members were determined to expose him to things that other tourists did not see, but after five minutes he had had his fill. To him, Pachinko seemed like just a bunch of people with little steel balls, rows of Japanese pinball-wizards, with lots of lights, smoke, tokens, and no evidence of a payout.

Dallin could not help but think, "Really, y'all like this thing?"

Other than Pachinko, the group's activities were awesome, and there were two things that Dallin especially took with him from these experiences. First, he was most impressed with the sense of group bonding that accompanied all these events, to the point where he felt guilty that these team members did not go home at night to be with their families. They did not. They all attended all the evening events, every evening.

"How will I ever be able to give them the same level of attention if they ever visit me in Albuquerque?" Dallin just knew he would not be able to do the same back home.

The second observation that stuck with Dallin was everyone's sense of cleaning up garbage at public events. "I know it's a strange observation, but even at sumo, somebody walked around the arena with a garbage bag and people dropped all their trash in the bags. There wasn't a speck of trash on the floor at the end of the events. Amazing, just amazing."

Returning to the training meetings, remember that Dallin was a little nervous about the team members' oral language skills. Back in Albuquerque, he avoided video chats because he often struggled to understand some team members' spoken English. However, in Tokyo, it turned out that the section leaders generally had strong English skills; and in all discussions, if something was not understood, there was always somebody to help explain and clarify things. So in the end communication was not an issue. There were times when Dallin felt as if he had to focus on the intent more than the actual words his coworkers used.

For example, in one meeting a team member asked if some-body was "pissed off," when he later learned that the team member's real intent was just to ask if that person was upset. Dallin learned that sometimes English phrases said by Japanese could come across sounding harsher than what the speaker had actually intended. Dallin started to catch on to this, and he was eventually able to interpret such comments in the tone intended.

Among other things, Dallin learned to slow down a bit, to repeat things more often, and to use visual cues to help move things along. He did find that while the team members had excellent written skills in English, their oral skills lagged behind. He discovered that the trick was to observe when people might be pretending to understand, when in reality they were getting a little lost.

Dallin also found out that it was helpful to take short breaks more frequently, and in doing so team members would help each other catch up on details that might have been missed. By the second week, Dallin was also catching more of the non-verbal cues that had seemed mysterious at first, such as people breathing through their teeth, taking long pauses before answering, bowing even when talking on the phone, and so on. In fact, he said he became so comfortable with the communication around him that he even started peppering his own presentations with a few Japanese phrases, such as "*Anō, eēto, chotto, sumimasen*" at the beginning of the sentence and "*Sō desho? Daijōbo desu ka? Shitsureishimashita*" at the end. He started his own phrasebook, and had about seventy-five phrases by the end of his stay. Ultimately, his two weeks of training and project initiation were extremely enjoyable and successful.

One other topic that Dallin worried about before the trip was his feet. Currently, he needs to wear orthotics, and he was concerned about what this might mean for him in Japan, given that in certain places he might be asked to take off his shoes. It worried him so much that before the trip, he e-mailed one of the section leaders to ask about it. But in the end, it was not a problem at all. In the few places where people took off their shoes, the team members had already brought shoe covers (similar to the ones that we sometimes see in hospitals). Dallin was relieved with the sympathy and care shown to him, and grateful for their understanding, even if it was simply a concession for a foreigner.

Finishing up, Dallin wanted to give a few other basic observations about his first visit to Tokyo. First, he liked Shinjuku Gyoen National Garden more than Yoyogi and Ueno Park. The dancers, performers, and bustle were all interesting, but he much preferred the serenity and peaceful feel that Japanese gardens brought. The same applied to the Meiji Shrine, which he enjoyed much more than Asakusa and the Senso-Ji Temple. He did have to admit, however, that the hustle and bustle of the Shinjuku subway station was mind blowing, that Akihabara was a perfect place to find gifts for his children back home, and that karaoke in private rooms was a brilliant idea! For Dallin, Tokyo was a great mix of modern and traditional, of massively noisy venues with thousands of people and quiet gardens with secluded areas, of gigantic skyscrapers and tiny rooms. He loved the contrasts. But he did come home with an appreciation for alone time.

"Some days, I just craved for a chance to be by myself, take a walk, and be alone. That just wasn't easy in the context of this trip."

The final takeaway for Dallin was that he was impressed with what these face-to-face meetings did for the team, and for him personally. "It's weird, for six years my only focus had been on the product; but now I know, for example, that Yoshinobu is hilarious, Tsutomu is a deep thinker, Seijo is super creative, and Takeshi has an incredible ability to summarize complex ideas." In realizing that there was immense value in having a team whose members had worked together for six years, Dallin left Japan with a sense that these working relationships now had a new depth.

"There were times in the past when I would feel myself being frustrated when the way we communicated affected our ability to follow up on work. That is to say, I know that I often found myself responding poorly to an issue. This was especially true of times when I was tired and was talking to them when it was late at night for me. Sometimes I just didn't have sympathy for their predicament. After this visit, I just know that I'll handle those situations better."

Finally, Dallin noted that he used to refer to these colleagues as "my Japanese team." Now, however, he noted that he prefers to refer to them as "our team in Japan." "I know it is a subtle difference, but I don't want to call them my Japanese team. They are simply members of our team who happen to be in Japan."

OBSERVATIONS AND COMMENTS
FROM AMERICAN EXPERTS

Scott Stegert
Vice President, Segment Head Asia, Continental Automotive
The experience of Dallin Bates is one that is not uncommon among Americans having their first real working experience in Japan. Until we experience otherwise, we naturally tend to assume most people are like us—in our habits, our working styles, even our values. Meeting and working in foreign settings can challenge these assumptions in ways we sometimes do not expect. But Dallin's patience and open-minded approach to his first experience in Japan will serve him well.

Initially, I am surprised that Dallin could have worked successfully with a team of thirty people in Japan for *six years* without once setting foot in the country. The fact that Dallin has been able to remotely lead a group in Japan (with little understanding of the culture) is remarkable. As a broad generalization, comparing Japan with the West, harmony has a greater emphasis in one's life and values—while individuality is typically not as high a priority. As a result, identifying local leaders (especially within foreign companies) can be a challenge.

Dallin's style of using written communication can be advantageous for both sides. Some extra time to choose one's words for clear understanding can make things easier. It is my experience that many Japanese folks are more comfortable writing English than speaking it. However, he will have to balance this against the time lag between conversations twelve time zones apart. Clarifying and getting things perfectly right is simply how things are done in Japan. In some working situations, trading e-mails once per day may not be workable.

Face-to-face communication is a critical part of any meaningful relationship in Japan. An introduction and polite conversation breaks the ice; shared experiences build trust; trust allows heart to heart communication; [and] heart to heart communication allows understanding and agreement. And practically *none* of this happens in formal business meetings. This happens after work, at restaurants, social events, and the like.

Formal business meetings (especially high-level meetings) can be as much ceremony as meaningful discussion. All the decisions have already been made behind the scenes. The meeting is to formalize the decision and agreement (almost *never* disagreement) in public.

This is the first mistake many Western businesspeople make (I did). We assume that meetings are places for discussion, debate, and coming to an agreement (everybody is like us, are they not?). Without understanding the cultural context, however, we can read the wrong meaning into what we see, and we can leave confused.

As a foreigner living in Japan, over time I noticed the theme of "harmony in all aspects of life" (historically called "*wa*"), repeated over and over. Even in the most discreet ways. Sometimes it can be beautiful; sometimes it can be frustrating. Some examples from Dallin's story:

- Written communication is sometimes preferred over verbal—it avoids discomfort for both the speaker and listener if the speaker is not fluent.
- Formal introductions—person-to-person recognition of the others' position and achievements. The *formality itself* is what makes it comfortable for both people to break the ice.
- Showing Dallin a great evening—seeking to build trust, understanding, and establish a harmonious working relationship.
- Baseball game—it seems like everyone knows their team's cheer and has their team's towel (but no face painters and no cowbell guy).
- Sumo—pillows are thrown when the *unexpected* wrestler wins. *Note:* Sumo is as much about the ceremony as it is

about the wrestling. Watch the wrestlers posturing *before* the match.

- Picking up at public events—this is just what everyone does, everywhere. Manners are the foundation of *wa*.
- Nonverbal cues—allow you to convey meaning without saying something that might make someone uncomfortable.

See if you can find more. . . . A fabulous country, a beautiful culture, wonderful people, and always something to learn—I would recommend Japan as an experience for anyone.

Howard Cash
President, Gene Codes Corporation and
Gene Codes Forensics, Inc.

In this vignette, I am first surprised that a major project could go on for six years without a visit from the project leader. Dallin's perspective is undoubtedly colored by the fact that he was accustomed to working from home. He certainly had experience working only electronically with the American part of his team, and may not have appreciated the extra value of face-to-face meetings for his Japanese collaborators and colleagues. On this topic, it seems significant that all seven section leaders had come to the company headquarters in Austin at the beginning of a project, but that Dallin had only ever met three of them. The implication is that while the Japanese partners were traveling 6,500 miles for a kickoff meeting, Dallin continued to work at home rather than travel one-tenth that distance. If not disrespectful, this could be seen as a faux pas or, at least, a diminished level of dedication. By example, the Japanese members of the team expressed their commitment to the relationship, and Dallin would have served the team and the project well by doing the same.

In our own experience, working with our most important Japanese partner, we had our earliest meetings at their US offices in San Francisco. This was a little easier for both sides, because they already had a business nexus in the States, and we scheduled our travel to San Francisco around the travel plans of their executives. Still, after a short while, I traveled to Japan as the president of my organization to meet with and develop relationships with our partners. The relationships that were formed on that trip still continue nearly twenty years later. More recently, when Japanese partners have come to visit our corporate headquarters in Ann Arbor, we have made it a point to fly in senior staff from our New York location to be part of the meetings.

One of the things that Dallin perceived quickly was an understood, fundamental respect for all team members. The confidence that his colleagues took from that foundation of respect gave them the freedom to engage in good-natured teasing without fear of insults. This might take much longer in a local, American collaboration; if a senior manager at a US manufacturer traveled to the location of a domestic supplier for an extended visit, the communications would commonly start out as formal, to the point of being constrained. The Japanese players in this story make a concerted effort to create comfortable social connections, building a path to less and less formal discussions, at least during off hours.

Dallin's experience was that sporting events made for good bonding opportunities. In the story, this included both participatory sports like golf and spectator sports like baseball. My own experience reflects those observations. I do not play golf myself, but my American team and I have made it a point when hosting our partners from Tokyo and Yokohama to take them to events like professional baseball games, and we hope to see a Japanese baseball game on a future visit.

Dallin probably earned the appreciation of his hosts with his effort to learn some Japanese phrases. Building on this visit, he would be well advised to keep using and developing his modest Japanese vocabulary. Similarly, he should capitalize on what he has learned about nonverbal communication and not slide back into his old communication patterns when he returns home. This might start with something as simple as putting a Post-It note on his computer screen, with a reminder to focus on active listening. He can make it a point to speak slowly and to repeat things back to demonstrate his own understanding.

Dallin should be conscientious about keeping the communication channels open and active. This can start with thank-you notes to the people with whom he spent time, acknowledging the fun times that they had had together, as well as the professional goals that were met. A phone call every six or eight weeks to discuss nonwork topics can keep a friendship robust.

Finally, in future meetings, Dallin should adopt the custom of presenting thoughtful, but not overly opulent, business gifts. By doing so, he will be showing not only friendship but also respect for the customs of his teammates.

Thomas Mally
Senior Manager, Vehicle Program Management
for Nissan Technical Center North America

Using written/digital documents for communication is easier than face-to-face verbal communication. There are several factors that make a significant difference between these methods:

1. The speed of comprehension is not an issue, because there is no pressure on the receiver of the information to quickly understand and provide a response during a conversation.
2. The ability of seeing the words versus having to understand the words. Factors such as dialect and the type of English (American, British, Australian, etc.) play a role in the ability to understand each other.
3. With digital applications to support us, there are many different ways to have information translated from one language into another. These tools allow the receiver to better understand and confirm what is being communicated before providing a response.

In Japan, there are many different formalities to be followed. In some cases, the people following them cannot answer why they exist; they have simply always been there. Because the population of Japan is very dense, there needs to be some inherent order for everybody to coexist in harmony. A lot of this cultural structure can also be seen in the city's cleanliness. There are not many trash bins around, so most trash is disposed of in the place of consumption. And if there are trash bins, then every item is thrown into a coordinated bin depending on the type of trash, such as plastic, paper, and others.

Formality is also followed in how Japanese people dress. Many jobs have matching uniforms that visually show what their specific tasks may be. This is also true in the office setting, where a businessperson or salaryman typically wears a dark suit with a white shirt and a tie. This translates to the female workers as they are also increasing as part of the workforce. In the past, women were treated very traditionally as housewives. Typically, if they did work, it would only be until they got married, or in some cases had their first child. Then they would stay at home to take care of the home and/or children.

Culturally, there are many different levels of respect in Japan. They range from hierarchy in an office setting to age or type of occupation outside the office. This is not just seen through experiences; it is also part of the language. Different versions of words are used to speak up a level, at the same level, or down a level, depending on your standing versus the person with whom you are communicating. This also includes the guest, who is respected and receives a tremendous amount of generosity from the hosts. In some cases, it can range from daily pick-ups to and from work so the guest does not need to worry about commuting to guided sightseeing tours on the weekend in the host's personal car on his or her personal time.

Even though many of the statements given above still hold true today, there does seem to be a shift happening within Japan. Whether it is the influence of other cultures or just a change nationally, you can see various examples of Japan's nontraditional side. Some examples include:

1. Celebration of holidays, such as Halloween and Christmas;
2. Expressing individualism through unique fashion styles (Lolita, Gyaru, Cosplay, Gothic, Hip-Hop etc.);
3. Increasing amounts of foreign vocabulary; however, in some cases it is a combination of foreign words to create a shorter, simpler version. Examples:
   a. personal computer → パーソナルコンピューター→パソコン (*pasocon*)
   b. convenience store → コンビニエンスストア→コンビニ (*combini*)

With Japan's dense population, especially in the city center, there is a limited amount of space to accommodate everybody comfortably. Under these conditions, it is sometimes difficult to find private, personal space. Most housing conditions are cramped, and certain rooms are set up with flexibility to serve as multipurpose spaces. This also makes it difficult for people to partake in certain hobbies or to entertain guests at home. For example, somebody that collects model trains does not have the space to set up the track structure, so in Japan they have a place where one can rent time at a store that has a huge track and scenery to run the trains. Similarly, instead of hosting a party at one's house, people will typically go out and meet for dinner and maybe rent a private karaoke room (or plan some other group activity), which would include drinks and food. Most karaoke rooms are set up with themes, so you can make a reservation based on your preferences.

OBSERVATIONS AND COMMENTS
FROM JAPANESE EXPERTS

Ko Unoki
Head of Strategic Alliances in Asia Pacific, Bayer
Yakuhin Ltd., and Former Senior Fellow, 21st
Century Public Policy Institute of the Federation of
Japanese Economic Organizations (Keidanren)
The rise and spread of information communications technology (ICT) has been manifested in the use of the internet; and its adjacent tools of networking have facilitated the creation of new business models and an unprecedented acceleration in the pace of global business transactions. In many industries, the barriers to entry have been lowered or eliminated on account of the internet, making it possible for an increasing number of new and smaller firms to enter the market without necessarily having the economies of scale or a vertically integrated structure that the corporate conglomerates born in the late nineteenth and twentieth centuries had in many instances built up or possessed. These new players are in many cases asset-light in structure

(i.e., have low fixed costs and overhead) and use ICT to facilitate horizontal specialization, which leads to the creation of intertwined supply and information networks that instantaneously connect suppliers, manufacturers, and consumers with each other. The lowering of the barriers to entry and the resulting increase in the number of new and nimble companies have led in several instances to an intensification of intra-industry competition, resulting in a lowering of industry profit levels. Industry profits have also been affected by ICT, as this has enabled producers and consumers to have almost immediate access to market information, making it difficult for companies to influence market prices. Yet, despite the rise of this ICT-centered brave new world that arguably may give birth to the utopian society envisioned by Karl Marx, where the exploitation of the working class will no longer exist as ICT inexorably drives marginal costs down toward zero and provides the opportunity for everyone to be simultaneously a producer and/or a consumer, the experience of Dallin Bates at Up in the Clouds, a company of the ICT age, arguably shows that regardless of the impact of ICT and the rise of new network-based business models, there is nothing more effective in building trust within or among organizations than old fashioned face-to-face interaction. Trust is a factor in business that can hardly be underestimated; after all, without trust companies cannot effectively build alliances, maintain supply-chain networks, or operate effectively.

Toward building trust, however, there is only so much that can be established by e-mail, video, or telephone conferencing. And this is especially the case when communication is done by people of different nationalities who do not have a common mother tongue or culture, making it at times difficult to accurately convey certain concepts that were developed within the scope of one language to another. In the case of interactions between Japanese and non-Japanese, for example, what must also be considered is the emphasis that many Japanese place on getting to *really* know the other side as a means of building mutual trust and strong long-term relations, something Dallin Bates found out in the gatherings with his Japanese colleagues at the *izakaya* during after-office hours. Personally, I have found that during these moments in the *izakaya* with our business colleagues is where the *honne*—real intentions, true thoughts, and individual personalities—are revealed, when everyone lets down his or her guard, in no small part thanks to the ice-breaking lubrication of several glasses of beer and sake. In this respect, ICT and its adjacent tools of e-mail and video and audio conferencing can perhaps never completely replace the face-to-face interaction upon which many Japanese insist and consider essential in building mutual trust.

Non-Japanese people and especially Westerners may consider spending after-office hours with business colleagues in the *izakaya* or other watering holes for tired corporate warriors as an inefficient way of doing business. But instead of brushing off in disdain what is essentially a custom of Japanese networking that still prevails in the ICT age, as the success of Dallin Bates had shown in his interactions with the Japanese, acceptance and tolerance of what may seem to be the idiosyncrasies of one culture have, arguably, a positive effect on building trust that would be beneficial for the long-term sustenance of business relations. In this respect, the example of Dallin Bates suggests that, while understanding and coming to terms with the nuts and bolts of ICT may be beneficial in building a competitive advantage in the twenty-first century and understanding foreign languages may help to bridge the communication gap among stakeholders and customers of different nationalities, the cultivation of a culture of tolerance and accommodation of other corporate and national cultures within business organizations and among individuals still remains a fundamental, if not the greatest, factor behind a successful business endeavor and in building long-term multinational business alliances and relationships.

Mitsuo Hirose
President of Maverick Transnational and
Sunsho Pharmaceutical Company
I have been a president of a subsidiary set up in the United States by a Japanese-affiliated company, Dai Nippon Printing America, Inc., as well as a subsidiary set up in Japan by the United States–affiliated company Johnson & Johnson Medical KK. From my

unique career, I have learned very much about the differences between the United States and Japan.

One of the biggest differences between these two countries are human relationships in the workplace. As shown in the vignette, coworkers in Japan spend a long time with their colleagues, even outside the office. American people might think this is an inefficient way of working, or may feel like they are forced to do so; but in many cases, the Japanese enjoy doing so, and it helps in carrying out their work efficiently in the office, too.

In a way, in Japan the workplace is seen as an extension of the family. This is the reason that the American versions of "efficiency" and "rationality," which are believed to be the "global way" in many Western countries, sometimes do not work as well in the Japanese workplace and market. American people might think "business is business," and they try to apply their individualistic and performance-based evaluation system in working with Japanese employees, and ignore the important function of personal bonding that fosters the group dynamics of the Japanese. Misunderstanding this point might be one of the reasons that many of the world's top American companies struggle to achieve success in the Japanese market. In my opinion, it is more "efficient" to use and take advantage of this Japanese group-oriented nature in business rather than to try and reform the system, because the Japanese system is one that has been nurtured through history, and it is difficult to change this in a short period of time.

In Japanese history, most companies started as small family businesses and grew gradually by keeping strong relationships between owners and employees, and also with local communities. The employees and the owners even lived together until recent times; and nowadays, too, many Japanese companies offer dormitories for unmarried employees and company housing for married employees. This is a successful and widely accepted system for building relationships with colleagues.

It is through such means that Japanese companies have been able to root their subsidiaries in a variety of different regional communities, where people take pride in their successes, regional dialects, local foods, and so on that shape each person's identity. The proof is that many of the oldest companies in the world are in Japan.

When I first became president of Johnson & Johnson Medical KK in Japan, although J&J was already the world's biggest medical company in the United States at the time, it had not been so successful in Japan. Because J&J took pride in its high-quality products, it tried to do direct sales and exclude existing distributors for cost reduction. Direct sales might work well in a country like the United States, but I soon realized that they would not work in the Japanese market, even if we had good products, because each Japanese region had its existing distributors that already had strong local bonds with their communities that had been cultivated over a very long time. It is time consuming and inefficient for a foreign newcomer to build a relationship with every hospital and pharmacy from the start. So what J&J's sales force did was to build good relationships with the strong local distributors and use their network for our sales. As a result, our sales strategy worked out well—sales doubled within two years, and went up twenty-three times in ten years.

As in this case, I strongly believe it is very important to learn the cultural and social background of the target country rather than just simply apply the "global way" in a given market. If you are going to take lead of a Japanese team, you need to have a deep understanding of its social system and the cultural background of the Japanese people in order to take advantage of its uniqueness for the business. In many cases in Japan, leaders who can be good intercultural mediators will work better than people with strong leadership skills.

Junji Taniguchi
Marketing Director for an Online Dress-Shirt
Company with 3D Tailoring
This is a story about a foreigner, or *gaijin*, visiting Japan for the first time to meet his associates. This is quite like a story we have seen many times in movies and other media venues. Having lived outside Japan, I felt some of Dallin's situations were familiar; however, there were a few aspects that I felt were no longer applicable to the Japanese work scene. Returning to Japan after

having lived in Thailand for seven years, I have since learned from contemporaries that there are fewer "night out" activities among young workers compared with their parents' generation. I understand that companies need to mention that there is no obligation for new recruits to participate in such events. It is not that they have other, more important matters; but the younger generation might feel pulled tight having to do things that have nothing to do with actually producing things. This change in policy is likely due to the fact that there are shortages of personnel due to lack of workers who are willing to work longer hours or weekends. This newfound freedom for the younger generation may vary across industries, but I feel that high-technology companies with relatively younger workers are more likely to have less traditional concepts, so I did find the entertainment scene obligations in the vignette a little unlikely. Also, high-technology companies that generally have younger workers are also known to keep late night hours—not because of the company's work schedule but because of their own lifestyle.

It may be different from company to company and from foreign person to foreign person, but what Dallin experienced in his sport entertainment sounds quite unique. Most companies I know no longer have the time or funds to be able to take a foreign person to sumo and baseball at the same time. Also, what was the season? I suppose Dallin was lucky to be able to experience both. I was a little disappointed that with the same funds and money, they did not take him to see Kabuki or other cultural venues to show more of Japan because he did seem to have the chance to visit Asakusa and visit Tsukiji to experience different kinds of sushi than what he experienced in Albuquerque.

Also, it was a little hard to believe that people in the high-technology field would spend as much time with him, as stated. I feel that the trend is that more and more people of such backgrounds value their time with families, due to their experience living or being educated abroad. I certainly would have had my family join in if I were going to a baseball game! I was puzzled to read the section regarding the Pachinko parlor, too, because parlors are getting less and less popular, particularly among young people. Karaoke parlors, too, are having such a hard time getting customers nowadays they are showing the latest movies rather than having customers sing.

Dallin's experience is certainly different from what I have experienced, probably because I am Japanese, even if I sometimes do not feel so Japanese inside from having lived abroad quite a lot. Because I am Japanese, I have never received the "welcome" banquet Dallin did, and would never expect to receive anything to the extent he did.

Overall, I was a little disappointed that after dealing with his colleagues for six years, Dallin had not ever visited his counterpart country, not for professional reasons but for personal ones. I believe cultural understanding goes both ways, and if he feels different in dealing with his counterparts, I felt that he needed to lean in a little more toward his counterparts in Japan.

OBSERVATIONS AND COMMENTS FROM THE AUTHORS

Each of the guest executives, both those from the United States and those from Japan, emphasizes the importance of face-to-face meetings and relationship building. All were surprised, even shocked, that after six years of working together remotely, Dallin had never met with many of the team members in a face-to-face exchange. Scott Stegert observes that face-to-face communication is critical in building meaningful relationships, and that it allows for ice-breaking, trust building, and having heart-to-heart communications, which lead to understanding and agreement. Howard Cash suggests that this personal interaction is so important that Dallin should have at least met with team supervisors in US cities when they were in the United States. Junji Taniguchi additionally observes that six years is long enough that Dallin should have even traveled to Japan even for personal reasons, just to be able to identify and better relate to his Japanese team. It may be that technology and virtual networks provide ample opportunities for remote communication. However, as Ko Unoki observes, old-fashioned, face-to-face interaction is key to building effective alliances.

We concur with these experts. This is not a simple matter of getting to know people. At some point in the six-year process, Dallin and his company should have recognized that this team was going to continue to work together. Especially given the fact that some of the Japanese team members were traveling to the United States, a positive step would have been to send Dallin to the same city for initial face-to-face meetings.

The irony, for Dallin and for many North Americans in general, is that remote communication is seen as cost-effective and efficient. From a Japanese perspective, however, short-term efficiency is also short lived. Compare this with the experience of Howard Cash, whose efforts to build foundations have resulted in relationships that have lasted for more than twenty years. Similarly, Mituso Hirose succinctly summarizes that the additional time spent in building human relationships is not inefficient—indeed, "Japanese enjoy doing so." His advice is to realize that when building relationships in the long run, it is more efficient to take advantage of Japanese group orientation.

Second, and closely related to the observations about relationship building, nearly all the guest executives comment about harmony. This is interesting because, from a North American perspective, "harmony" is a word that is seldom used in the context of a work environment, and it is not a word that was specifically used in the case study. Scott Stegert juxtaposes Japanese harmony against North American individuality. Thomas Mally observes that the demands of a dense population in limited space create a society where harmonious interaction becomes important. Mitsuo Hirose reminds readers that in Japan the workplace in seen as an extension of the family; welcoming Dallin in the manner the Japanese colleagues did was welcoming him into the family. Moreover, Mitsuo Hirose further recommends that this understanding leads to an understanding of Japan as a social system, rather than a one-size-fits-all global way of doing things. From our perspective, these executive comments dovetail well with our discussion in chapter 4, on contexting and listener talk. Take time to understand the context and interpret what the other is trying to imply and say.

A third area where all the executives comment on the case relates to the linguistic advantages and disadvantages of written versus oral communication. Scott Stegert concurs that written communication often allows both parties more time to choose words and more time to decipher what is said. Thomas Mally adds that many Japanese are aided by being able to see the written words and by having access to translation support. At the same time, both recognize that the time lag of written communication can be detrimental when dealing with time-sensitive issues. Also related to oral language, Howard Cash gives Dallin kudos for learning some Japanese. He further recommends that Dallin now leave a Post-It note on his computer screen as a reminder of lessons learned, such as speaking more slowly and repeating himself more often. As authors, we also realize that a person in Dallin's position may not focus exclusively on becoming fluent in Japanese. However, given that this is *his* team, and that they have worked together for six years, Dallin would benefit from the experience of learning to speak Japanese, and we encourage him to do so.

There are a few other comments from the guest executives that we highlight. Junji Taniguchi mentions that nowadays there are fewer nights out than there used to be, and that this is especially true for younger executives. The trend is to spend less time with colleagues and more time with family. We understand where Junji is coming from. We also realize that in the vignette, Dallin and his team were experiencing the unique experience of meeting in Japan for the first time, after six years of having already worked together. This dynamic, we believe, was part of the reason why Dallin received, in Junji's words, a "welcome banquet." Next, Howard Cash recommends that Dallin enter a phase of writing thank-you notes, giving out gifts, and even calling work associates every so often to discus nonwork topics. All these suggestions coincide well with Mitsuo Hirose's observation that personal bonds foster group dynamics, and that this is more important than mere "business is business" and "performance-based evaluation."

Another observation deals with Dallin's orthotics. We know Dallin personally. We also know how concerned and obsessed he is about his feet. Still, we feel that Dallin was probably unaware of how large of a concession he was asking for when he sent the e-mail to one of the section leaders. We can only imagine all the discussions, decisions, and allowances that were made in order to accommodate his request.

Finally, there are a couple of items that our guest executives did not mention, which we would like to highlight. Dallin mentions in the vignette that he was concerned about how he could reciprocate if his Japanese team were to visit him in Albuquerque. Our recommendation is that he provide a very personalized American experience by inviting his Japanese team to his house for a barbeque. Notice that a visit to a person's home is not a common event among Japanese. In North American culture, however, an invitation to a home to have a backyard barbeque is quite common. Dallin's Japanese team would certainly enjoy such a reception.

For those readers who want to discuss these issues further, consider the following topics and questions for discussion:

1. In what ways do you or do you not think of Up in the Clouds as an international company? In terms of the LESCANT approach, what does this tell us about social organization?
2. Ko Unoki observes that there is a disconnect between North American perceptions of an efficient use of time as compared with Japanese perceptions of the benefits of team building—for example, time spent at the *izakaya*. How do you respond to this dichotomy?
3. In the vignette, Dallin had to get used to nonnative use of English. For example, one team member used the term "pissed off" when what he really meant was simply being upset. What recommendations can you give to help native speakers of English deal with such nonnative patterns?
4. To what do you believe Mitsuo Hirose was referring when he compared the North American tendency to look at the quality of products and direct sales with the Japanese focus on the bonds you make with those with whom you work?
5. Scott Stegert made observations about the assumptions that North Americans make about the purpose of meetings

(focusing on discussions, debates, and the desire to come to an agreement). How do you respond to these observations in light of Japanese patterns?

6. Returning to the discussion of loyalty and *amae* in chapter 5, on authority, what examples can you draw from this vignette that can be analyzed from the perspective of *amae*?

7. Returning to the discussion of *uchi-soto-kankei* in chapter 3, on social organization, what examples can you draw from this vignette that can be analyzed from a perspective of inside and outside faces?

INTRODUCTION

1. US Central Intelligence Agency, *CIA Factbook*, www.cia.gov/library /publications/the-world-factbook/.
2. US Census Bureau, "Foreign Trade," www.census.gov/foreign-trade /statistics/highlights/top/index.html; Government of Canada, "Bilateral Relations," www.canadainternational.gc.ca/japan-japon /bilateral_relations_bilaterales/index.aspx?lang=eng.
3. Data for both are from US Central Intelligence Agency, *CIA Factbook*.
4. *Forbes*, "The World's Biggest Public Companies," www.forbes.com /global2000/list/#industry:Trading%20Companies.
5. David A. Victor, *International Business Communication* (New York: HarperCollins, 1992).
6. Haru Yamada, *Different Games, Different Rules: Why Americans and Japanese Misunderstand Each Other* (New York: Oxford University Press, 1997).

CHAPTER 1

1. For data on TOEIC scores, see "2015 Report on Test Takers Worldwide: The TOEIC Listening and Reading Test," Educational Testing Service, www.ets.org/s/toeic/pdf/ww_data_report_unlweb.pdf.
2. For the story on Japanese TOEFL scores, see Jun Hongo, "Abe Wants TOEFL to Be Key Exam," *Japan Times*, March 25, 2013, www .japantimes.co.jp/news/2013/03/25/national/abe-wants-toefl-to-be -key-exam/#.VstVipMrKgR.
3. For the story on low scores of Japanese test takers, see "Disappointing Levels of English," *Japan Times*, March 28, 2015, www .japantimes.co.jp/opinion/2015/03/28/editorials/disappointing -levels-english/#.VstW25MrLUp.
4. For English proficiency levels in Japan, see "EF English Proficiency Index: Country Fact Sheet," *Education First*, 2016, http://www.ef.co .uk/epi/regions/asia/japan.
5. For data on the frequency of last names, see "The Expanded Dictionary of Japanese Family Names" (in Japanese), *Houbunkan*, www .houbunkan.jp/shopping/20201/index.shtml.

CHAPTER 2

1. For data on inhabitable space, see Thomas Brinkhoff, "Urban Population," World by Map, http://world.bymap.org/UrbanPopulation .html.

2. "Fukushima Nuclear Crisis Estimated to Cost ¥11 Trillion: Study," *Japan Times*, August 27, 2014, www.japantimes.co.jp/news/2014 /08/27/national/fukushima-nuclear-crisis-estimated-to-cost-%C2 %A511-trillion-study/#.V5-1YJMrIoo.

3. For data on fish consumption, see "Fish Consumption Per Capita in Japan," HelgiLibrary, 2016, www.helgilibrary.com/indicators/fish -consumption-per-capita/japan.

4. "Japan's Self-Sufficiency Rate Fails to Meet 45% Target," *Japan Times*, August 7, 2015, www.japantimes.co.jp/news/2015/08/07 /national/japans-food-self-sufficiency-rate-fails-meet-lowered-45 -target/#.V5-3bZMrL_Q.

5. For population data, see "Statistical Handbook of Japan," Statistics Japan, www.stat.go.jp/english/data/handbook/c0117.htm.

6. David Levinson, *Encyclopedia of Homelessness* (Beverly Hills, CA: Sage, 2004).

7. For data on population declines, see "Japan's Population Declines for the First Time since 1920s: Official Census," *The Guardian*, February 26, 2016, www.theguardian.com/world/2016/feb/26/japan -population-declines-first-time-since-1920s-official-census.

8. Kathy Matsui, *Womenomics 3.0* (New York: Goldman Sachs, 2010).

9. "Modern Immigration Wave Brings 59 Million to US, Driving Population Growth Through 2065: Views of Immigration's Impact on US Society Mixed," Pew Research Center, September 28, 2015, www .pewhispanic.org/2015/09/28/modern-immigration-wave-brings -59-million-to-u-s-driving-population-growth-and-change-through -2065/.

10. Stephen Smith, "Why Tokyo's Privately Owned Railways Work So Well," *Atlantic City Lab*, October 31, 2011, www.citylab.com /commute/2011/10/why-tokyos-privately-owned-rail-systems-work -so-well/389/.

11. "女性専用車男が乗ってもOK" (Women-Only Cars: If Men Get On It, It's Legally OK), *President Online*, November 16, 2011, http:// president.jp/articles/-/5126.

12. Leo Lewis, "All-Women Trains Are Only Way to Defeat Bottom Pinchers," *The Times* (London), November 24, 2004.

13. Kyuya Fukada, *Nihon Hyakumeizan* (Tokyo: Shinchosha, 1964).

CHAPTER 3

1. This is not to be confused with 華族 *kazoku*, a peerage system used between 1869 and 1947.

2. James Brooke, "Here Comes the Japanese Bride, Looking Very Western," *New York Times*, July 8, 2005, www.nytimes.com/2005 /07/08/world/asia/here-comes-the-japanese-bride-looking-very -western.html?_r=0.

3. Jeffrey Hayes, "Divorce in Japan," Facts and Details, http://factsanddetails.com/japan/cat18/sub117/item616.html.

4. "Hitonami o motomeru kara kekkon surukara kekkon shinai e" (People want to be like everyone else moves answers, from "Want to marry" to "Don't want to marry"), Blogos, October 19, 2013.

5. Vikas Mehrotra, Randall Morck, Jungwook Shim, and Yupana Wiwattanakantang, "Adoptive Expectations: Rising Sons in Japanese Family Firms," *INSEAD Preliminary Studies*, February 28, 2011, http://dx.doi.org/10.2139/ssrn.1777548.

6. Mayumi Hayashi, "The Care of Older People in Japan: Myths and Realities of Family 'Care,'" *Policy Papers–History & Policy* (Kings College & University of Cambridge), June 3, 2011, www.historyandpolicy.org/policy-papers/papers/the-care-of-older-people-in-japan-myths-and-realities-of-family-care.

7. There were about 39,000 children in various child care institutions in Japan in 2013. In 2012, just 12.0 percent were in the care of foster parents. This contrasts sharply with 93.5 percent in Australia and 77.0 percent in the United States. For the details, see Osaki Tomohiro, "Japan's Orphans Neglected: HRW," *Japan Times*, May 1, 2014, www.japantimes.co.jp/news/2014/05/01/national/japans-orphans-neglected-hrw/#.VuRDpxh5XXl.

8. 私立学校の振興, Shiritsu Gakkoo no Shinkou," Ministry of Education, Culture, Sports, Science, and Technology (Private Schools Promotion), May 1, 2010.

9. Hideki Maruyama, *Moral Education in Japan* (Tokyo: National Institute for Educational Policy Research of the Ministry of Education, Culture, Sport, Science, and Technology, 2013).

10. Ministry of Education, Culture, Sport, Science, and Technology, *Kokoro no Noto* (Notes of the Heart) (Tokyo: Ministry of Education, Culture, Sport, Science, and Technology, 2011).

11. Michael Blaker, Paul Giarra, and Ezra F. Vogel, *Case Studies in Japanese Negotiating Behavior* (Washington, DC: US Institute of Peace Press, 2002).

12. Sumo now has more than fifty-five foreign-born athletes. The road has not been easy, however, and restrictions on the number of foreigners in a stable were instituted in 1992. In 2002 a strict policy of one foreign-born person per stable was put into place; in 2010 it was confirmed.

13. For information, see "Global Gender Gap Report," World Economic Forum, http://reports.weforum.org/global-gender-gap-report-2014/rankings/.

14. For recent Japan rankings, see "Gender Gap Index 2014," World Economic Forum, http://reports.weforum.org/global-gender-gap-report-2014/economies/#economy=JPN.

15. For more information, see Kathy Matsui, "Womenomics 4.0: Time to Walk the Talk," Goldman Sachs, May 30, 2014, www.goldmansachs.com/our-thinking/pages/macroeconomic-insights-folder/womenomics4-folder/womenomics4-time-to-walk-the-talk.pdf.

16. For information regarding the need of nurses, see Kisaku Seno, "Why Foreign Nurses Are Good for Hospitals in Japan," ABS-CBN News, December 18, 2014, http://news.abs-cbn.com/global-filipino /12/18/14/why-foreign-nurses-are-good-hospitals-japan.

17. For recent articles about robot-manned hotels, see Monisha Rajesh, "Inside Japan's First Robot-Staffed Hotel," *The Guardian*, August 14, 2015, www.theguardian.com/travel/2015/aug/14/japan-henn-na -hotel-staffed-by-robots.

CHAPTER 4

1. Edward T. Hall, *The Silent Language* (New York: Doubleday, 1959).

2. Haru Yamada, *Different Games, Different Rules: Why Americans and Japanese Misunderstand Each Another* (New York: Oxford University Press, 1997).

3. Susan Cain, *Quiet: The Power of Introverts in a World That Can't Stop Talking* (New York: Crown, 2012), 129.

4. Yasuo Kitahara, "KYshikinihongo: Romajiryakugonazehayarunoka" (KYstyle Japanese: Why Romanized Japanese Acronyms are Popular) (Tokyo: Taishukan, 2008).

5. We thank Mina Ito for these insights.

6. To view a dramatic rice cake pounding, see, e.g., "Dramatic Japanese Rice Cake Pounding," *Lens on Japan*, YouTube, January 25, 2011, www.youtube.com/watch?v=T44R78e2Dms.

7. Roger Shuy, *Language Crimes: The Use and Abuse of Language Evidence in the Courtroom* (Cambridge: Blackwell, 1993).

8. Ishihara Shintaro, *The Japan That Can Say No* (New York: Simon & Schuster, 1991).

CHAPTER 6

1. There is a Japanese notion called *gaman*, which means withholding one's feelings so as not to offend the other. Among many Western countries, withholding one's emotions is often discouraged because it is generally perceived as repressive, and not good for one's physical and mental health.

2. This is possibly due to the lack of immigration; whereas there is a strong expectation in many Western countries for immigrants to assimilate in all social manners, the Japanese stereotype of a *gaijin* foreigner is that they will not be able to do as the Japanese do. This can be infuriating for the many non-Japanese who have acquired native or near-native fluency in Japanese communication and interaction. Equally, it is also frustrating for second-generation Japanese Americans and Japanese Brazilians who are expected to conform to Japanese customs more quickly than any other foreigners.

3. P. Ekman, W. V. Friesen, and P. Ellsworth, *Emotion in the Human Face: Guidelines for Research and Integration of Findings* (Elmsford, NY: Pergamon Press, 1972); J. D. Boucher and G. E. Carlson, "Recognition of Facial Expressions in Three Cultures," *Journal of*

Cross-Cultural Psychology 11 (1980): 263–80; C. E. Izard, *The Face of Emotion* (New York: Appleton-Century-Crofts, 1980).

4. D. Matsumoto, T. Consolacion, H. Yamada, R. Suzuki, B. Franklin, S. Paul, R. Ray, and H. Uchida, "American-Japanese Cultural Differences in Judgments of Emotional Expressions of Different Intensities," *Cognitive Emotion* 16 (2002): 721–47.

5. Anjanie Kang-Lee, Shoji Itakura, and Darwin Muir, "Cultural Display Rules Drive Eye Gaze during Thinking," *Journal of Cross-Cultural Psychology* 37, no. 6 (2006): 717–22.

6. Takahiko Masuda, Phoebe C. Ellsworth, Batja Mesquita, Janxin Leu, Shegehito Tanida, and Ellen Van de Veerdonk, "Placing the Face in Context: Cultural Differences in the Perception of Facial Emotion," *Journal of Personality and Social Psychology: Attitudes and Social Cognition* 94, no. 3 (2008): 365–81, at 375.

7. Rochelle Kopp, "Why Do Japanese Fall Asleep in Meetings?" *Japan Intercultural Consulting*, October 13, 2011, www.japanintercultural.com/en/news/default.aspx?newsID=101.

8. Peter Backhaus, "The Japanese Traffic Light Blues: Stop on Red, Go on What?" *Japan Times*, February 25, 2013, www.japantimes.co.jp/life/2013/02/25/language/the-japanese-traffic-light-blues-stop-on-red-go-on-what/#.VqVB2OYYHSw.

CHAPTER 7

1. Scott M. Stringer, "The Hardest-Working Cities," Economic Brief, Office of the New York City Comptroller, March 2015, http://origin-states.politico.com.s3-website-us-east-1.amazonaws.com/files/Embargoed%20Hardest%20Working%20Cities%20Study.pdf.

2. Toshijuki Kobayashi, Emi Morofuji, and Yoko Watanabe, "Sleeping Time Keeps Decreasing, Male Housework Time Is Increasing: From the 2010 Japanese Time Use Survey," NHK Broadcasting Culture Research Institute, April 2011, www.nhk.or.jp/bunken/english/reports/pdf/report_110401.pdf.

3. Witold Rybczynski, "Waiting for the Weekend," *The Atlantic*, August 1991, www.theatlantic.com/magazine/archive/1991/08/waiting-for-the-weekend/376343/.

4. Victoria Woollaston, "Sleeping Habits of the World Revealed: The US Wakes Up Grumpy, China Has the Best Quality Shut-Eye, and South Africa Gets Up the Earliest," *Daily Mail*, April 17, 2015, www.dailymail.co.uk/sciencetech/article-3042230/Sleeping-habits-world-revealed-wakes-grumpy-China-best-quality-shut-eye-South-Africa-wakes-earliest.html; "Night Owls and Early Birds," Sleep Cycle Alarm Clock, April 26, 2015, www.sleepcycle.com/night-owls-and-early-birds-of-the-world/.

5. Geert Hofstede, *Cultures and Organization: Software of the Mind* (London: McGraw-Hill, 1991).

6. "Tohoku Shinkasen Speed Increase: Phased Speed Increase After the Extension to Shin-Aomori Station," East Japan Railway

Company, November 6, 2007, www.jreast.co.jp/e/press/20071101/index.html.

7. "Japan's Maglev Train Breaks World Speed Record with 600 Km/H Test Run," *The Guardian*, April 21, 2015, www.theguardian.com/world/2015/apr/21/japans-maglev-train-notches-up-new-world-speed-record-in-test-run.

8. Greg Rosalsky, "Why Are Japanese Homes Disposable? A New Freakonomics Radio Podcast," Freakonomics Radio, February 27, 2014, http://freakonomics.com/podcast/why-are-japanese-homes-disposable-a-new-freakonomics-radio-podcast-3/.

Christianity, 74–75, 198
chronometers, 202
chrysanthemum symbol, 181, *181*
Chūbu region, 34*f*, 35
Chūgoku region, 7, 34*f*, 36–37
class systems, 128–29
climate, 56–58
closed eyes, 115, 120, 165
clothing. *See* dress and
    adornment
cloud platform software, 209,
    210. *See also* case study of
    technology company
collaborative communication,
    135–42
collective decision making, 137
color associations, 176–78
communication and contex-
    ting, 93–122; collaborative,
    135–42; ethnic diversity in,
    96–97; inverse correlation
    of context and content,
    95–98; LESCANT approach,
    described, xvi–xxii; overview,
    xx, 93–95; recommenda-
    tions for, 119–20; regional
    variations in, 148; speaker
    talk in, xx, 98–100, 102; talk
    vs. silence in, 100–104; and
    temporal conception, xxii;
    in workplace, 98, 215–16. *See
    also* business communication;
    feedback; Japanese phrases
    and terms; listener talk; mis-
    communication; nonverbal
    communication and behavior
concrete conception of abstract
    thought, 22–24
conformity to rules, xviii, 54–55
Confucianism, 125–27, 156, 200
consensus-building in decision-
    making, 82–83, 135–36, 138–
    39, 193, 195
content, inverse correlation with
    context, 95–98
contexting. *See* communication
    and contexting
contractions, 27

conversational space, 112–14, 120
cosplay, 90, 169–71, *171*
cram schools, 80
crime rates, 55–56, 81
cross-cultural communication.
    See communication and con-
    texting; *specific languages*
crowd management, 54–56;
    bumping into people, 173–74
crypts, 50
cultures: high-context, xx,
    95–96, 98–99; individualistic,
    64–65, 66–67, 69, 71; long-
    term oriented, 200, 203; low-
    context, xx, 95–96, 98–99;
    monochronic, 192–94, 206–7;
    others-centered, 65–67,
    71, 155–56; polychronic,
    192–95, 207. *See also* social
    organization

dams, 44
daruma (papier-mâché dolls),
    185, *185*
daylight savings time, 197–98
deadlines, 193–94, 195
decision making: approval sys-
    tem in, 140–42, *141*; collective,
    137; *nemawashi* (consensus-
    building) in, 82–83, 138–39,
    145, 193, 195; temporal con-
    ception in, 196–97
deferential language (*keigo*), 21,
    22
Deming, William Edwards, 83
demographic environment,
    47–49, 49*f*
depopulation trends, 48
designer clothing, 167
dining out, 60, 171, 185, 213
diphthongs, 28–29
disasters. *See* natural disasters
diversity. *See* ethnic diversity
divorce, 75–76
Dōgen Zenji (monk), 76
Doi, Takeo, 130
dress and adornment, 166–72;
    cosplay apparel, 90, 169–71,

high-context cultures, xx, 95–96, 98–99
hiking, 60
Himiko (shaman), 86
hiragana syllabary, 16–17, 18
Hirai, Kaz, *158*, 159
Hirose, Mitsuo, 226–28, 231, 232
Hofstede, Geert, 200
Hokkaidō region: English proficiency in, 7; geography and demographic features, 34*f*, 36; nonverbal communication in, 149; temporal conception in, 197; tourism in, 36, 40
holiday celebrations, 169, 180, 223
homelessness, 48
homes. *See* housing
Honda Motor Company, 82, 89–90
Honshū region, 33–36, 34*f*
hō-ren-sō system of business communication, 136–38
horizontal writing (*yokogaki*), 13–14, *14*
hōshin kanri (strategic policy employment system), 136, 142–44, 143*f*
hospitals, 77, 89
House of Camellia garden, 56
house slippers, 167–68, *167–68*
housing, 51–53, 203–4, 224, 227; addresses, 59
hugging, 155, 173
humble language (*kenjōgo*), 21
husband–wife bond, 126
hydroelectric dams, 44

ICT (information communications technology), 224–25, 226
ideograms, 15–16, 24
idioms, 27
illustrators, 159
immigrant populations, 48–49, 49*f*, 89, 148, 162, 238*n*2
individualistic cultures, 64–65, 66–67, 69, 71

Industrial Revolution, 192, 194
information communications technology (ICT), 224–25, 226
infrastructure, xviii
"in-language," 94
inside–outside interactions, 67–71; in business relationships, 68–69; in education, 69; elevator etiquette, 66; in families, 69, 73, 131–32; formality levels for, 22; haptics for, 173–74; interpretation of events based on, 70–71; kanji characters in organization of, 68; names and titles in, 8, 11; permeability of, 70, 90
intercultural communication. *See* communication and contexting; *specific languages*
international exchange programs, 79
interruption, guided, 20
investments, return on, 139, 144–45
Ishihara, Shintaro, 114
Islamic State, 70
island regions of Japan, 32–37, 34*f*
isolationism, 42
Itakura, Shoji, 164

Japanese Broadcasting Corporation, 198
Japanese feudal era, 127–30
Japanese language, 1–30; ambiguity of meaning in, 24–26; articles of speech in, 24–25; communication strategies, 26–29; comparison with Chinese language, 15–16; concrete conception of abstract thought in, 22–24; diphthongs in, 28–29; English proficiency by native speakers of, 4–7; formality in, 21–22; names and titles in, 7–12, 73; as near-orphan language, 2–3; onomatopoeia in, 17–18;

Matsui, Kathy, 48, 87

mausoleums, 50

meetings: after-work gatherings, 185, 192, 195, 225–26; closed eyes in, 165; formal, 219; listener talk in, 113; preparation for, 28; scheduling, 179, 193; social organization of, 83–84

Meiji Restoration, 82, 127, 192

Meiji Shrine, 217

men: affect displays by, 162; bowing techniques for, 155, 156–57; dress for, 223; father–son bond, 126; homeless, 48; husband–wife bond, 126; marriage age for, 75; names and titles for, 9–10; and proxemics, 174; in workplace, 87, 88, 213, 223

merchants, class status of, 128

metatalk, 112–14, 118, 120

metronomes, 202

micromanagement, 138

midlevel bows, 158

miscommunication: and English language, 25; and gestures, 151, 152; and oculesics, 163

Mitsubishi UFJ Financial Group, 83

Miyazaki, Hayao, 39

monochronic time, 192–94, 206–7

monorails, 54, 54

moral education, 80

mountain regions of Japan, 37–41, 60

Muir, Darwin, 164

multigenerational living, 77

Nagano Olympics (1998), 35

names and titles, 7–12, 73

Naruhito, 60

national flower. See cherry blossoms

natural disasters: earthquakes, 35, 40–41, 44, 50, 60, 204; tsunamis, 36, 40, 44; volcanic eruptions, 41

navigation systems, 59, 196

needs, anticipation of, 133–35

negations in listener talk, 114–17

nemawashi (consensus-building), 82–83, 138–39, 145, 193, 195

newspapers, 13–14

New Year's Day ceremonies, 169, 180

Nikko, 202

9, as unlucky number, 180

Nixon, Richard, 117

nodding, 4, 109, 149–50

nontask sounding, 104

nontouching (ahaptic) society, 172–73

nonverbal communication and behavior, 147–90; challenges for, 147–48, 188; dress and adornment in, 166–72, *166–72*; ethnic diversity in, 148, 159, 162, 173; haptics, 172–74; oculesics, 163–65, *164*; overview, xxi; proxemics, 174–75, *176*; recommendations for, 187–88; regional variations in, 148, 166, 173. *See also* gestures; kinesics; passive nonverbal communication

North America, compared to Japan: adaptor acceptability, 160–61; affect displays, 160, 162; authority and power, 127, 134, 137–38; business meetings, 83–84, 113; cheerleaders, 162; color associations, 177–78; contexting, xx, 96–99, 119; cosplay, 170; dress and adornment, 166, 171; education, 80–81; families, 73; gender equality, 87; gestures, 151, 152, 154; haptics, 172–74; hierarchical authority, 124–25, 135; housing, 51–52, 203; illustrators, 159; kinesics and regulators, 149, 150–51; listener talk, 109, 110, 113–14; long-term orientation ranking, 201; lucky and unlucky numbers,

unlucky numbers, 178–80, *179*
Unoki, Ko, 224–26, 230
urban population, 45–47
utopian society, 225

vehicles, 59
vertical writing (*tategaki*), 13–14
Victor, David, xvi
videoconferencing, 199, 211, 215,
   225, 226
volcanoes, 41

watchmaking, 201–2
water boundaries of Japan,
   41–44
wedding ceremonies, 74–75,
   74–75
women: bowing techniques for,
   155, *156–57*; dress for, 223; education for, 79; hand-holding
   between, 173; husband–wife
   bond, 126; marriage age
   for, 75; names and titles for,
   9–10; and proxemics, 174;
   in social organization, 86–87;
   in sports, 85–86; transportation for, 55; in workplace, 48,
   87–88, 213, 223
word order, 18–20
workplace: after-work gatherings, 185, 192, 195, 225–26;
   bowing in, 155, 157, 158–59;
   communication and con-
   texting in, 98, 215–16; commute time to, 198; dress and

adornment in, *166*, 166–67,
   213, 223; English proficiency
   in, 4, 27, 29; eye contact in,
   163, *164*; formality in, 21–22;
   hours in workweek, 198; men
   in, 87, *88*, 213, 223; names
   and titles in, 11; punctuality at,
   202, 207; religious influences
   on, 198; seniority in, 87, 124,
   125, 127; social organization
   in, 81–84; strategic policy
   employment system, 136, 142–
   44, *143f*; temporal conception
   in, 192, 193–95, 196, 199, 212;
   uniforms in, 171–72, *172*, 223;
   urban office space, 51; women
   in, 48, 87–88, 213, 223. *See
   also* business relationships;
   meetings
World Economic Forum, 86
wrestling. *See* sumo wrestling
written Japanese, 12–18; complexity of, 12–13; kanji, 15–16,
   18; *rōmaji* (Roman letters), 12,
   14–15, 17; syllabaries in, 16–18;
   tategaki (vertical writing),
   13–14; *yokogaki* (horizontal
   writing), 13–14, *14*

Yamada, Haru, xx, 6, 7, 98–99,
   108, 111, 112–13
yellow, cultural associations
   with, 177
Yoshida, Jiro, 203, 204
yukata apparel, 57, 169

Orlando R. Kelm, PhD, is an associate professor of Hispanic linguistics at the University of Texas at Austin, where he teaches courses in Portuguese and Spanish, focusing mainly on business language and the cultural aspects of international business communication. He also serves as the associate director of business language education for the University of Texas at Austin's Center for Global Business. His research and publications center on the cultural aspects of international business and pedagogical applications of innovative technologies in language learning, focusing mainly on Latin America and Brazil. Together with coauthor David A. Victor, he published the first volume in this series, *The Seven Keys To Communicating in Brazil: An Intercultural Approach* (Georgetown University Press, 2016).

David A. Victor, PhD, is a tenured professor of management and international business at Eastern Michigan University, as well as a consultant, author, and editor. He teaches courses on managing world business communication, international management, and international business and offers a series of seminars on doing business in various countries, including Brazil. As a consultant, he has run training programs and coached the leaders of more than 200 companies and organizations, ranging from global 500 companies to governments and nongovernmental organizations. Among his many publications is the groundbreaking *International Business Communication* (HarperCollins, 1992), which introduced the LESCANT Model used as the framework for this book.

Haru Yamada, PhD, is a sociolinguist and an expert on international business communication. She pioneered the study of listener-driven communication featured in this book, and she has published books in both English and Japanese—*Different Games, Different Rules* (Oxford University Press, 1997) and 喋る アメリカ人聴く日本人 (Seiko Shobo, 2003)—as well as articles in academic journals and commercial magazines in both print and digital media. As a consultant and an editor, she enjoys helping international business professionals and students gain the global edge.